Global Challenges

Global Challenges

War, Self-Determination, and
Responsibility for Justice

Iris Marion Young

polity

First published in 2007 by Polity Press

Polity Press
65 Bridge Street
Cambridge CB2 1UR, UK

Polity Press
350 Main Street
Malden, MA 02148, USA

ISBN-10: 0-7456-3834-1
ISBN-13: 978-07456-3834-8
ISBN-10: 0-7456-3835-X (pb)
ISBN-13: 978-07456-3835-5 (pb)

A catalogue record for this book is available from the British Library.

Typeset in 10.5 on 12 pt Times
by SNP Best-set Typesetter Ltd, Hong Kong
Printed and bound in Malaysia by Alden Press Ltd

For further information on Polity, visit our website: www.polity.co.uk

Contents

Acknowledgments

The essays in this volume have been presented at many venues in North America, Europe, and South Africa, and I am grateful to the audiences that have stimulated their refinement. In each text I thank individuals who gave me comments and provided research assistance. Here I would like to thank David Held for encouraging me to collect these into a single volume. I also thank Daniele Archibugi for agreeing to have a revised version of an essay we authored together included in this volume.

All of the essays have been previously published. I am grateful to the following publications for their permission to reprint somewhat revised versions of the essays: "Hybrid Democracy: Iroquois Federalism and the Postcolonial Project" was first published in Duncan Ivison, Paul Patton, and Will Sanders, *Political Theory and the Rights of Indigenous Peoples*, Cambridge University Press, 2000; "Two Concepts of Self-Determination" was first published in Austin Sarat and Thomas R. Kearns, eds, *Human Rights: Concepts, Contests, Contingencies*, University of Michigan Press, 2001; "Self Determination as Nondomination: Ideals Applied to Palestine/Israel" was first published in *Ethnicities*, vol. 5, no. 2, June 2005; "Power, Violence, and Legitimacy: A Reading of Hannah Arendt in an Age of Police Brutality and Humanitarian Intervention" was first published in Martha Minow, *Breaking the Cycles of Hatred: Memory, Law and Repair*, ed. Nancy Rosenblum, Princeton University Press, 2002; "Envisioning a Global Rule of Law," with Daniele Archibugi, was first published in James Sterba, ed., *Terrorism and International Justice*, Oxford University Press, 2003; "The Logic of Masculinist Protection: Reflections on the Current Security State" was first published in *Signs: Journal of Women in Culture and Society*, vol. 29, no. 1, 2003; "Decentering the Project of Global Democracy" was first published in Daniel Levy, Max Pensky, and John Torpey, eds, *Old Europe, New Europe, Core Europe*, Verso, 2005; "Reflections on Hegemony and Global Democracy" was first published in *Theoria: A Journal of Social and Political Theory*, no. 103, April 2004; "Responsibility, Social Connection, and Global Labor Justice" was first published under the title "Responsibility and Global Justice: A Social Connection Model," in *Social Philosophy and Policy*, 2006.

Finally, as always, I thank David Alexander and Morgen Alexander-Young for their supportive critical thinking and their loving friendship.

Introduction

On February 15, 2003, I turned on the morning news as I prepared to go to a rally in the Pakistani–Indian neighborhood of Chicago to protest the Bush Administration's determination to invade Iraq. I learned that millions of people had already streamed into the streets of Sydney, Tokyo, Delhi, Berlin, Madrid, and Johannesburg, and that millions more would be chanting and carrying signs in São Paulo, Managua, Vancouver, and dozens of other cities. Knowing that I was part of an international protest movement rolling across the world changed my experience of marching with a few thousand people down Devon Street. At least ten million people in scores of cities marched for peace on that weekend.

In a statement published a few months later also signed by Jacques Derrida, Jürgen Habermas declared that the protest marches of that weekend showed that there is a transnational public sphere. A public sphere consists in a discursive space mediating strangers in which claims and criticisms can be made with the knowledge that they are heard by many others, including political leaders and other powerful actors. Increasingly today, such public discourse and criticism is transnational. Those who speak truth to power and the anonymous auditors to whom they speak do not take officials of their own nation-states to be the sole or even primary target of their political expression. Publics in Paris and London aimed to speak not only to Tony Blair, but to George W. Bush and the United Nations General Assembly. Europe itself, according to Habermas, has emerged as a single political entity with a single public sphere.

In "Decentering the Project of Global Democracy," reprinted here, I criticize Habermas for confining his observations and interest to

Europe. I agree that significant social movement activity in the twenty-first century reveals transnational public communication, which the weekend of February 15 shows to be global, not merely European. Indeed, it can be argued that movements in the global South have led the creation of a global public sphere.

The essays in this volume, even those written before that weekend, all intend to join in the spirit of February 15. They are inspired by contemporary social movements that call multinational corporations to accountability and question the global military hegemony of the United States. They aim, however, not merely to applaud the anger and hope of these movements, but more importantly, to offer concepts for analyzing a range of events and issues that these movements address and to give arguments for some of their specific claims. In this introduction, I review several themes that the essays treat under the headings of war, self-determination, and global justice.

War

More than two hundred years ago Immanuel Kant envisioned an order of perpetual peace. Peace, he said, is not simply the absence of war, but rather a settled and regulated relationship of cooperation among states. Kant envisioned a confederation of states as the legal realization of such relationships. When the end of the Cold War was declared in the years after the fall of the Berlin Wall, many people expressed new hopes for a perpetual peace. In the United States we heard talk of a "peace dividend": with the motive for amassing weapons and armies gone, our government would reduce military spending and shift the funds to more humane purposes. Because a clash of ideologies no longer defined international politics, relations among states and peoples would now become more rule-bound.

The US-led war against Iraq of 1991 dashed those hopes for some people, but confirmed them for others. This was a war authorized by the United Nations. Some commentators thought that institutions of global governance and cooperation such as those in the United Nations system should be strengthened by thorough reform and a greater commitment of resources to them by member states. Although the world was shocked by ethnic cleansing in Croatia and Bosnia, civil war in Somalia, and genocide in Rwanda, during the 1990s numerous scholars, political commentators, and activists continued to envision and work for transnational institutions to regulate states and amplify the voices of the world's less powerful peoples in international discussions.

Since the attacks on the World Trade Center and the Pentagon in September 2001, considerably less energy has been devoted to imagining institutions of just and democratic transnational cooperation, especially concerning the elimination of war. It seems that some who once embraced projects of disarmament and conflict resolution without war have decided that when the dangers of violence come from non-state actors we cannot afford such imaginings. At the same time, current US foreign policy decision-makers have seized the moment to act on their long-standing disdain for international institutions, including the United Nations. They have concocted a doctrine of justified preemptive war that few international lawyers accept, and appear to be pursuing an agenda of military expansionism under the banner of humanitarianism. Here, at the beginning of 2006, this agenda seems fraught with difficulty and unpopular with American voters along with many others in the world.

Each of the essays in Part I of this book analyzes moral issues concerning a recent US-led war – against Serbia, Afghanistan, and Iraq – and finds in each case that the war was wrong. As a group, they intend to challenge the attitude that war is a tool of conflict resolution that must remain in international relations. Institutions that keep international peace would certainly be difficult to put and keep in place, and even if they were implemented there would be violators that law enforcers would have to deal with. We cannot abandon hope for a regime of perpetual peace, however, because that hope can motivate at least ameliorative action. Thus, all the essays in this volume endorse a project working for more settled institutions of international governance than currently exist. Apparently, some people think that such a project denies the realities of deep conflict between people or that some people simply wish to do evil things. There is no contradiction, however, between being realistic about the way things are and determined to try to improve those realities.

Those who constituted the global public sphere on the weekend of February 15 urgently wanted to stop a war that we thought was morally wrong and politically foolish. While we did not stop the war, our actions helped render it illegitimate in the eyes of most of the world. Widespread public protest is important for reasons of legitimation or falsifying claims to legitimation, among others. Especially leaders who claim to act on behalf of democratic values must stand before a world public forum and gain their support in order to claim legitimacy for their acts. Thus, in spite of its disdain for the institution, the Bush Administration sought the approval of the United

Nations Security Council for the war against Iraq. Without many of their citizens supporting their stances in the streets, the governments that refused to grant this legitimacy to the war might not have been so united and so bold.

Even when military action appears to be authorized by international public opinion and institutions, however, it may not be justified. "Power, Violence, and Legitimacy" reflects on such a distinction between legitimacy and justification in war. Beginning from such a distinction suggested by Hannah Arendt in "On Violence," I argue that legitimacy concerns authorization but justification also concerns consequences. I liken the 1999 war against Serbia to a police action in domestic affairs. Serbia was judged by much of the world, especially NATO, as an "outlaw" state. By oppressing and threatening Albanians in Kosovo, Serbia violated norms of international law and order. When UN authorization of military action against Serbia could not be achieved, NATO acted as the international police to enforce these international norms.

In domestic law enforcement situations, police often attempt to justify their use of violence by appeal to their legitimate authority and their right to make their own judgments about the acceptability of violent means. Sometimes they may be justified when they violently restrain, shoot, or kill suspected law breakers. Citizens often question these claims, however, and a concept of "police brutality" has evolved to name their unjustified and unacceptable use of violence. I argue that we should sometimes invoke a similar idea in international affairs.

I wrote "Envisioning a Global Rule of Law" with Italian theorist of international relations, Daniele Archibugi, in response to the war against Afghanistan. We argue that responding to the terrorist attacks of September 11 with conventional state-to-state military action misconceives our current situation. Rather than bring response to such criminal violence under the rubric of war, we argue, it should be conceived as international law enforcement. The sovereign state paradigm mitigates against the kind of international cooperation that can try to prevent violent crime as effectively as possible while at the same time guaranteeing basic liberties.

"The Logic of Masculinist Protection: Reflections on the Current Security State" reflects on two trends together: the curtailment of civil liberties in the United States and its aggression abroad. In this essay I am particularly interested in how the Bush Administration has mobilized consent to these connected policies by presenting the President as the protector of citizens. With appeals to the state as protector, I argue, political rhetoric draws on gendered ideas of benevolent hierarchy that are antidemocratic in their implications. I suggest that such appeals account for how easily measures to curtail civil liberties contained in the USA Patriot Act and other recent acts by the US federal government could be accepted by the American people. The government implicitly makes a bargain with the people: if you want protection, then you must allow us more discretion to decide whose behavior to monitor and how. I argue that this is not a good deal; citizens in a democracy should not be treated like children, but as decision-makers equal in status to public officials. The attitude that there is an inevitable trade-off between security, on the one hand, and rights of liberty and democracy, on the other, seems to have aided the creation of secret and not so secret detention centers by the US government and the belief of many of its officials that they are entitled to hurt and terrorize detainees for the sake of pursuing that end.

"The Logic of Masculinist Protection" also raises critical questions about the attempts to justify the war against Afghanistan by appeal to women's liberation. The Bush Administration adopted a stance of "saving brown women from brown men" in pursuing that war. Too many women continue to suffer violence at the hands of men in every country of the world today. Obstacles to the ability of women to make a decent living, or attain to positions of power and prestige, remain in place in most of the world, to a large degree because women continue to do most of the unpaid care work that gets done. There is no question, however, that women as a group are worse off in some places than others. Afghanistan was one such place before 2001, and to a large degree it remains one. I argue, nevertheless, that American and other Western feminists should be wary of adopting the mantle of protectors and saviors of women in Asia and Africa, especially when this involves military action. The cloak brings with it an imperialist history that is difficult to shake off.

The most angry of the essays in this volume, "Reflections on Hegemony and Global Democracy," claims that the Bush Administration has acted as a global dictator in going to war against Iraq against the will of most of the rest of the world. At the moment of that writing it seemed to me that ambitions of global dictatorship better described these attitudes and actions than does Empire. A dictatorship is a ruling power that imposes its own political desire and interests on others even in the face of their objections or protest. I conjure the idea of global dictatorship in order to invoke the ideal of its opposite, global democracy. The institutions of stronger global cooperation and regulation that we should envision and work for have to be thought of as democratic. Among other things, this means that they do not replace institutions through which peoples exercise a right of self-determination, but provide means through which self-determining peoples can be represented in transnational decision-making on terms that insulate smaller or less powerful groups from domination and exploitation.

Self-determination

Each of the three wars whose rightness I challenge in this book was justified at least partly on humanitarian grounds. In each case the United States and its allies said they were aiding oppressed people – the Albanians in Kosovo, and the people of Iraq and Afghanistan. Humanitarianism is fast becoming the primary justification for military action, especially from the United States. Some discussions of human rights and war go so far as to suggest that principles of state sovereignty are obsolete, and that intervention for humanitarian ends is always morally permissible or even obligatory. I certainly would not claim that the international community should never use military force to save people who are being slaughtered by their governments or neighbors. I do think that such action should be genuinely multilateral, approved by global democratic processes, and be likely to succeed in preventing harm. Those are conditions difficult to meet.

The world community should be wary, however, of humanitarian justifications for war. When the claim that the United States and Britain had to attack Iraq in order to protect the world from Iraq's weapons was exposed as false, the United States and Britain justified their action primarily as liberating the people from a ruthless dictator. Such an appeal in principle would justify going to war against any authoritarian government. When I was in South Africa in April 2003, people asked me why the United States wasn't aiming to topple Robert Mugabe in Zimbabwe. They thought that he is another example of a ruthless dictator. The problem is that there are too many potential sites of intervention on these grounds. Any hope of world order evaporates if we affirm that outsiders are justified in removing governments by military force whenever they are cruel dictatorships.

Why? As John Stuart Mill argued one hundred and fifty years ago, and others repeated in the twentieth century, military intervention violates principles of self-determination. However much they hate the dictatorship, the people living under it usually hate their foreign saviors as much or more. A stronger global rule of law should not entail that people lose a right of self-determination. Recognition of an equal right of peoples to self-determination can provide some cushion for smaller and economically less advantaged peoples against the turbulence and power inequalities that globalization exacerbates.

Many advocates of cosmopolitan ethics and stronger global governance institutions pay little attention to principles of self-determination for peoples. Some doubt that such a vision is compatible with such principles. If we assume that self-determination is equivalent to Westphalian ideas of sovereignty, they may be right. Three of the papers in this volume offer an alternative theory of self-determination, which I suggest is compatible with and ideally part of institutions of transnational governance.

Two of these papers begin with claims of indigenous peoples. "Hybrid Democracy: Iroquois Federalism and the Postcolonial Project," considers the structure and operation of the Iroquois federation before and during the eighteenth century as interacting with the birth of the United States. I suggest that an understanding of the spirit of these governance practices among six self-determining peoples can help us today to imagine international relations with more recognized regulation of peoples who retain strong institutions of self-governance.

"Two Concepts of Self-Determination" explains the conceptual shift that must be made to make such ideas coherent. I take a practical cue from two distinct but not contradictory aspects of indigenous politics today: most indigenous people claim that their rights of self-determination have not been fully recognized, and yet they do not usually seek the status of independent nation-states. I argue that the most politically useful understanding of self-determination today would define it not as noninterference, but rather as nondomination. Conceptualizing self-determination as nondomination challenges an equation of self-determination with sovereignty, in the sense of having final authority over a unified and bounded jurisdiction in which outsiders have no say. A conception of self-determination as nondomination agrees prima facie that outsiders ought not to interfere, but with an important caveat. In an interdependent world there are many circumstances in which the decisions and actions of outsiders affect insiders and those of insiders affect outsiders; these circumstances often call for procedures to regulate the relationship between prima facie self-determining entities.

Relying on a notion of relational autonomy, I argue for a conception of self-determination that involves institutionalized procedures for negotiating between self-determining units when their activities affect one another's basic interests. In institutional terms, such procedures would imply some version of federalism at a global level and at more regional and even local levels. As a general idea, federalism refers to governance procedures in whose design member groups participate, and whose purpose is to enable fair cooperation among them.

"Self-Determination as Nondomination: Ideals Applied to Palestine/Israel" takes some steps toward theorizing alternative forms of federalism. Most federalist theories and practices make three assumptions about the form of federal institutions: that federal institutions relate vertically to the constituent units, overriding their decisions; that constituent units should be large contiguous territories; and that all constituent units should have the same rights and duties. None of these assumptions is necessary to the concept or design of federalism, I argue. If we open the political imagination to conceiving relationships among federated units in new ways, we may be able to conceive some institutional solutions to conflicts that now appear intractable. We can think of federated units as local jurisdictions, or as encompassing a noncontiguous jurisdiction, as providing ways that units relate horizontally more than vertically, or as having different rights and duties. The essay proposes an interpretation of proposals for a bi-national federated political solution to conflict between Israeli Jews and Palestinians as an example of such political imagination.

Understood as nondomination, then, a principle of self-determination both recognizes rights of self-governance, and affirms that such rights entail obligations on the part of self-governing units to respond to claims by outsiders that they are harmed by activities of the unit. Federated institutions need not be conceived as constituting a center whose rules override those of the constituents of a federal system. Instead, they can be designed as regulated practices of negotiation and cooperation among units. With such an understanding of federalism, we can imagine more federated relations among locales and regions in the world quite distinct from any notion of a single global state. The ideas of global, regional, and local governance that I put forward in these essays should not be taken as full-blown political proposals, but rather as critical methods that dislodge unproductive habits of thinking about issues of sovereignty, self-determination, and interdependence.

Global justice and democracy

Democracy at a global level in principle means the same thing that it means at any other level. To the extent that there are and should be institutions of global regulation and governance, their constitution and decisions should be made with the participation of all the world's people. The movement that the media often labels as "antiglobalization" is often called by its participants an "anti-corporate globalization" movement. Many proponents argue that they are not against but in principle for more transnational interaction and cooperation. Their problem is that currently international and multinational institutions are dominated by elite powerful interests, especially transnational capital, and to a significant extent operate in the service of those interests. Of the many public and private institutions that regulate aspects of global interaction, few are democratic in their decision-making structure or spirit.

In the last two decades social movements have created a sporadic global public sphere in which activists demand global democratization and enact it to the extent that they can use their public voices to hold powerful actors to account and sometimes have been able to influence those actions. Activist groups and nongovernmental organizations that conducted large meetings at the sites of several United Nations conferences on environment, human rights, and women's issues helped create and sustain a global public sphere before which state leaders found themselves being held to account. Beginning in the mid-1990s, groups such as 50 Years Is Enough organized opposition to the devastating effects of loan conditionalities imposed on states borrowing from the International Monetary Fund and the World Bank. The Jubilee 2000 movement for debt cancellation and the World Social Forum had some success in raising global popular awareness about international power relations and their effects on the world's poorest people. The calls for cancellation of debts owed by the world's poorest countries have been answered at least in words by international government organizations, such as the G8 nations.

The purpose of appeals to global democracy ought to be to promote justice across the globe. Even official voices today call for policies in which wealthier parts of the world redistribute material resources to address the causes and consequences of the absolute poverty in which hundreds of millions of people live. Issues of global justice concern not only global poverty, but economic inequality more broadly, as well as the fair distribution of risks and responsibilities in addressing global environmental issues, the treatment of refugees and migrants, the differential effects of multinational investment decisions on fragile societies, and the shape of the transnational division of labor. There is no guarantee that wider public discussion of policy issues within and between states, and an increased effective voice for less powerful states and peoples in making decisions about them, will decisively undermine global injustice. The primary reason to democ-ratize global institutions and decision-making, however, is to increase the chances that these decisions will promote global justice.

Issues of global justice concern not only the sites of state policy and international organizations. Voices in the global public sphere direct their demands and criticism also at powerful non-state actors such as multinational corporations. Global civil society can and should be an arena of political, social, and economic contention, and action that undermines injustice. The last essay in this volume, "Responsibility, Social Connection, and Global Labor Justice," reflects on the meaning of one such global justice movement in civil society, the antisweatshop movement. I construe this movement as having made a puzzling claim about responsibility. Activists in North America and Europe have claimed that institutions that sell goods manufactured in facilities with horrible working conditions, often in Asia or Latin America, and consumers who buy them, should take responsibility for criticizing and changing the workers' circumstances. The claim is puzzling because according to most common ideas of responsibility, the far away institutions and consumers have not caused the conditions, and for that reason should not be held respon-sible for them. The appeal to take responsibility has nevertheless apparently resonated with many people who have joined or supported the movement, which has succeeded in shaming some retailers into changing some of their practices and has established nongovernmental and noncorporate monitoring operations.

"Responsibility, Social Connection, and Global Labor Justice" pro-poses a theory of responsibility to correspond to this practice. I dis-tinguish a social con-nection model of responsibility from a more standard model of responsibility, which I call the liability model, as a more appropriate understanding of the responsibility of individual and collective agents in relation to structural injustice. While the focus of this paper is on global justice, I argue that this model of responsibility applies generally to all questions of responsibility in relation to structural injustice.

Conclusion

In response to events of the last two decades, there has been an ex-plosion of political theorizing concerning international relations. The essays in this volume leave many subjects of global justice and democracy untouched. Their particular contribution consists in raising critical questions about three areas where the normative and practical challenges we face are great: humanitarian justifications for war, a properly formulated conception of self-determination as part of ideals of democratic global governance, and ideals of democratic global governance for the sake of promoting justice. I bring to these issues clear alternatives based in, among other things, feminist, indigenous, and workers' rights-inspired perspectives.

Part I

Self-Determination

1

Hybrid Democracy: Iroquois Federalism and the Postcolonial Project

On the eve of the bicentennial of the Constitution, the United States Congress passed a resolution commemorating the influence of the Iroquois Confederacy on the founding institutions. A year later a New York State public school curriculum review panel recommended teaching that the Iroquois system of governance had an impact on the development of the institutions and practices of the State of New York and the United States. These are noble and overdue gestures of recognition of Native Americans. It seems that most historians of the period, however, flatly reject the claim that Indian governance forms influenced the American Constitution. Critics of multiculturalism regularly point the finger at the Iroquois influence claim to demonstrate the mad excesses of the movement. No less a guardian of historical pedagogy than Nathan Glazer, however, asserts that teaching children that Indians contributed to the founding of American institutions may be a good thing even if scholars contest a claim to direct influence on the Constitution.[1] Clearly, passions run high on this question, which splinters American identity itself.

In this essay[2] I situate this debate in the postcolonial project. Anyone interested in justice today must face the project of undoing the legacies of colonialism. Understood as a project, postcoloniality does not name an epoch at which we have arrived, one where colonialism is in the past. On the contrary, precisely because the legacies of colonialism persist, progressive intellectuals and activists should take on the task of undoing their effects. The postcolonial project has an interpretive and institutional aspect. Institutionally, postcoloniality entails creating systems of global democratic governance which can meet the demands of the world's indigenous peoples for self-determination. Because the existing international system of nation-states cannot meet those demands, commitment to justice for indigenous peoples entails calling those states systems into question. In the last two sections of the essay I will review other reasons for questioning the system of state sovereignty, and offer a model of governance based on decentered, diverse, democratic federalism instead. This institutional condition presupposes the interpretive aspect of the postcolonial project. Development of the institutional imagination and commitment to confront the colonial legacy depends partly on rereading the history of modernity, democracy, and the building of nation-states from the point of view of colonized peoples considered as actors and not merely as those acted upon.[3] Drawing on the methods of postcolonial interpretation offered by Homi Bhabha, particularly his notion of "hybridity," I use the Iroquois influence debate as a lens through which to reread some elements of the history of colonial and republican America for the sake of our contemporary self-understanding. Among other things, I find in this rereading an example of the interaction of distinct peoples without sovereign borders that can help us imagine a postsovereign alternative to the existing states system.

Hybridizing historical consciousness

Homi Bhabha suggests that narratives of national identity are predicated on the obligation to forget the multidimensional cultural interaction producing societies and institutions, especially in the colonialist interactions of European peoples with other peoples of the world.

> The anteriority of the nation, signified in the will to forget, entirely changes our understanding of the pastness of the past, and the synchronous present of the will to nationhood. . . . To be obliged to forget – in the construction of the national present – is not a question of historical memory; it is the construction of a discourse on society that *performs* the problem of totalizing the people and unifying the national will.[4]

The postcolonial critic can confront colonial power's disavowal of its situatedness and multiplicity by reinterpreting modern history as *hybrid*. One story of World History describes a lineal progression where universal values of liberty, democracy, technology, and economic development born in Western Europe spread around the world through the power and knowledge of European nations. In this story the colonized peoples of the world usually appear as objects of action, those upon whom the power and influence of the West is exercised, usually for good, sometimes for ill. While the story includes the encounter and conflict of cultures, it does not depict the ideas, practices, institutions, and events of the Europeans as objects of and influenced by the subjectivity of the non-European Others.

Understanding colonial history as hybrid, according to Bhabha, means reversing the linearity of the official story, and allowing "strategies of subversion that turn the gaze of the discriminated back upon the eye of power."[5] Events and institutions in any locale may appear as products of cultural interaction where Europeans are as much influenced as influencing and the temporality and spatiality of action themselves are multidimensional.

> If the effect of colonial power is seen to be the *production* of hybridization rather than the noisy command of colonialist authority or the silent repression of native traditions, then an important change of perspective occurs. The ambivalence at the source of traditional discourses on authority enables a form of subversion, founded on the undecidability that turns the discursive conditions of dominance into the grounds of intervention.[6]

The furnaces of modern national and empire building either absorb cultural difference in their alchemy or expel them. A hybridizing strategy inserts the subjectivity of colonized people into the imperial narrative, allowing the reflective emergence of a "time lag" between the moment of signification and its hearing. History becomes then not the narrative of a single subject or national identity, but the encounter of cultural difference. Neither one nor the Other, the pluralized stories enact intersubjectivity, subjects as relationally constituted, with an interactively constituted world in between.[7] Among other things, this interpretive strategy upsets colonial dualities reiterated still today: self/Other, inside/outside, civilized/savage, citizen/alien, modern/primitive.

Bhabha's ideas are inspired partly by a Lacanian theory of discourse which I do not feel entirely competent to interpret or apply. I do not think that I do his work violence, however, to carry a somewhat simplified version into a reflection on the interaction between indigenous peoples and the thirteen British colonies in North America and the meaning of this interaction for a postcolonial project that can do justice, among other people, to the living descendants of North Ameri-can indigenous people. Hybridizing the story of that relationship, as I see it, involves affirming colonial North America as a terrain of interaction, constructing American subjectivity as ambiguous, and fashioning a relational understanding of government jurisdictions. It could be argued, of course, that indigenous people have always related colonial history as hybrid in this sense. That is one reason to attend to indigenous voices in the effort to generalize a hybrid story to Europeans and their descendants.

Iroquois colonial interaction and the influence thesis

Several contemporary scholars have contributed to the argument that the founders of the political institutions of the United States were influenced by Native American ideas and institutions, including Jack Weatherford, Robert Venables, and José Barreiro.[8] I find the work of Donald Grinde and Bruce Johansen the most comprehensive. Their book, *Exemplar of Liberty*, is both amply documented and the subject of serious criticism by other historians of the period. I rely primarily on it for an account of the relationship between British colonists and Native Americans.[9]

Contact between native peoples and British settlers in North America produced profound changes on both sides. Each group found the others strange, and they made war on each other often enough, but some members of both Native American and colonial groups also learned from and admired the strangers. Roger Williams, for example, learned several Indian languages and much about Indian culture and politics. Grinde and Johansen suggest that this knowledge contributed to Williams's design of the government of Rhode Island in the mid-seventeenth century. While conflict between Indians and colonists erupted repeatedly in the two centuries before the American Revolution, the same epoch also saw widespread cooperation, trade, and treaty negotiation. Colonists felt obliged to reach treaties with Indians about land and resource use, military alliance, and other affairs because they recognized the Indians as well-organized self-governing peoples. Daily life activities were commonly governed by village councils and all group meetings. Many groups of North American Indians were organized into complex confederated governance systems each of which might have included tens of thousands of people inhabiting and moving across vast unbounded territories.

Long before European settlers appeared at the shores of North America, five nations of the Iroquois – Mohawk, Oneida, Onondaga, Cayuga, and Seneca – formed a federation which espoused peace and brotherhood, unity, balance of power, the natural rights of all people, impeachment and removal, and the sharing of resources. (The Tuscarora people joined the confederacy in the eighteenth century.) They developed an open set of decision-making practices that relied on deliberation, public opinion, checks and balances, and consensus.

People in any one of the federated groups might raise an issue to the confederacy, and then the Onondaga chiefs would meet to determine whether the issue should be considered by the Grand Council of the Confederacy. One of the chiefs operated as keeper of the council fire, with the power to call a council. Debate of an issue began with the Mohawk representatives. After they agreed on a position the issue was discussed by the Senecas, and then by the Oneida and Cayuga people. Once the Oneidas and Cayugas reached a position, the issue was discussed again by the Mohawks and the Senecas. Finally the issue was sent back to the Onondaga, who at this stage had a power analogous to judicial review. They could raise objections to a proposal if they believed it was inconsistent with the Great Law of Peace. Iroquois principles included relative equality and participation. Male chiefs were chosen by women leaders, who also had the power to impeach and replace them. When issues were under discussion by the Grand Council the people in the separate regions and villages often engaged in public discussion and debate. The people could propose laws to the council on their own.

What *federalism* meant to the Iroquois, then, was an assumption of self-determination for the member nations at the same time as a commitment to procedural unity with the other five nations and the willingness to have any issue considered for federal decision-making. Indian governance can be considered *democratic*, moreover, at least because of the following attributes: leaders were chosen on merit, although they usually came from designated families; they were expected to respond to public opinion, and in extreme cases could be impeached if they abused their power; issues and policy proposals could come from anywhere in the federation; decision-making relied on deliberation both within and among member nations and included mechanisms of review.

As I read it, Grinde and Johansen construct a broad and a narrow frame for a story of the hybrid constitution of American democracy. While it is not certain how much colonists knew of the details of Iroquois or other Indian governance systems, many did observe Indian meetings and had to adapt to Indian protocol in their trading or treaty negotiation. Some colonists and European visitors described the Indians as living without law because they lacked formally written principles and procedures, and they variously interpreted this as a sign of either backwardness or blissful freedom. Others, however, observed a complex government, and compared Indian oratorical powers to those of the Romans. Some admired the consultation, participation, and search for consensus they observed in Indian decision-making bodies, and some saw in the Iroquois Confederacy the virtues of united strength that preserved a high level of local self-determination.

Grinde and Johansen argue that the agency and political intelligence of Indians had an impact not only on colonists, but also on some of those in the home European countries. Colonists and European visitors wrote detailed ethnographies and travelogues about diverse Indian peoples. While these may not have been terribly accurate in their descriptions of Indian institutions, they were influential in Europe. Some compared Iroquois and other Indian political practices to those of the Greeks, and commented on Indian statecraft and regard for individual autonomy. John Locke constructed his image of the state of nature partly with the lives of these native peoples in mind; that state is one without civil society, on Locke's account, but also one of natural liberty and the light of natural reason. Enlightenment fathers of modern constitutionalism and democracy such as Montesquieu and Rousseau constructed their romanticized fantasies of Indian lives in their effort to promote ideas of liberty and equality and criticize the corruption and subjection of European societies. In "Huron, or Pupil of Nature," for example, Voltaire, the prerevolutionary French republican, put a scathing critique of French aristocracy and hypocracy into the mouth of a Huron leader. In the broad frame of Grinde and Johansen's story, then, the Enlightenment political philosophers that influenced the American founders to establish a democratic republic were themselves conditioned by real and imagined interaction with Native Americans.

Grinde and Johansen argue that independence-minded colonists looked to Indian imagery and practices in their project of distancing their loyalty from England and developing the symbols of patriotic American loyalty. By the time of the American Revolution, many British colonists had only a distant feeling for England. By examining engravings and paintings, as well as records of patriotic societies, and written accounts of revolutionary meetings and rallies, Grinde and Johansen document the significant degree to which the British colonists sought to construct an American national identity through the use of Indian imagery.

The rebels of the Boston Tea Party dressed as Indians less in order to disguise themselves, Grinde and Johansen argue, than to signify their assertion of liberty. Pamphlets and banners during the revolutionary and republican period repeatedly used images of Indians or symbols derived from Indian visual art to signify American freedom, equality, and democratic self-government. The famous snake of the New Hampshire flag is an original Indian symbol, for example, as is the eagle grasping a cluster of arrows that appears on the dollar bill of the United States. Most conspicuous in this story of Euro-American appropriation of Indian imagery, however, are the Tammany societies. Founded as a secret brotherhood of revolutionary patriots, these clubs took their name from a Delaware leader. Their "meetings" frequently consisted of these Euro-Americans dressing as Indians, singing songs and dancing in their own fashion "as" Indians, and pledging their loyalty to the American republic. The Tammany societies continued as patriotic associations until well into the nineteenth century.

The more narrow story that Grinde and Johansen construct of an influence of the Iroquois Confederacy on the evolution of American political institutions goes like this. The British colonists relied on support of Indians in their military confrontations with the French in the mid-eighteenth century. At a treaty meeting in 1744 the Iroquois leader Canassteago recommended to the colonists that they form a federation of their governments, as the Iroquois people had done. An admirer of the Iroquois people and their federation, Benjamin Franklin published a report of this meeting, including this speech, which was widely distributed. Ten years later the Seneca leader Tryonoga, also called Hendrick, attended the conference in Albany where the British colonies drew up their first Plan of Union. Benjamin Franklin was one of the main designers of the Albany Plan.

While the Continental Congress sat in Philadelphia in 1775 and 1776, delegations of Iroquois came to observe and delegations of colonists went to meet with the Iroquois several times. The emerging Euro-American nation sought and received a pledge of neutrality from the Iroquois in their war with Britain. During many meetings the colonists discussed political and economic affairs with these and other Indian groups.

On Grinde and Johansen's account, the Articles of Confederacy which were adopted by the Continental Congress had an earlier iteration in the Albany Plan of Union, which in turn was influenced by the Iroquois Great Law of Peace. When they debated what provisions the new Constitution of the United States should contain, the American revolutionaries discussed ideas of the Iroquois federation among others. John Adams, for example, included a discussion of Indian political institutions in his comprehensive survey of governments of the world. Adams urged the framers of the Constitution to study

Indian governance systems thoroughly. Some speeches to the Continental Congress in the years leading up to the passage of the Constitution invoked Iroquois ideas and imagery. Thus, Grinde and Johansen claim that the ideas and practices of Iroquois federalism had an indirect influence on the founding, as one of the many streams that flowed into the American democratic current.

Critics of the claim that American political institutions have a hybrid history focus almost exclusively on the claim that specific elements of the final US Constitution can be directly or indirectly traced to the Iroquois Great Law of Peace. These critics appear to take the historical question to be: did some or many of the representatives to the Constitutional Congress have the structure or procedures of the Iroquois Confederacy in mind when they debated about the structures and procedures of the United States? Whatever the founders knew of the Indian governance systems, they argue, this knowledge had next to nothing to do with their debates. Some of those who seemed to mention Iroquois institutions positively such as John Adams, moreover, were on the losing side of the federalist debate. While Benjamin Franklin may have thought well of Iroquois political institutions and these may have influenced his writing of the Albany Plan of Union, that Plan was merely a military alliance and not the constitution of a full-blown government. The founders were most influenced by European ideas, the critics assert, including European models of federation. I agree with the critics in this debate that there seems little reason to say that those who voted into law the Constitution of the United States were directly influenced by the design of the Iroquois Federation.[10] Debating that particular question, however, seems to me rather beside the point. The more important issue is whether the American settlers and their descendants eventuating in the generation of the Founders had their views of freedom and the possibilities of self-rule partly shaped by their interaction with and study of native peoples. On this point the record seems clear: the influence of this interaction is strong.

In light of the strong disagreement over whether and how to assign influence of Native American governance systems in the formation of the United States Constitution, it is surprising that the two sides appear to agree on so many other claims. There is little question, for example, that from the time of first settlement many Europeans had significant contact with Native Americans, learned much about their ways of life, and that perhaps as many admired them as feared or loathed them. In many regions of North America British and French settlers, along with African slaves, created a hybrid society from the complex encounter of very different cultures.[11] Not an insignificant number of Europeans joined Indian groups over the course of the two centuries before the American founding, and not an insignificant number of Indians adopted European dress, language, and ways of living, and some were educated in colonial or European institutions of higher learning. Colonists and British officials negotiated hundreds of treaties with Indian groups, evidence that the Europeans regarded Indians with a certain level of respect, even as in many cases they succeeded in manipulating the treaty process to their own advantage. One of the most adamant critics of the claim that the Iroquois Federation influenced the US Constitution, Elisabeth Tooker, nevertheless agrees that at the time of seeking independence from England the colonists looked to images of Indians to help inspire commitment to independence and nation-building. Treaty and other diplomatic negotiations between colonies and Indians indicate that each regarded the others as distinct political formations, but unified sovereign states in the modern sense did not exist on the continent.[12] Among other things, the founding of the United States of America began the process of creating such a modern unified sovereign state, a process which spelled disaster for the Indians.[13]

Most of the scholarly and journalistic reaction to work like that of Grinde and Johansen focuses on the truth or falsity of the Iroquois influence thesis. That focus, it seems to me, avoids the importance of the account that Grinde and Johansen make and the evidence they supply of the hybrid play of political ideas and symbols running between Native Americans and Europeans and colonists. From the perspective of a hybrid interpretation of colonial history, and for the purposes of the argument for a postsovereignty global democratic polity that I will make below, I summarize the significance of work like that of Grinde and Johansen as follows. By proposing that Indians served for American revolutionaries as exemplars of liberty, Grinde and Johansen deconstruct the modern Western discourse which positions the Native Americans as the excluded Other in comparison with which the Europeans confirmed their cultural superiority. On this hybrid interpretation, the Indians regard the Europeans as obsequious servants to distant lords and social conventions, while they know freedom. On this interpretation, Native Americans stand for an alternative to monarchist European structures, an alternative internalized in a plural European–American discourse.

Even if evidence does not support the claim that the Iroquois Federation directly and in specifics influenced the evolution of American government, the *question* of a relationship between the Iroquois government and the United States government remains important for the way it hybridizes the idea of democracy. Many people in

European or European-settled countries implicitly and sometimes explicitly construct democracy as a specifically Western value. In their struggle for independence and self-determination some colonized and formerly colonized peoples of Africa and Asia themselves promulgate the claim that democracy is a specifically European set of institutions not appropriate to truly independent non-Western states. If democracy means institutions of formal legislatures, elected by citizens in a multiparty competition, a system of administrative bureaucracies to apply the laws, and a system of courts to interpret and enforce them, then democracy is a specifically modern and Western invention. But even the Western lineage of democracy is not confined to this image. Athenian democracy, for example, for centuries romanticized as the most authentic of all democracies, fits this description in almost no respect. By asking the question, in what ways are the ideas and practices of American democracy similar to the governance system of the Iroquois Federation, we pluralize our possible understandings of democracy. In today's search for new human possibilities of self-government, participation, and societal cooperation, we ought to look to Indian governance practices, some of which have a living legacy in contemporary government institutions of indigenous North and South Americans, among other indigenous peoples. Nor is it absurd for new democracies in Africa to reflect on some traditional village practices as alternatives to modern Western forms of democracy that offer resources for forging postcolonial African democracies.[14] Iroquois institutions in particular valued deliberation, an orientation to collective problem solving, and local self-governance in the context of a strong federation. Contemporary democratic theory is much occupied with each of these democratic values, and in the next section I will elaborate on the last. The project of rethinking democracy for a postcolonial age, I am suggesting, benefits from a hybrid vision of the history of societies and governments that refuses the traditional/modern, savage/civilized dichotomies.

The Iroquois influence debate encourages a popular reinterpretation of European Americans as not only the agents of American history, but also as those in relation to whom Native Americans have acted. In this hybrid mode, when we think of American society and identity as a product of the interaction of Native and European cultures, the very meaning of being American becomes decentered and relational. I shall argue that such a relational and decentered notion of subjectivity and polity contributes to reconceptualizing self-determination and global governance.

The story of interaction between settlers and indigenous people in the mid and late eighteenth century in America, finally, provides a concrete image of federated and political interaction among distinctly identifying groups without the developed centralizing and disciplinary institutions of the modern nation-state. While the postcolonial project does not advocate recreating such plural intercultural conditions, it can learn from them. Mid-eighteenth-century America was the site of a bloody war of sovereign supremacy between two European states, France and England, affecting both Indians and colonists. In the midst of the conditions of war, however, the thirteen colonies conducted negotiated interaction with each other and with diverse Indian governments. The Indian peoples had complex negotiated and federated interactions with one another as well.

The Great Law of Peace spelled out a complex set of rules for deci- sion-making about those matters members of the federation thought concerned them all, such as war and peace or territorial dispute. These rules were designed in part to ensure the equality and contin- ued autonomy of the federation members as they participated in the wider decisions. Other Indian peoples on the continent also thought of themselves as self-governing, and many participated in other fed- erated relationships. At this time, each of the thirteen colonies had its own system of governance; the seat of government of each was quite far from the others, and settlers outside the cities were quite dispersed. While colonists and Indians considered themselves as dwelling in distinct territories, there were no strict borders separat- ing them. Instead, the places where jurisdiction was clear shaded into wider borderlands of common use and sometimes dispute. Colonial territories, moreover, might be "within" Indian territories and vice versa. Some of the Lenni Lenape (or Delaware), for example, dwelt on either side of some of the settlements of the Commonwealth of Pennsylvania. So it was with the Seneca and the Pennsylvanians and the New Yorkers. Under these circumstances of territorial ambiguity, political autonomy, relative equality of power and interfusion, coop- erative relations among the Indian groups, the colonial groups, and between Indians and colonial groups, when they existed, relied on dialogue and negotiation.

I do not wish to romanticize the relations among native peoples of this period, or between the native peoples and the European- descended settlers. Then as now, there was plenty of violence, exploitation, and corruption in intergroup affairs. The point is only to find in the past grounds for bracketing ossified assumptions about jurisdiction, governance, and the relation of self-determining peoples. To the extent that indigenous peoples and other peoples who reject the state sovereignty model of government today live out this recollection in their current governance and intercultural relations, these grounds may also lie in the present.

Moral challenges to sovereignty

The postcolonial project begins after World War II, when one after another the international community of states recognized new sovereign states in the territories of former European colonies. The borders of many of these states were relatively arbitrarily drawn, often gathering peoples who considered themselves distinct under the rule of one state dominated by one of the groups. It can be argued that much of the violence on the Asian and African continents is traceable to this process of sovereign state creation. Ideals and practices of a global regime constituted by sovereign states, however, are coming under increasing normative and practical challenge.

As I discussed earlier, an institutional aspect of the postcolonial project consists in conceiving and bringing about a postsovereignty global governance system. The legitimate claims of indigenous peoples today for self-determination cannot be fully met within the existing system of global governance that assumes the nation-state as the primary international actor. Consonant with these claims, we need to envision a more federated system of global governance with both stronger global regulation than currently exists and more regional and cultural autonomy. Before sketching some principles for such a global federated democracy, I will review some other reasons for challenging the principle of sovereignty in international affairs.

I distinguish the concept of sovereignty from that of *state* institutions. States are public authorities that regulate the activities of those within their jurisdictions through legal and administrative institutions backed by the power to sanction. While only states can be sovereign, they need not be, and many strong state institutions currently exist at a jurisdictional level lower than sovereign states. State institutions are capable of being subject to review or override without losing their status as states. They can share jurisdiction with other states, and their jurisdiction need not encompass all the activities in a territory.

A *sovereign* state wields central and final authority over all the legal and political matters within a determinate and strictly bounded territory.[15] Sovereignty entails a clear distinction between inside and outside. Within a sovereign state there are often partial and lesser governments and jurisdictions, but the sovereign government exercises a higher and final authority over them. The sovereignty of the state is partially constituted by the states outside it, moreover, who recognize it as a legitimate sovereign state. This recognition entails a principle of nonintervention; for a state to have final authority implies that no other state and no transnational body has the authority to interfere with the actions and policies of sovereign state.[16]

Some writers claim that states today no longer have sovereignty in the sense I define here, and perhaps never did. It is questionable, that is, whether states today really exercise centrally coordinated power that is systematically connected over domains of government, and that they exercise it as a final authority. State power today, some claim, is in fact much more fragmentary and limited than the commitment to sovereignty would have one believe.[17] Whatever the factual situation of state powers, however, the *idea* of sovereignty still carries much weight among political leaders and scholars, regarding the relation of states to both internal organization and jurisdictions, and international relations. Many today continue to believe that states *ought* to be sovereign, and that, to the degree that their sovereignty is under challenge or in a process of fragmentation, steps should be taken to reinforce a system of strong sovereign states. Others disagree, and promote either internal devolution or the external evolution of transnational authorities. I shall argue that a principle of state sovereignty lacks moral legitimacy, regarding both external and internal affairs.

External challenges

Considerations of global justice call into question the legitimacy of claims by states that they alone have the right to attend to affairs within their borders and have no obligations to peoples outside their borders. Charles Beitz, Thomas Pogge, and Onora O'Neill, among others, argue that there are no privileged grounds for limiting the scope of evaluations of justice to relations between people within nation-states. Moral evaluation of social relations in terms of justice and injustice apply wherever social institutions connect people in a causal web. To the extent that people assume the actions of distant others as background to their own, they stand with them in relations of justice. The scope and complexity of economic, communication, and many other institutions in the world today constitute a sufficiently tight web of constraint and interdependence today that we must speak of a global *society*.[18] Principles of justice apply to relations among persons, organizations, and state institutions in diverse reaches of global society. These claims of justice constitute a double challenge to the moral boundaries of states. Agents outside of states have some claim to judge and regulate the activities of states over affairs within their jurisdictions, on the one hand; states and their members, on the other hand, have obligations to people outside their borders. Considerations of economic regulation, human rights intervention, environmental protection, and migration are among those that raise profound issues of justice that challenge sovereignty in this double way.

The principle of sovereignty gives to states the right and power to regulate for the benefit of their own members. States ought positively to pursue economic gain for their own citizens at the expense of other people in the world if necessary, so long as they do not forcefully invade and conquer the territories of other sovereign states. They have the right to exclude persons from entry into their territory in order to preserve the privileged access their members have to resources and benefits there. States or their citizens owe no general obligation to others outside, whatever their needs or level of relative deprivation. Any efforts states or their members make to help needy people elsewhere in the world are superogatory.

Several moral arguments can be offered against this view of the right of nonintervention in states' policies and their right to be indifferent to the circumstances of those outside their borders. Charles Beitz questions the moral right of states to keep for themselves all the benefits derived from the natural resources that happen to lie within their borders. Resources such as fertile land, economically valuable minerals, and so on, are by no means evenly distributed about the globe. Because the placement of resources is morally arbitrary, no state is entitled to treat them as its private property to be used only for its own benefit. Because certain resources are necessary for the productive capacity of all societies, they must be considered a global commons. Their use and the benefits of their use should thus be globally regulated under a cooperative framework of global justice.[19]

The global resources argument is one example of a challenge to the sovereignty claim that outside agents have no claim to regulate the actions of states over activities that take place within their jurisdiction. The state of production, finance, and communications in the world has evolved in such a way that many actions and policies internal to a state nevertheless sometimes have profound effects on others in the world. A moral challenge to a principle of nonintervention has come most obviously from environmental concern. States' internal forestry policies, their kind and level of industrial pollution regulation, and similar policies produce consequences for the air quality and climate of many outside their borders. Economic and communicative interdependence, moreover, generate certain international moral claims over other kinds of internal policies. Financial policies of the German or Japanese states, for example, can seriously affect the stability of many other economies. Such interdependencies as these call for some form of international regulatory scheme that aims for stable and just cooperation.

Many argue, furthermore, that current distributive inequality across the globe raises questions of justice that require a globally enforced redistributive regime. The fact that some peoples live in wasteful affluence while many more in other parts of the world suffer from serious deprivation itself stands as prima facie ground for global redistribution. But these facts of distributive inequality alone do not make a very strong case for global economic regulation. More important is the history of dependence and exploitation between the now poor and now rich regions of the world, and the continuance of institutional structures that perpetuate and even help enlarge global privilege and deprivation. Many scholars argue that the current wealth of Europe and North America compared to societies of Africa, Latin America, and South Asia is due to a significant degree to the colonial relations among these regions whereby the former looted the latter for three centuries. While the poorer regions of the world today are composed of independent states with the same formal sovereignty rights as any other states, many argue that the colonial economic relations between North and South persist.[20] The economies of the South depend on capital investment controlled from the North and most of whose profits return to the North. Their workers are often too poorly paid by multinationals or their local contractors to feed their families, and farmers and miners of the South obtain very unfavorable prices on a global resource market. Such deprivation has forced most governments of the Southern Hemisphere into severe debt to Northern banks and to international finance agencies such as the World Bank. This indebtedness severely restricts the effective sovereignty of Southern states, because powerful financial institutions have effective power to control their internal economic policies, all for the sake of preserving the existing system of international trade and finance and the benefits it brings primarily to some in the North.

The issue is not simply distributive inequality, and that some people in some parts of the world are seriously deprived while others in other parts of the world live very well. Rather, the global institutional context sets different regions in relations of dependence and exploitation with others, and this institutional system reproduces and

arguably widens the distributive inequalities. Redress of unjust deprivation and regulation of the global economy for the sake of promoting greater justice thus calls for institutional change, and not merely
a one-time or periodic transfer of wealth from richer to poorer
people.

In the absence of such institutional change, many question the
moral right of states to limit immigration. According to Joseph
Carens, for example, excluding people from a relatively rich country,
which people wish to enter from elsewhere in order to better their
lives, is little different from the preservation of a feudal privilege. By
the mechanism of immigration control, people whose privilege
derives from birth are able to protect that privilege from encroach-
ment by others who happen to have been born elsewhere.[21]

Internal challenges

Internally, the idea of sovereignty entails that a state has ultimate
authority to regulate all the activities taking place within a specific
territorial jurisdiction. This often seems to mean, by implication,
that the same form of law, regulation, and administration ought to
apply to all the peoples and locales within the territory. Both these
aspects of internal sovereignty are morally questionable, however,
because they do not sufficiently recognize and accommodate the
rights and needs of national and cultural minorities. Political recognition for distinct peoples entails that they are able to practice
their culture and that they can affirm their own public culture in
which to express and affirm their distinctness. To the degree that
peoples are distinct, moreover, they have prima facie rights of self-
governance. These points entail that peoples who dwell with others
within a wider polity nevertheless limit the sovereignty of that wider
polity over their activities.[22] The limitation of sovereign authority of
a wider polity over groups and locales may vary in kind or degree,
from local or group-based autonomy over nearly all affairs, to self-
governance over only a small range of issues, such as family law or
the management and utilization of particular resources. As those
examples indicate, moreover, local self-determination may vary
according to whether it is legislative or administrative or both.
Despite the strong claims of most states to be sovereign over all the
activities in a territory, the sovereign power of many states today is
already limited or restricted in many ways that recognize or accommodate national, cultural, and religious differences within their
claimed jurisdictions.[23]

Many of these challenges come from indigenous peoples. Most of the world's indigenous peoples claim rights of self-determination against the states that claim sovereign authority over them. These claims are difficult or impossible for states organized in the existing states system to accommodate, because they involve claims about the rights to use land and resources, and the right to develop governance practices continuous with precolonial indigenous practices, which are often at odds with the more formal and bureaucratic governance systems of modern European law. The struggles of most indigenous peoples for culture rights and self-determination reveal asymmetries between the indigenous peoples' societies and the European societies that colonized them. This cultural and institutional clash continues to provoke many states to repress and oppress the indigenous peoples.

Despite unjust conquest and continued oppression, however, few indigenous peoples seek sovereignty for themselves in the sense of the formation of an independent, internationally recognized state with ultimate authority over all matters within a determinately bounded territory. Most indigenous peoples seek significantly greater and more secure self-determination within the framework of a wider polity.[24] Most seek explicit recognition as distinct peoples by the states that claim to have jurisdiction over them, and wider terms of autonomy and negotiation with those states and with the other peoples living within those states. They claim or seek significant self-government rights, not only with respect to cultural issues, but with respect to land and access to resources. They claim to have rights to be distinct political entities with which other political entities, such as states, must negotiate agreements and over which they cannot simply impose their will and their law.

Roger Maaka and Augie Fleras detail one model of such indigenous self-determination in the context of a wider polity, which they refer to as "soft" sovereignty.[25] They explicitly eschew a notion of sovereignty as noninterference, and instead articulate a model of the relations of distinct peoples in which they engage with one another as equals on an ongoing basis.[26]

Indigenous peoples remain colonized people. Despite the locality of their claims, they have forged a global social movement which has achieved significant success in the past two decades in gaining recognition for the legitimacy of their claims. In some regions of the world they have had some successes in motivating some social and political changes to accommodate their needs and interests. Properly recognizing the claims of indigenous peoples today, however, requires challenging the international system of sovereign states. Indigenous peoples world-wide have long been aware of the incompatibility of their claims to justice with the concept of state sovereignty that predominates in international relations. Especially in the last two decades, they have organized across different parts of the world, and have succeeded to some extent in having the uniqueness of their claims recognized by international bodies such as the World Court and the United Nations. Their social movements have prompted some reforms in the policies of some states that claim to have jurisdiction over them. Despite these successes, many nation-states continue to repress indigenous movements. Their accommodation to indigenous demands for self-determination requires a degree of institutional change that most states are unwilling to allow, especially if other states in the international system are not doing so. Thus, indigenous peoples' movements are both a source of ideas and action beyond the system of sovereign states, and at the same time show the limits of that system.[27]

Decentered diverse democratic federalism

I have argued that the postcolonial project entails envisioning governance without sovereignty, partly because the predominant meaning of sovereignty cannot be kept in place and justice also be done to indigenous people. With some others who question the sovereignty principle, I suggest that we can draw some inspiration for an imagination of the future of global governance from the past before states as we know them had fully evolved. In particular, I have suggested that a revaluation of the meaning of Native American federated governance and the pre-state relations of colonists and Native Americans aids this project.[28]

While many share the criticisms of the system of sovereign states that I have summarized, they assume that we must continue to work within that system because we lack alternatives. In this concluding section I sketch a vision of global governance with local self-determination that I call, in accordance with its major principles, *decentered diverse democratic federalism*. This vision should not be construed as a proposal for concrete institutional design, but rather as a set of principles that social movements and policy makers should keep in mind in their work. In articulating the vision I draw on the work of Gerald Frug, David Held, and James Tully, among others.

A long-time advocate of increasing powers of local governance in the United States, Gerald Frug points out that most concepts of decentralized democracy assume what he calls a centered subject.

They assume that a unit of government, whether a state or a locale, is an independent, bounded jurisdiction with sole authority over matters in its purview. Most visions of decentralized democracy, that is, implicitly transfer the idea of sovereignty from nation-states to smaller units. Such a concept of the centered subject, however, is problematic at any level. Despite the interdependence I alluded to above, this concept of autonomy tries clearly to separate a realm of our business from an outside realm that is none of our business, and where outsiders should mind their own business and leave us alone.

Certain feminist and postcolonial theories question this "sovereign self," and propose to substitute the notion of a relational self which recognizes the constitution of selves by interaction with others and their interdependencies.[29] In the theory of a relational self, freedom or autonomy does not consist in separation and independence from others, or complete control over a self-regarding sphere of activity in which others have no right to interfere. Instead, on the relational account, a subject is autonomous if it has effective control over its own sphere of action and influence over the determination of the conditions of its action, either individually or with others in collective decision-making processes.

Frug proposes to extend this ideal of the relational self and the *decentered* subject to the empowerment of local government. Instead of assuming that decentralized units must be centered, bounded, and separated from their neighbors in self-regarding and self-interested pursuit of local well-being, he proposes that more empowered localities should be understood as situated subjects. While locales or other units are or ought to be self-determining, at the same time we should recognize that the web of global, national, and regional interactions draws all of us into relationships such that actions or events in one locale often have profound consequences for others, and that much about our local context is constituted by our relationship to those outside. While local and regional self-determination are important values, no jurisdiction ought to be sovereign. To reflect this, Frug calls for strong federated and negotiated regional governments in which local governments and their citizens directly participate.[30] I propose to extend this principle of federalism to the relationship between peoples at both regional and global levels.

The first element in a vision of global democracy, then, is local self-determination, but without sovereign borders. I take the claims of self-determination within the context of a wider polity made by many indigenous peoples as a model of what such local governance might mean. Regions, peoples, even nongovernmental organizations can each be thought of as having claims to self-determination, but none ought to be sovereign. This means rejecting a conception of self-governance as noninterference, clearly separating a realm of our business from a realm outside that is none of our business, and where those outside must keep out of our business. Whether at the level of individual persons, locales, local regions, nations, or continents, self-determination subsidiarity decisions should be made and carried out at the most local level possible. Others have a right to make a claim to be party to a decision and its execution, or to review them, only if they can show that the issue and decision materially affect them. When issues and actions are thus mutually affecting, parties should make the decision together. Thus a principle of self-determination, as distinct from the principle of sovereignty, gives prima facie right of noninterference with participatory rights in collective decision-making in those many cases when the prima facie autonomy is justifiably overridden.

Thus, with David Held,[31] Thomas Pogge, and others, I envision a principle of local self-determination enacted in the context of global governance structures. Both international distributive justice and self-determination would be better served by more global central-ization of some of the powers that supposedly sovereign states cur-rently have, and at the same time more regional and local control at the level below that of current nation-states. While these may sound like contrary goals, the experience of some groups within the Euro-pean union, for example, offers some grounds for thinking that more global regulation can enable more local control as compared with the current states system. Locales can relate directly to global authorities in order to challenge and limit the ability of nation-states to control them. I imagine a global system of regulatory regimes to which locales, regions, and states relate in a nested, federated system. The global level of governance is "thin," in the sense that it only lays down rather general principles with which all jurisdictions must comply. Interpretation and application of the principles, as well as any governance issues that do not come under the principles, are left to local jurisdictions. Public administration, according to this vision, is local and regional, which is to say that each locale has the power to decide for itself how it complies with the general regulatory principles.

My purpose is not to design global governance institutions, but only to set out and argue for a few principles of postcolonial gover-nance. In that spirit, I envision at this "thin" level of global gover-nance seven kinds of issues about which moral respect and international justice would seem to call for a global regulatory regime: (1) peace and security, (2) environment, (3) trade and finance,

(4) investment and capital utilization, (5) communications and transportation, (6) human rights, including labor standards and welfare rights, and (7) citizenship and the movement of peoples.[32] Each of these issue areas already has an evolving regime of international law which could be built upon to create a global regime with greater enforcement strength and resources for carrying out its purpose. For the most part, however, states are the subject of what international regulation exists. An important aspect of decentering governance through global regulatory regimes would consist in making at least some of the activities of non-state organizations, such as indigenous groups, municipalities, corporations, non-profit service associations, and individuals directly addressed in global regulation, with state, regional, and local governments serving as the tools of implementation.

I do not envision a single sovereign government – a world state – which legislates regulation in these areas. I share with many others a fear and suspicion of the very idea of a single centralized government entity on a global scale. At a global level more than any other a principle of the separation of powers is vital. Thus, I imagine that each regulatory regime has a functional jurisdiction legally separate from those of the others, each with its own regulative function. Each provides a thin set of general rules that specify ways that individuals, organizations, and governments are obliged to take account of the interests and circumstances of one another. The visionary founders of the United Nations hoped that its institutions would evolve this way, and some of these institutions would still have the potential to do so if they had the support of most of the world's governments and their people.

Held imagines global governance with nested levels of jurisdiction. Government would start with the presumption that an issue or conflict should be dealt with in locales or in associations not territorially based. If conflict is not resolved or if additional agents have a legitimate stake in the issue, then the governance structure would kick up to a more comprehensive level, and so on to a level of global judgment and regulation. Within such a nested set of governance relationships there would be no reason to eliminate that level of organization now called the nation-state. The uniformity, centrality, and final authority of that level, however, would be seriously altered. Decentered federalism allows sovereignty at no level. While there is a presumption of local or associational self-determination, outsiders have a right to claim that they are affected by a unit's or agent's business, and problems and conflicts should be worked out through federated democratic negotiations and decision-making that create larger units.

With Held, I envision regimes of global federation as *democratic*. Some might regard this as the most farfetched of all the elements in the vision. To the degree that more global coordination and negotiation occurs today transcending the level of existing states, most are deeply undemocratic. The growing global power of private corporations and financial institutions is explicitly undemocratic. The tribunals of international law have few channels of democratic accountability. Scholars and journalists bemoan the "democratic deficit" they observe in the operations of today's most complex and thoroughly developed transnational governance body, the European Union. Most of its policies have been developed and implemented by a relatively small group of state-based elites, with little or no opportunity for the participation of ordinary citizens and locales.[33] Especially because of the power and structure of the Security Council, the United Nations is not a democratic institution. Some might claim that at this level democratic participation and accountability is simply not possible.

Of course, there are huge questions of institutional design for making decentered global federalism democratic, and I cannot begin to address those. At the level of vision, here are some things to bear in mind. First, one of the reasons to insist on localism, the devolution of sovereign authority onto more local units, is to promote democracy. Participation and citizenship are always enacted best at a local level. Democratic federated regimes of global regulation, however, do require institutions of representation and policy deliberation at levels far removed from the local. A global environmental regulatory decision-making body would not need to be any *more* removed from ordinary citizens than national legislatures currently are. For once we move beyond a local level, any polity – national, hemispheric, or global – is an "imagined community" whose interests and problems must be discursively constructed as involving everyone, because people do not have experience of most of the others in the polity. This problem is no greater for transnational and global regulation than it is for the existing nation-state. Institutions of representation must be constructed with mechanisms of popular and public accountability in regional and global regimes. Postcolonial possibilities of transportation and communication, finally, enable the formation of public spheres composed of active citizens in global civil society. By means of strong local organization, ordinary citizens have organized knowledgeable and obstreperous civic publics around many major international treaty negotiations and policy conferences in the last decade.

With James Tully, finally, I envision decentered democratic global federalism as *diverse*. In *Strange Multiplicity* Tully looks to premodern political and legal relations to fuel our imagination on alternative legal discourses and institutions.[34] As I have done earlier in this essay, he reflects on the hybrid moment of intercultural communication between indigenous peoples and Europeans on the North American continent before the emergence of nation-states. Aboriginal peoples were able to approach the European settlers to negotiate treaties and agreements in part because they had long histories of dealings with other aboriginal peoples whom they recognized as distinct, and had institutions and practices for negotiating arrangements of cooperation and accommodation (as well as fierce institutions of war when they chose not to accommodate or cooperation broke down). Tully extrapolates three "constitutional conventions" from this example of treaty constitutionalism, which he believes can be generalized as ideals for a postcolonial politics: mutual recognition, consent, and continuity. Parties to negotiation on terms of cooperation and joint regulation must first mutually recognize one another as distinct but not closed political entities, with their own interests, modes of discourse, and ways of looking at the world. In their negotiations they do not seek once and for all agreement on a general set of principles, but rather they seek to reach agreement on issues of distribution or institutional organization on particular matters of contention or uncertainty. In the process of negotiated interaction they maintain continuity with their pasts, each party's distinctness is affirmed, they seek to maintain continuity with previous agreements, and to forge new links with new agreements that will have some lasting effect, though they are always also revisable by means of new negotiations.

Tully describes what emerges from such a process of interaction and negotiation among distinct groups as "diverse federalism." The local groups join together in federated arrangements which may be quite large and govern many aspects of societal life. As a federation, however, they maintain strong presumption of local or group-based self-governance. The federated relation to wider legal arrangements is diverse in several respects. A polity in the mode of diverse federalism publicly recognizes the diversity of peoples, ways of life, modes of thinking, and forms of self-government that make it up. When units of the federated polity dialogue and negotiate about matters of interactive or joint concern, they do not assume a single common idiom of discussion, a self of common premises, or a single common way of expressing themselves. Instead, they try to be open to the diverse discourses and assumptions of one another in order to understand how they are similar and how different. The relationships in which the diverse units and groups stand to the federation, finally, are not necessarily uniform. Agreements and regulations may apply to different units in different ways and degrees, or indeed, some may not apply at all.

The postcolonial project entails, I have suggested, challenging the linearity of Western history and recognizing the history of both the colonizers and the colonized as hybrid. Most places, institutions, practices, are constituted through intercultural interaction without a bounded self. Politically, the postcolonial project entails recognition of the claims of indigenous peoples today for self-determination and challenges the existing international system which, by means of the institutions of state sovereignty, preserves privileges for people in the North at the expense of those in the South. I have sketched some ideas of decentered democratic diverse federalism as a system of global governance with local self-determination as an alternative to that states system.

2

Two Concepts of Self-Determination

In a speech he gave before a 1995 meeting of the Open-Ended Inter-Sessional Working Group on Indigenous Peoples' Rights established in accordance with the United Nations Commission on Human Rights, Craig Scott appealed to a meaning of self-determination as relationship and connection rather than its more common understanding as separation and independence.

> If one listens, one can often hear the message that the right of a people to self-determination is not a right for peoples to determine their status without consideration of the rights of other peoples with whom they are presently connected and with whom they will continue to be connected in the future. For we must realize that peoples, no less than individuals, exist and thrive only in dialogue with each other. Self-determination necessarily involves engagement with and responsibility to others (which includes responsibility for the implications of one's preferred choices for others). . . . We need to begin to think of self-determination in terms of peoples existing in relationship with each other. It is the process of negotiating the nature of such relationships which is part of, indeed at the very core of, what it means to be a self-determining people.[1]

Scott's plea is very suggestive, but he neither develops a critical account of the concept of self-determination from which he distinguishes his own, nor does he explain the meaning, justification, and implications of the concept he proposes. In this essay[2] I articulate these two interpretations of a principle of the self-determination of peoples, and argue for a relational interpretation along the lines that Scott proposes. Like Scott, my motive in this conceptual work is to contribute to an understanding of the specific claims of indigenous peoples to self-determination. I believe the concept of self-determination I advocate, however, applies to all peoples and relationships among peoples.

First I briefly review the current status of a principle of self-determination in international law and recent developments of indigenous peoples. Then I elaborate the historically dominant interpretation of a principle of self-determination for peoples, which continues to hold the minds of many who write on the subject. This concept of self-determination equates it with sovereign independence, where the self-determining entity claims a right of nonintervention and noninterference. Drawing particularly on feminist critiques of a concept of the autonomy of the person as independence and noninterference, I argue that this first concept of self-determination ignores the relations of interdependence peoples have with one another, especially in a global economic system. Again following the lead of feminist theories of autonomy, I argue for a relational concept of the self-determination of peoples. I draw on Philip Pettit's theory of freedom as nondomination to argue that peoples can be self-determining only if the relations in which they stand to others are nondominating. To ensure nondomination, their relations must be regulated both by institutions in which they all participate and by ongoing negotiations among them.

Self-determination and international politics

Neither the United Nations Charter nor the 1948 Declaration of Human Rights mentions a right of self-determination. The General Assembly resolution 1541 appears to be the origin of the post-World War II discourse of self-determination. Passed with the project of decolonization in view, that resolution defines self-government as entailing either independence, free association with an independent state, or the integration of a people with an independent state on the basis of equality. It implicitly entails the "salt water" test for ascertaining whether a people deserves recognition of their right to self-determination: they have a distinct territory separated by long global distances from a colonial power from which they claim independence. Recognition of self-determination in these cases entails recognition of separate independent sovereign states if that is what the former colonies wish.

Between the era of postcolonial independence and the early 1990s the international community showed great reluctance to apply a principle of self-determination to disputes among peoples in territorial contiguity. In two decades fewer than ten new states were established and recognized under such a principle. As international law on human rights has evolved, some scholars argue that many of the issues of freedom and self-governance that people in the world raise can be treated under individual human rights principles, without invoking a collective principle of self-determination – such as rights of minorities against discrimination and persecution, rights to participate in the governance of the state, rights of cultural practice and preservation.

Some international agreements since the 1950s, however, elaborate further a principle of self-determination for peoples. The Covenant on Economic, Social and Cultural Rights and Covenant on Civil and Political Rights, which was drafted in 1966 and went into force in 1976, states a principle of self-determination in Article 1. All peoples have the right to self-determination, which means freely to determine their political status and pursue economic, social, and cultural development. The Helsinki Final Act of 1975, the Conference on Security and Cooperation in Europe, also reaffirms the right of a people to be free from external influence in choosing its own form of government.[3]

A principle of self-determination for peoples, then, has been increasingly recognized as applying to all peoples, and not only those in the territories of the former European colonies of Africa and Asia. Continued and wider affirmation of a principle of self-determination in international documents encourages indigenous groups and other displaced, oppressed, or dominated groups to press claims against states that claim to have jurisdiction over them both directly and in international fora. Hotly contested, of course, is just what counts as a "people" who have a legitimate claim to self-determination. This is a crucial question which I believe cannot be settled by means of a once and for all definition. Peoples are not natural kinds, clearly identifiable and distinguishable by a set of essential attributes. Although I shall not argue this here, I believe that the relations among peoples and their degrees of distinctness are more fluid, relational and dependent on context than such a substantial logic suggests.[4]

Instead of addressing the important and contentious question of what a people is, here I will assume that there are some groups in the world today whose status as distinct peoples is largely uncontested, but which do not have states of their own and make claims for greater self-determination. Among such groups are at least some of those called indigenous peoples.

I bracket the question of what is a people in order to focus on the question of what counts as self-determination. For while a principle of self-determination appears to have acquired a wider scope in international law in recent decades, it appears at the same time to have lost clarity and precision as a concept. Since the era when former colonies obtained state independence, the international community has been very reluctant to allow a principle of self-determination to ground or endorse claims of separation, secession, and the formation of new states. The break-up of the Soviet Union and Yugoslavia into separate sovereign states is a grand exception, mainly explicable by a cynical desire in the West to weaken a former world power once and for all. Claims by minority groups that they are wrongly dominated by dominant groups in nation-states seem to be getting more hearing in international political discussions. At the same time, the dominant opinion among global powers gives a strong priority to the preservation of existing state territories. Thus, the opinion seems to be widely held among scholars and practitioners of international law that if certain peoples have rights to self-determination, this does not entail rights to secede from existing nation-states and establish their own independent sovereign states with exclusive rights over a contiguous territory. Such clarity on what self-determination does not imply today, however, produces confusion about what it does imply. It is to this question that I aim to contribute moral and political theoretical arguments of clarification.

The claims of indigenous peoples

For more than twenty years United Nations commissions have met to discuss the claims and status of the world's indigenous peoples. This work has culminated in the UN Draft Declaration of the Rights of Indigenous Peoples, which was discussed at the 1995 meeting I cited above,[5] and has been revised several times since.

At issue in world fora and in documents such as the Draft Declaration are both the definition of indigenous peoples and to whom the definition applies. Just who counts as indigenous is fairly clear in the case of the American settler colonies and in the settler colonies of Australia and New Zealand. They are the people who inhabited the land for centuries before the European settlers came, and who live today in some continuity with the premodern ways of life of their ancestors. The United Nations, however, also recognizes some other peoples in Europe, Asia, and Africa as indigenous, a designation which some states contest for some of "their" minorities. Still other groups which the United Nations does not recognize as indigenous would like to be so recognized. Just who should and should not count as indigenous people, as distinct from simply ethnic groups, is a contentious issue. Although this question is also important, I will bracket it as well. I will assume that descendants of the pre-Columbian inhabitants of North and South America count as indigenous people, as well as the Aboriginal people of New Zealand and Australia. While I believe there are others who ought to have rights of indigenous people, in this essay I will not develop criteria for classifying a people as indigenous and apply these criteria. Although I begin my thinking about the principle of self-determination by reflecting on the claims of (at least some) indigenous people, ultimately I believe that the conception of self-determination which I recommend ought to apply to all peoples. Thus, for the argument of this essay it is neither necessary to find an ironclad definition of *indigenous* nor to sort out which peoples are and which are not indigenous.

The UN Draft Declaration specifies that indigenous peoples have a right to autonomy or self-government in matters relating to their internal and local affairs, including culture, employment, social welfare, economic activities, land and resources, management and environment.[6] Nothing in the Declaration implies that indigenous peoples have a right to form separate states, and few if any indigenous people actually seek to form separate states. Most seek explicit recognition as distinct peoples by the states that claim to have jurisdiction over them, and wider terms of autonomy and negotiation with those states and with the other peoples living within those states. They claim or seek significant self-government rights, not only with respect to cultural issues, but with respect to land and access to resources. They claim to have rights to be distinct political entities with which other political entities, such as states, must negotiate agreements and over which they cannot simply impose their will and their law.[7]

Although indigenous peoples rarely seek to be separate states, they nevertheless claim that their legitimate rights of self-determination are nowhere completely recognized and respected. Every region of the world has its own stories and struggles of indigenous peoples in relation to the states that have emerged from colonization, and a full review of these claims and struggles would take me away from the conceptual work that is the main task of this essay. Thus, I will focus on the example of indigenous peoples related to the United States. Native Americans have a relatively long history of self-government institutions recognized by the United States government, and in the last twenty years native self-government has been more actual than ever before. Nevertheless, Native Americans typically claim that the United States government has never recognized their rights to self-determination, and that they are not so recognized today. The United States Congress reserves the right to recognize a group as a tribe, a status which accords it self-government rights. At any time, the Congress believes itself to have the power to rescind tribal status, and it has done so in the past, most notably during the period in the 1950s when the Indian Termination Act was in effect. Congress continues to act as though it has ultimate legislative authority over Native Americans. In the Indian Gaming Act of 1988, Congress for the first time ever required Native peoples to negotiate with US state governments regarding the use of Indian lands.

Some US public officials believe that Indians should not have distinct and recognized self-government and legal jurisdiction, and have led efforts to cripple Indian sovereignty. In a recent attack of fall 1997, Senator Slade Gorton (Rep., Washington) led a move to make the allocation of funds to tribal governments conditional on their waiving their current immunity from civil lawsuits filed in United States courts. This effort, hidden within the bill allocating funds to the National Endowment for the Arts and for national parks, was defeated. Even if it had passed it would likely not have stood up to treaty-based court challenge. It nevertheless shows how thin the line may be between self-government and subjection for Native Americans today.

My interest in rethinking the concept of the self-determination of peoples, then, begins from this apparent paradox. Indigenous peoples claim not to have full recognition of rights of self-determination, but most do not claim that allowing them to constitute separate states is necessary for such recognition. The dominant meaning of the concept of self-determination today would seem to require sovereign statehood. What is a meaning of the concept of self-determination that would correspond to the claims of indigenous peoples? I will argue that a concept of self-determination as relational autonomy in the context of nondomination best corresponds to these indigenous claims.

Self-determination as noninterference

Although some international political and legal developments of recent decades have brought it into question, the most widely accepted and clearly articulated meaning of self-determination defines it as independent *sovereignty*. An authority is sovereign, in the sense I have in mind, when it has final authority over the regulation of all activities within a territory, and when no authority outside that territory has the legitimate right to cancel or override it.[8]

This concept of self-determination interprets freedom as non-interference. In this model, self-determination means that a people or government has the authority to exercise complete control over what goes on inside its jurisdiction, and no outside agent has the right to make claims upon or interfere with what the self-determining agent does. Reciprocally, the self-determining people have no claim on what others do with respect to issues within their own jurisdictions, and no right to interfere in the business of the others. Just as it denies rights of interference by outsiders in a jurisdiction, this concept entails that each self-determining entity has no inherent obligations with respect to outsiders.

Only states have a status approaching self-determination as noninterference in today's world. When the principle of self-determination was systematized in the early twentieth century and then again after World War II, world leaders created or authorized the formation of states according to criteria of viability and independence. For a state to be sovereign or self-determining, and thus to have a right of noninterference, it was thought, it must be large enough to stand against other states if necessary, and have the right amount and kind of resources so that its people can thrive economically without depending on outsiders. Thus, the world powers that created states after World War I were concerned that no state be land locked and that states recognized as sovereign have sufficient natural resources to sustain an independent economy. The powers creating states in the decades after World War II also brought these standards of viability for independent living to bear on their work, usually seeking to make states large, though not always succeeding. Some today who worry about applying a principle of self-determination to peoples, such as the indigenous, continue to take the ability to be economically independent as a condition of such exercise of self-determination.

Some political theorists argue that state sovereignty considered as final authority and the enjoyment of noninterference is eroding today, and may have never existed to the extent that concept supposes.[9] Some think that global capitalism and international law increasingly circumscribe the independence and sovereignty of states.[10] Here, I am less concerned with whether any peoples or governments actually have self-determination as noninterference than with evaluating the normative adequacy of the concept, especially in light of indigenous peoples' claims. I argue below that noninterference is not a normatively adequate interpretation of a principle of self-determination.

My argument relies on two different but I believe compatible efforts to theorize a concept of individual autonomy which criticize the primacy of noninterference and offer alternative accounts. The first comes from feminist political theory and the second from neo-republican theory. Both theories suggest that the idea of freedom as noninterference does not properly take account of social relationships and possibilities for domination. The form of their arguments can be extended, however, from the relations among individuals to relations among peoples.

The concept of freedom as noninterference presupposes that agents have a domain of action that is their own which is independent of need for relationship with or influence by others. The status of autonomous citizenship presupposes this private sphere of individual property. From this base of independence, on this account, individual agents enter relationships with others through voluntary agreements. Except where obligations are generated through such agreements, the freedom of individuals ought not to be interfered with unless they are directly and actively interfering with the freedom of others. The ideal of self-determination, on this view, consists in an agent's being left alone to conduct his or her affairs over his or her own independent sphere.

Critics of liberal individualism since Hegel have argued that this image of the free individual as ontologically and morally independent fails to recognize that subjects are constituted through relationships, and that agents are embedded in institutional relations that make them interdependent in many ways. Relational feminist critics of the equation of freedom with noninterference draw on both these insights. In contrast to an account of the subject as constituted through bounding itself from others, a relational account of the subject says that the individual person is constituted through his or her communicative and interactive relations with others. Individuals acquire a sense of self from being recognized by others with whom they have relationships; they act in reference to a complex web of social relations and social effects that both constrain and enable them.[11]

On this account, the idea that a person's autonomy consists in control over a domain of activity independent of others and from which others are excluded except through mutual agreements is a dangerous fiction. This concept of self-determination as noninterference values independence, and thereby devalues any persons not deemed independent by its account. Historically, this meant that only property-holding heads of household could expect to have their freedom recognized. Women and workers could not be fully self-determining citizens, because their position in the division of labor rendered them dependent on the property holders. Feminist criticism argues, however, that in fact the male head of household and property holder is no more independent than the women or workers he rules. The appearance of his independence is produced by a system of domination in which he is able to command and benefit from the labor of others. This frees him from bodily and menial tasks of self-care and routine production, and helps increase his property, so that he can spend his time at politics or business deals. In fact, the more powerful agents are as embedded in interdependent social relations as the less powerful agents. Feminists argue that contemporary discourse of the freedom of individuals understood as noninterference continues to assume falsely that all or most persons are or ought to be independent in the sense that they can rely on their own sphere of activity to support them and need nothing from others.

Feminist theory thus offers an alternative concept of autonomy, which takes account of the interdependence of agents and their embeddedness in relationships at the same time that it continues to value individual choices. In this concept, all agents are owed equal respect as autonomous agents, which means that they are able to choose their ends and have capacity and support to pursue those ends. They are owed this because they are agents, and not because they inhabit a separate sphere from others. The social constitution of agents and their acting in relations of interdependence means the ability to be in such separate spheres is rare if it appears at all. Thus, an adequate conception of autonomy should promote the capacity of individuals to pursue their own ends in the context of relationships in which others may do the same. While this concept of autonomy entails a presumption of noninterference, especially with the choice of ends, it does not imply a social scheme in which atomized agents simply mind their own business and leave each other alone. Instead, it entails recognizing that agents are related in many ways they have not chosen, by virtue of kinship, history, proximity, or the unintended consequences of action. In these relationships agents are able either to thwart one another or support one another. Relational autonomy consists partly, then, in the structuring of relationships so that they support the maximal pursuit of individual ends.

In his reinterpretation of ideals of classical republicanism, Philip Pettit offers a similar criticism of the idea of freedom as noninterference.[12] Interference means that one agent blocks or redirects the action of another in a way that worsens that agent's choice situation by changing the range of options. In Pettit's account, noninterference, while related to freedom, is not equivalent to it. Instead, freedom should be understood as nondomination. An agent dominates another when he or she has power over that other and is thus able to interfere with the other *arbitrarily*. Interference is arbitrary when it is chosen or rejected without consideration of the interests or opinions of those affected. An agent may dominate another, however, without ever interfering with that person. Domination consists in standing in a set of relations which makes an agent *able* to interfere arbitrarily with the actions of others.

Thus, freedom is not equivalent to noninterference both because an unfree person may not experience interference, and because a free person may be interfered with. In both cases the primary criterion of freedom is nondomination. Thus when a person has a personal or institutional power that makes him or her able to interfere with my action arbitrarily, I am not free, even if in fact the dominating agent has not directly interfered with my actions. Conversely, a person whose actions are interfered with for the sake of reducing or eliminating such relations of domination is not unfree. In Pettit's account, it is appropriate for governing agents to interfere in actions in order to promote institutions that minimize domination. Interference is not arbitrary if its purpose is to minimize domination, and if it is done in a way that takes the interests and voices of affected parties into account. Like the feminist concept of relational autonomy, then, the concept of freedom as nondomination refers to a set of social relations. "Nondomination is the position that someone enjoys when they live in the presence of other people and when, by virtue of social design, none of those others dominates them" (p. 67).

In sum, both the feminist and neorepublican criticisms of the identification of freedom with noninterference are mindful of the relations in which people stand. A concept of freedom as noninterference aims to bound the agent from those relations, and imagines an independent sphere of action unaffected by and not affecting others. Because people and groups are deeply embedded in relationships, many of which they have not chosen, they are affected by and affect one another in their actions, even when they do not intend this mutual effect. Such interdependence is part of what enables domination, the ability for some to interfere arbitrarily with the actions of others. Freedom then means regulating and negotiating the relationships of people so that all are able to be secure in the knowledge that their interests, opinions, and desires for action are taken into account.

Relational interpretation of self-determination

We are now in a position to fill out Craig Scott's claim, which I quoted above, that we should think of the self-determination of peoples in the context of relationships. For the moment I will keep the discussion focused on the situation of indigenous people in the Americas and the antipodes. Because of a long and dominative history of settlement, exchange, treaty, conquest, removal, and sometimes recognition, indigenous and nonindigenous peoples are now interrelated in their territories. Webs of economic and communicative exchange, moreover, place the multicultural people of a particular region in relations of interdependence with others far away. In such a situation of interdependence, it is difficult for a people to be independent in the sense that they require nothing from outsiders and their activity has no effect on others.

I propose that the critique of the idea of freedom as noninterference and an alternative concept of relational autonomy and nondomination are not only relevant to thinking about the meaning of freedom for individuals. They can be usefully extended to an interpretation of the self-determination of a people. Extending any ideas of individual freedom and autonomy to peoples, of course, raises conceptual and political issues of what is the "self" of a people analogous to individual will and desire, by which it can makes sense to apply a concept of self-determination to a people at all. Extending political theoretical concepts of individual freedom to a people appears to reify or personify a social aggregate as a unity with a set of common interests, agency, and will of its own.[13] In fact, however, no such unified entity exists. Any tribe, city, nation, or other designated group is a collection of individuals with diverse interests and affinities, prone to disagreements and internal conflicts. One rarely finds a set of interests agreed upon by all members of a group that can guide their autonomous government. When we talk about self-determination for people, moreover, we encounter the further problem that it is sometimes ambiguous who belongs to a particular group, and that many individuals have reasonable claim to belong to more than one. Since a group has neither unanimity nor bounded unity of membership, what sense does it make to recognize its right to self-determination?

It is certainly true that group membership is sometimes plural, ambiguous, and overlapping, and that groups cannot be defined by a single set of shared attributes or interests. This is why it is sometimes difficult to say decisively that a particular collection of individuals counts as a distinct people. Such difficulties do not negate the fact, however, that historical and cultural groups have often been and continue to be dominated and exploited by other groups, often using state power to do so. Nor do these ambiguities negate the fact that freedom as self-government and cultural autonomy is important to many individuals who consider themselves belonging to distinct peoples.

Any collection of people that constitutes itself as a political community must worry about how to respond to conflict and dissent within the community, and whether the decisions and actions carried out in the name of a group can be said to *belong* to the group. For this reason the "self" of a group that claims a right to self-determination needs more explication than does the "self" of individual persons, though the latter concept is hardly clear and distinct. Insofar as a collective has a set of institutions through which that people make decisions and implement them, then the group sometimes expresses unity in the sense of agency. Whatever conflicts and disagreements may have led up to that point, once decisions have been made and action taken through collective institutions, the group itself can be said to act. Such a discourse of group agency and representation of agency to wider publics need not falsely personify the group or suppress differences among its members. Most governments claim to act for "the people," and their claims are more or less legitimate to the extent that the individuals in the society accept the government and its actions as theirs, and even more legitimate if they have had real influence in its decision-making processes. This capacity for agency is the only secular political meaning that the "self" of collective self-determination can have.

Self-determination for indigenous peoples, as well as other peoples, should not mean noninterference. The interpretation of self-determination that models it on state sovereign independence equates a principle of self-determination with noninterference. For the most part, indigenous peoples do not wish to be states in that sense, and while they claim autonomy they do not claim such a blanket principle of noninterference. Their claims for self-determination, I suggest, are better understood as a quest for an institutional context of nondomination.[14]

On such an interpretation, self-determination for peoples means that they have a right to their own governance institutions through which they decide on their goals and interpret their way of life. Other people ought not to constrain, dominate, or interfere with those decisions and interpretations for the sake of their own ends, or according to their judgment of what way of life is best, or in order to subordinate a people to a larger "national" unit. Peoples, that is, ought to be free from domination. Because a people stands in interdependent relations with others, however, a people cannot ignore the claims and interests of those others when their actions potentially affect them. Insofar as outsiders are affected by the activities of a self-determining people, those others have a legitimate claim to have their interests and needs taken into account even though they are outside the government jurisdiction. Conversely, outsiders should recognize that when they themselves affect a people, the latter can legitimately claim that they should have their interests taken into account insofar as they may be adversely affected. Insofar as their activities affect one another, peoples are in relationship and ought to negotiate the terms and effects of the relationship.

Self-determining peoples morally cannot do whatever they want without interference from others. Their territorial, economic, or communicative relationships with others generate conflicts and collective problems that oblige them to acknowledge the legitimate interests of others as well as promote their own. Pettit argues that states can legitimately interfere with the actions of individuals in order to foster institutions that minimize domination. A similar argument applies to actions and relations of collectivities. In a densely interdependent world, peoples require political institutions that lay down procedures for coordinating action, resolving conflicts, and negotiating relationships.

The self-determination of peoples, then, has the following elements. First, self-determination means a presumption of noninterference. A people has the prima facie right to set its own governance procedures and make its own decisions about its activities, without interference from others. Second, insofar as the activities of a group may adversely affect others, or generate conflict, self-determination entails the right of those others to make claims on the group, negotiate the terms of their relationships, and mutually adjust their effects. Third, a world of self-determining peoples thus requires recognized and settled institutions and procedures through which peoples negotiate, adjudicate conflicts, and enforce agreements. Self-determination does not imply independence, but rather that peoples dwell together within political institutions which minimize domination among peoples. It would take another essay to address the question of just what form such intergovernmental political institutions should take; some forms of federalism do and should apply. Finally, the self-determination of peoples requires that the peoples have the right to participate *as peoples* in designing and implementing intergovernmental institutions aimed at minimizing domination.

I have argued for a principle of self-determination understood as relational autonomy in the context of nondomination, instead of a principle of self-determination understood simply as noninterference. This argument applies as much to large nation-states as to small indigenous groups. Those entities that today are considered self-determining independent states in principle ought to have no more right of noninterference than should smaller groups. Self-determination for those entities now called sovereign states should mean nondomination. While this means a presumption of noninterference, outsiders may have a claim on their activities.

Understanding freedom as nondomination implies shifting the idea of state sovereignty into a different context. Sovereign independence is neither a necessary nor a sufficient condition of self-determination understood as nondomination. As I have developed it above, a self-governing people need not be able to say that it is entirely independent of others in order to be self-determining; indeed, I have argued that such an idea of independence is largely illusory. For these reasons, self-governing peoples ought to recognize their connections with others, and make claims on others when the actions of those others affect them, just as the others have a legitimate right to make claims on them when their interdependent relations threaten to harm them.

Those same relations of interdependence mean, however, that sovereign independence is not a sufficient condition of self-determination understood as nondomination. The people living within many formally independent states stand in relation to other states, or powerful private actors such as multinational corporations, where those others are able to interfere arbitrarily with actions in order to promote interests of their own. For some people, formal sovereignty is little protection against such dominative relations. The institutions of formal state sovereignty, however, allow many agents to absolve themselves of responsibility to support self-governing peoples who nevertheless stand in relations of domination.

Thus, the interpretation of self-determination as nondomination ultimately implies limiting the rights of existing nation-states and setting these into different, more cooperatively regulated relationships. Just as promoting freedom for individuals involves regulating relationships in order to prevent domination, so promoting self-determination for peoples involves regulating international relations to prevent the domination of peoples.

Applying a principle of self-determination as nondomination to existing states, then, as well as to peoples not currently organized as states, has profound implications for the freedom of the former.

States ought not to have rights to interfere arbitrarily in the activities of those peoples in relation to whom they claim special jurisdictional relation. In the pragmatic context of political argument within both nation-state and international politics, many indigenous groups do not challenge the idea that the autonomy rights they claim are or will be within the framework of nation-states. Some appear to recognize that nation-states presume a right of noninterference in their dealings with "their" autonomous minorities.[15] If self-determination for peoples means not noninterference but nondomination, however, then nation-states cannot have a right of noninterference in their dealings with indigenous minorities and other ethnic minorities. Small, resource poor, relatively weak peoples are most likely to experience domination by larger and more organized peoples living next to or among them than from others far away. The nation-state that claims jurisdiction with respect to a relatively autonomous people is likely sometimes to dominate such people. If a self-determining people has no public forum to which it can go to press claims of such wrongful domination against a nation-state, and if no agents outside the state have the authority and power to affect a state's relation to that people, then that people cannot be said to be self-determining.

Thus, a principle of self-determination for indigenous peoples can have little meaning unless it accompanies a limitation on and ultimately a transformation of the rights and powers of existing nation-states and the assumptions of recognition and noninterference that still largely govern the relation between states.[16] There are good reasons to preserve the coordination capacities that many existing states have and to strengthen these capacities where they are weak. Nevertheless, the capacities of diverse peoples to coordinate action to promote peace, distributive justice, or ecological value can in principle be maintained and enlarged within institutions that also aim to minimize the domination that states are able to exercise over individuals and groups.

Illustration: the Goshutes versus Utah

Let me illustrate the difference between a concept of self-determination as noninterference and a concept of self-determination as autonomy in regulated relations by reflecting on a particular conflict between a Native American tribe and some residents of the state of Utah.

According to a report in the New York Times,[17] the Skull Valley Band of Goshutes have offered to lease part of their reservation as the temporary storage ground for high-level civil nuclear waste. The State of Utah's territory surrounds this small reservation, and state officials have vowed to block the border of the reservation from shipments of nuclear waste. The Skull Valley Band of Goshutes asserts that they have sovereign authority over the reservation territory and the activities within it, and that the State of Utah has no jurisdiction over this activity. The State of Utah, on behalf of counties near the reservation, claims that they have the responsibility to protect the health and welfare of the citizens of Utah. Since the storage of nuclear waste carries risks of potential harm that people in counties surrounding the reservation would bear along with those living on the reservation, the State of Utah feels obliged to assert its power.

So far as I understand the law of tribes and the United States, the Goshutes do have a right to make this decision through their own government mechanism, and to issue their own guidelines to a waste storage operation that wishes to lease their land. They are obliged neither to consult the State of Utah nor to abide by the regulations of the US Environmental Protection Agency. Just this sort of legal independence makes Indian reservations attractive as potential sites for the treatment or storage of hazardous wastes from the point of view of the companies that operate such facilities. Sometimes, companies are willing to pay handsomely for the privilege of working with Indian groups in order to bypass what some regard as unnecessarily complex and time-consuming state and federal regulatory processes. For their part, some Indian groups such as the Skull Valley Band find in such leasing arrangements one of only a few opportunities to generate significant income with which they can improve the lives of their members and develop reservation infrastructure.

The Goshutes, I have said, do have self-determination rights in this situation. They are a distinct and historically colonized people with a right to preserve their cultural distinctness and enlarge their well-being as a group through their own forms of collective action. On the interpretation of this right of self-determination that I reject, they may simply deny that the State of Utah and US federal government have a right to interfere with their decision to lease the land for a nuclear waste storage site. On this interpretation, they can rightfully say that this decision is entirely their business and is none of the business of the State of Utah.

There is no denying, however, that the siting of a nuclear waste storage facility has potential consequences for people living in Utah counties near the reservation. They can be just as adversely affected as those on the reservation if the facility leaks radioactive material into the ground, water, or air. In my account of self-determination, the Goshutes and the citizens of Utah are in a close and ongoing relationship. This relationship, in this case partly defined by geographical proximity, obliges the Goshutes to take the interests of potentially affected citizens of Utah into account.

The apparent approach of the State of Utah to this controversy, however, is to challenge any right to self-determination. The State of Utah apparently would like to have the power to override the Goshute decision, to impose state government power and regulations over this group. It seems that between the two groups we face the alternatives of either recognizing the right of the Indian band to do what it wishes with its territory or recognizing the right of a larger entity around it to exercise final authority over that territory.

More generally, the United States Congress has recently held hearings on the question of whether US tribal sovereignty should not be revised or eliminated. There are many in the United States who believe that disputes such as this nuclear siting dispute are best addressed by eliminating jurisdictional difference. All the people in a contiguous territory in this case ought to be subject to the same laws and procedures of decision-making. On this account, a state ought to be the overriding, unifying, and final authority, with no independent entities "within" it. When that state is recognized by the international community as an independent sovereign state, such as the United States or New Zealand, then that sovereign state has a right of self-determination understood as noninterference. Such a right of noninterference applies particularly to the right of that state to make its own decisions about how it will rule over "its" minorities who claim rights of self-determination in relation to it. All states recognized as independent sovereign states in international law today, at the moment have such a right of noninterference with respect to "their" indigenous peoples. Hearings considering the question of whether to continue the current system of tribal self-determination assume that the United States has such a right.

From the point of view of indigenous people, even those that presently have significant autonomy rights in relation to the states that claim jurisdiction over them, this right of states is illegitimate. The only recourse they have within the logic of national sovereigntists is to assert for themselves the right of autonomy as noninterference. Political stand-off, then, is the typical result of this position.

Self-determination understood as relational autonomy, on the other hand, conceives the normative and jurisdictional issues in this dispute as follows. The Skull Valley Band of the Goshutes should be recognized as a self-determining people. This implies that they have self-government rights and through that government they can make decisions about the use of land and resources under their jurisdiction which they think will benefit their members. Thus, they may decide to lease land for nuclear waste storage. They do not have an unlimited right of noninterference, however, concerning their activities. Communities outside the tribe who claim potential adverse effects to themselves because of tribal decisions have a *claim* upon those activities, and the Goshutes are morally obliged to hear that claim. Intergovernmental relations ought to be structured such that, when self-governing entities stand in relationships of contiguity or mutual effect, there are settled procedures of discussion and negotiations about conflicts, side effects of their activities, and shared problems. Because parties in a dispute frequently polarize or fail to respect each other, such procedures should include a role for public oversight and arbitration by outside parties with less stake in the dispute. Such procedures of negotiation, however, are very different from being subject to the authority of a state under which more local governments including the indigenous governments stand, and which finally decides the rules.[18]

Final question: the rights of individuals

I have argued that international law ought to continue to recognize a principle of self-determination for peoples, and should interpret this principle differently from the traditional principle of noninterference and independence. I have argued for an alternative interpretation of self-determination as relational autonomy in the context of institutions that aim to prevent domination. Some critics suspect claims to self-determination, and recognizing such claims, because they worry that this gives license to a group to oppress individuals or subgroups within the group. If a people has a right to govern its affairs its own way, some object, then this allows discriminatory or oppressive practices and policies toward women, or members of particular religious groups, or castes within the group, to go unchallenged. This sort of objection has little force, however, if we accept a concept of self-determination conceived as relational autonomy in the context of institutions that minimize domination.

My articulation of a principle of self-determination as involving nondomination instead of noninterference above focused on the relationship between a group and those outside the group. If we give priority to a principle of nondomination, however, then it should also apply to the relation between a group and its members. The self-determination of a people should not extend so far as to permit the domination of some of its members by others. For reasons other than those of mutual effect, namely reasons of individual human rights, outsiders sometimes have a responsibility to interfere with the self-governing actions of a group in order to prevent severe human rights violations. This claim introduces a whole new set of contentious questions, however, about how human rights are defined, who should decide when they have been seriously violated by a government against its members, and the proper agents and procedures of intervention. These important questions are beyond the scope of this essay. A relational concept of self-determination for peoples does not entail that members of the group can do anything they want to other members without interference from those outside. It does entail, however, that insofar as there are global rules defining individual rights and agents to enforce them, all peoples should have the right to be represented *as peoples* in the fora that define and defend those rights. Thus, the sort of global regulatory institutions I have said are ultimately necessary to prevent domination between peoples should be constituted by the participation of all the peoples regulated by them.

3

Self-Determination as Nondomination: Ideals Applied to Palestine/Israel

Few political commentators today think that every distinct people can and should have a sovereign state exclusively its own. Yet writings on the self-determination of peoples for the most part continue to assume a paradigm of self-determination that mirrors the sovereign state. In this paradigm, a self-determining people dwells together in a relatively large territory in which only members of their group reside, and this homogenous territory is contiguous and bounded; the self-determining people exercises strong self-government rights over this territory. This autonomous region may not be sovereign, but rather may stand in formalized relation to a larger state. This paradigm of self-determination has guided many political events and international interventions of the last quarter century – from the ethnic cleansings of Croatia to the United Nations protectorates of Kosovo and East Timor. Acting under this paradigm of self-determination sometimes brings as much justice as there can be under the circumstances. Where groups with conflicting claims to exclusive sovereignty over a territory reside side by side within that territory, however, as in Northern Ireland or republics of the former Yugoslavia, adhering to this paradigm tends to produce injustice and perpetuate cycles of violence.

One reason for such a consequence lies in the lack of correspondence between this model of self-determination as self-government over a homogeneously occupied large, contiguous bounded territory, on the one hand, and the actual situation of conflicting peoples, on the other. Most sizeable territories are inhabited by several peoples who consider themselves distinct, and they are usually dispersed across these territories in smaller enclaves, towns, villages, or neighborhoods next to towns or neighborhoods in which members of groups from which they differentiate themselves reside.

Most peoples that regard themselves distinct from other peoples dwell in proximity to others from whom they differentiate themselves. The form of such differentiation, moreover, is often fluid, and there are often at least some individuals who are "hybrid" in the sense that they identify with multiple groups. Rather than base a conception of self-determination on the assumption that peoples are separate or separable, then, it behooves those of us interested in peace and justice to conceptualize self-determination as compatible with the fact that groups often dwell together in territories; for this reason they often have shared problems, and the activities of those in one group often affect the possibilities of action for others.

In this essay I offer a conception of self-determination as compatible with being together-in-difference.[1] Whereas the more standard concept assumes self-determination as noninterference, I conceptualize self-determination as nondomination. Principles of nondomination imply relationships between self-determining units and the joint regulation of such relationships. To understand the application of this model, I suggest that we should assume the situation and claims of indigenous people as the norm rather than the exception. This model of self-determination implies federalism as a mode of being together with other self-determining units. Many discussions of federalism, however, assume that autonomous units are large, homogeneously occupied, contiguous territories. Suspending this assumption opens ways of conceiving federal relations as more local, plural, and horizontal.

To illustrate how this concept of self-determination might contribute to imagining alternatives in a situation of group political conflict, I apply the analysis to the situation of Palestine/Israel.[2] I suggest that a vision of dispersed Jewish and Palestinian jurisdictions, organized in a federal system whose constitution minimizes the possibility of domination may have some advantages over other visions of the region's future. The main purpose of this example is not to make concrete proposals for moving the Palestinian–Israeli conflict toward just peace. It is to show how the conception of self-determination I propose might fuel the political imagination anywhere that groups are interspersed with one another but claim exclusive rights to sovereignty over a territory.

Indigenous people as paradigmatic

If we refocus the lens for looking at the normative requirements
of self-determination from assuming a large homogeneously concentrated people in a relatively large, contiguous, bounded territory, to
understanding distinct peoples as more dispersed and mixed geographically alongside one another, then it is useful to take the claims
of indigenous people for self-determination as paradigmatic rather
than exceptional. The claims of indigenous people for self-
determination have in the last quarter century achieved considerable
legitimacy in the international community as well as in the domestic
politics of many states. Despite the effort of some states to implement
policies aimed to accommodate indigenous claims for self-determination, almost no indigenous people anywhere in the world believe
they have achieved full self-determination. In an apparent paradox,
however, almost no indigenous people take as their political goal
secession from the state which now claims jurisdiction over them
to establish their own sovereign state. I suggest, if we articulate a
concept of self-determination that corresponds to the aspirations of
most indigenous people, that this concept can be useful more generally to considering political conflicts that involve peoples who
perceive themselves as distinct, but who dwell side by side or
are interspersed over contiguous lands. Such a concept of self-
determination is likely to be more useful under such circumstances,
which describe many conflicts in the world, than is the idea of a separate contiguous bounded territory over which the self-determining
people has exclusive control.[3]
   Other features of the situation and claims of indigenous people
make this a useful paradigm for theorizing self-determination. In
every place where the category of indigenous is relatively uncontested, particularly in North and South America, Australia and New
Zealand, the indigenous people have suffered histories of serious
injustice and domination under colonialism. In most of these places,
indigenous people as a group are among the least well off in the
society, and continue to suffer discrimination and exploitation. Colonialist and modernist domination have disrupted the traditional
languages and cultural practices of many of these groups, but they
nevertheless managed to retain enough of them to engage in projects
of cultural renewal when repression lessened. The claims to self-
determination that indigenous people make gain some of their legitimacy in the eyes of others from a judgment that this history of
domination was wrong and that the current deprived status of most

indigenous people, both as individuals and groups, requires their own autonomy to be ameliorated.

Almost nowhere do indigenous people form a territorially concentrated large group. Partly because of traditional nomadic or village band life, and partly because of colonial policies of creating reserves, indigenous people usually live dispersed in relatively small clusters across the territory of the nation-state to which they are currently related. Their national identity, moreover, is usually defined in terms of these traditional bands which understand themselves as related to particular locales. Maori in New Zealand, First Nations in Canada, Aboriginals in Australia, or Indians in the United States are all political categories which have evolved as indigenous people politically organize with one another in order to protest and engage with the white settler state. In each case, the peoples who claim self-determination for themselves are smaller, dispersed local groups who usually dwell alongside nonindigenous peoples.

Some theorists of nationalism and multiculturalism try to mitigate possible conflict between the claim of distinct peoples for self-determination and the desire of states to maintain control over activities in a territory by arguing that nationalist claims are best recognized through systems of cultural autonomy. On this view, liberal nationalism consists in guaranteeing that national minorities have governing power over the generation, expression, and transmission of national culture – ability to speak their own language without suffering disadvantage, freedom of religion and self-government over religious institutions, the constitution of autonomous schools, and the like.[4] In this view of minority rights, self-determination claims do not need to involve control over land and resources. Almost no indigenous people think that institutions of cultural autonomy are sufficient to give them self-determination, important as these are. Their claims necessarily involve control over land and resources, not only because their identities are tied to place, but also because they judge that their material improvement as individuals and groups requires having land and resources about which they as a group make autonomous decisions.[5]

Indigenous peoples' claims for self-determination thus raise the following questions. What does it mean for groups to be self-determining but not on the model of nation-state sovereignty? How can groups that are relatively small and territorially dispersed among others who understand themselves as belonging to different groups be self-determining without necessarily ruling over a large territory in which they are concentrated and from which they have the right to exclude others? How can such dispersed self-determination be recognized, especially when the group requires control over land and resources to be self-determining? How should relations between these groups and the nonindigenous among whom they dwell be conceived?

Let me note one final feature of indigenous politics of self-determination as it often plays out today. Indigenous claims for self-determination often involve claims for redistribution or subsidy of their governmental and social service institutions, and some states have taken steps to respond to these claims. To be self-determining and for their people to flourish, indigenous people generally insist that the states against which they claim self-determination and to some extent international institutions ought to enable the realization of their self-determination rights by at least partly funding their governments and their government services including bureaucratic staff, equipment, schools, health services, and similar public services. Some nonindigenous people in the affected states believe this is contradictory: the indigenous people cannot both claim self-determination of cultural expression and economic development and expect the wider society to subsidize their government activities and services. Without such support, however, in many cases the indigenous group would have little means to exercise their rights of self-determination. Thus, a final question is: is there a conception of self-determination in which such subsidy, where needed, is coherent? While this set of questions arises most obviously in connection with claims of indigenous people to self-determination, I suggest that their answers can illuminate the normative meaning of self-determination for most peoples.

Some Palestinian advocates think that their claims of justice might be well furthered by trying to achieve recognition under international law as indigenous people.[6] I make no judgment about whether this is a worthy political strategy, nor do I wish to take a position on whether Palestinians qualify as indigenous under the current definition of international law.

I am suggesting, as I said above, that the indigenous paradigm is more useful for exploring the question of what self-determination might mean normatively for Palestinians rather than the nation-state sovereignty paradigm. The situation of Palestinians now residing in Israel, as well as those residing on the West Bank, in Gaza, in East Jerusalem, in Jordan, Syria, and Lebanon, has certain similarities with the situation of many indigenous people. Many were forced to move during a process of colonization. Israeli regions such as Galilee and the Negev contain predominantly Arab populations adjacent to and surrounded by Israeli Jewish state power and development. Many Palestinians are concentrated in the Gaza strip, surrounded by hostile forces and cut off from many material benefits and freedom to move and associate. Other Palestinians are more dispersed, living in relatively small villages across territories in the West Bank or Israel where Jews and other non-Palestinians live; or they dwell in neighborhoods and enclaves in mixed cities such as Jerusalem, Tel Aviv, or Haifa. Cultural autonomy is an important part of a claim of Palestinian self-determination, and many Palestinians lack cultural autonomy. Like indigenous people, however, Palestinian claims to self-determination cannot be accommodated without autonomy with respect to land and resources as well as culture. The exercise of self-determination for Palestinians, finally, requires redistributive transfers to enable their governmental and social services.

To reiterate, I have discussed the situation and claims of groups referred to as indigenous people because their situation and claims are often taken to be anomalous in international relations. I invoke the example of indigenous people to suggest that their situation and claims appear anomalous only under the paradigm of self-determination as separate and exclusive nation-state sovereignty. This paradigm has been coming under increasing strain both because processes of globalization impinge on sovereignty from without and group rights movements challenge singular sovereignty from within. Thus I suggest that, if we conceptualize a concept of self-determination which responds to the situation and claims of indigenous people, such a concept might serve as a better general paradigm of self-determination. In the next two sections, I propose such an alternative concept of self-determination and argue that it implies institutions of horizontal federalism. Then in the final section I will return to the case of Palestine/Israel, to show how this conception of self-determination might guide institutional vision for the region.

Two concepts of self-determination

Even though many theorists and political actors today question the idea that the realistic response to most claims of nations or peoples to self-determination is to establish a separate sovereign state for each people, most writings on self-determination assume the model of state sovereignty as their paradigm. I refer to this as the noninterference model of self-determination.[7] In this interpretation, for a group to be self-determining means that it controls a sphere over which others have no authority. The noninterference model makes a strong distinction between inside and outside. The self-determining group dwells inside a single territorial jurisdiction over which self-governing institutions have sole authority. For the group to be self-determining means primarily that outsiders do not interfere with the decisions and actions that those governing institutions make over what goes on inside the jurisdiction.

The noninterference model of self-determination is certainly plausible. Autonomy, whether of an individual or a group, certainly means having the right to run one's own affairs and to challenge others who try to run them instead. There are, however, several drawbacks to the noninterference model of self-determination. A major reason groups seek self-determination is to protect against domination by others. The noninterference model fulfills the purpose only imperfectly, however, and sometimes not at all. When enacted, this model protects against the direct interference by an outside agent in the decisions and actions of an autonomous unit. A noninterference model assumes that these autonomous units can be and are properly separate and need have no interaction other than what they voluntarily enter into. As I noted earlier, however, the world's peoples are often geographically mixed, or dwell in close proximity to one another, within physical and social environments that jointly affect them. The peoples who have or claim self-determination are inevitably related to one another. They have numerous economic and social interactions where each affects the others, and each risks being adversely affected by actions of the others because of their relationship. Because agents and groups are often closely related in common contexts where their actions affect one another, and because they are often unequal in resources or power or both, some of the weaker units may be vulnerable to domination by more powerful units, not because they directly interfere, but because they determine conditions under which the weaker party is forced to act.

Forms of domination such as this are common among supposedly sovereign entities in the world today. Arguably, the United States stands in a dominative relation to Mexico, for example, even though the United States only infrequently tries to interfere in the internal processes of Mexican sovereignty. The United States government and private organizations based in the United States are able to constrain options of both the Mexican government and many private actors under its jurisdiction just because activities in each society are interdependent, and because the power relationship between the two societies is unequal in many respects.

The noninterference model of self-determination, moreover, does nothing to protect insiders from domination by the governing institutions or by other insiders. A concept of self-determination that means primarily noninterference with the internal affairs of a sovereign government implicitly allows for domination within, to the extent that it forbids outsiders from interfering if they observe such internal domination. Some contemporary human rights theorists worry, for example, that a strong noninterference model of self-determination must turn a blind eye to traditions and practices through which men dominate women.[8] Inasmuch as most autonomous jurisdictions contain ethnic minorities vulnerable to domination by majorities, moreover, a noninterference model of self-determination implicitly gives such majorities license to dominate internal minorities.

Arguably, a pure noninterference concept of sovereignty has never existed in practice. International law and practices of international governance in the late twentieth and early twenty-first century, moreover, increasingly involve forms of transnational authority constraining the actions of sovereign states and forms of negotiation and cooperation between entities within different states. Both theorists and political actors in international affairs nevertheless continue to take noninterference as the primary meaning of the concept of self-determination.

I propose a different model of self-determination, one that puts the objective of mutual respect and the avoidance of domination more at the center. Self-determination means autonomy. The self-determining entity should be able to set its own ends and be able to act toward their realization, within the limits of respect for and cooperation with other agents with whom one interacts and with whom one stands in relation. Conceived as nondomination, self-determination entails a *presumption* of noninterference.[9] Prima facie, outside agents should stay out of the business of self-determining units. Because some of these autonomous agents are inevitably related to one another in wider contexts of shared environments, overlapping influence and affect, and in the way they define themselves, a conception of self-determination should take such relations into account. When groups stand together in their difference they must be mindful that sometimes their efforts to enact their own projects may have potentially adverse effects on other agents. Outside agents who believe that the actions of an autonomous agent affect them adversely can legitimately make a claim on the affecting agent to have a right to negotiate with them about the terms of their relations and the actions that may harm them. Self-determining entities need to join a decision-making body to work out procedures for adjudicating such claims and potential conflicts. To the extent that self-determining units dwell together in a common environment, moreover, they are liable to face some common problems. What it means to face such problems autonomously, then, is that they have institutions through which they are able to discuss those shared problems and decide on joint actions to address them. Within such institutions, self-determining entities ought to have equal status and mutual respect.

The prima facie principle of noninterference in the internal jurisdiction of a self-determining unit may be suspended, then, in order that the common decisions of units be enacted to prevent domination by one of the units of another. Noninterference is also suspended, moreover, in order to prevent some members of a self-determining unit from dominating members internally. The autonomous units that potentially can harm one another by engaging in their own self-regarding activities should participate in a process that decides when such intervention to prevent domination is called for. Promoting self-determination as nondomination, finally, requires providing positive support for units that are weak or poorly resourced, to a level that enables them meaningfully to pursue their way of life, autonomy, and competence to interact and negotiate with other self-determining units.

Institutional design implications: horizontal federalism

Under circumstances where distinct peoples or units are spatially, economically, and environmentally interdependent, self-determination as nondomination requires relations of joint governance among self-determining units. Under these circumstances, self-determination as nondomination *entails* federalism. Most generally, federalism designates a system of "self-rule plus shared rule."[10] In principle, federalism is "an attempt to find equilibrium between centripetal and centrifugal forces, between conflicting needs for unity and diversity, for putting together and keeping apart."[11]

The claim that self-determination as nondomination entails federalism means that self-determination isn't yet realized by a people having a jurisdiction of their own, but also requires having regulated relations with other jurisdictions. *Why* does this understanding of self-determination *entail* federalism? Because the people or unity claiming self-determination dwells together with others – on lands together or next to each other, in a common regional environment of relatively dense social and economic interaction. Together, they sometimes face common problems. They are economically interdependent on issues such as trade, the demand for labor, the effects of production and finance on their people, and in the distribution of resources and opportunities.

Even though interdependent in these and other ways, peoples that dwell together are often unequal in their resource base, wealth, or capacity for asserting their interests. All these factors underlie a potential for conflict between the goals and interests of the units, and they also generate efficiency needs for joint action to address the problems. If these mutually affecting units do not have regulated means of settling conflict fairly, if they do not have ways of preventing interdependence from becoming an unequal dependence, or if they do not have mechanisms for ongoing cooperation, then domination of some of the formally autonomous units by another or others is likely to ensue. Federalism is the general name for governance arrangements between self-governing entities in which they participate together in such cooperative regulation. When one people from one group live in the same territories as others, or when the groups are close, self-governing units, they cannot be fully self-determining unless the differently defining peoples participate together in processes that regulate their inevitable and in many ways involuntary relationship.

Federalism is a genus with several possible species. Both theoretical literature about federalism and most existing federations operate with a model influenced by the concept of self-determination as noninterference. They assume that the units of a federation are each single, relatively large, contiguous, bounded territories. In most models of federalism, furthermore, these self-governing units do not relate to one another directly, but rather only through a central, federal government in which each of them is represented. The federal rules determine what are the powers of the central government and what are those of the federated units. In most federal systems, finally, the definition of the powers of each of the self-governing units is the same. Each element of this typical model of federalism can be questioned as necessary to or most desirable for a system of self-rule with shared rule that can correspond to a concept of self-determination as nondomination.

Asymmetry versus symmetry

The last of the conditions I have mentioned has been brought into question by proponents of asymmetrical federalism. A federation is symmetrical when its constitution defines identical rights and powers for each of the constituent units with relation to the central government and to one another. The United States embodies a symmetrical federalism. Canada, on the other hand, has been moving toward an asymmetrical federalism in which the jurisdictional powers of Quebec differ in certain respects from those of the other provinces. Given the historical, geographical, or power relationships between some federated units, there can be good reasons to define their jurisdictional powers differently, and/or to differently define their relationships to the federal governance processes. Some people believe that asymmetrical federalism is inherently unfair because it departs from a standard of formally equally treatment. Where there are differences of culture, history, or power among federating units, however, an asymmetrical federalism may in fact be more fair than a constitution that accords the same rights and powers to each unit.

Horizontality versus decentralization

Typically, systems called federal consist of a constitutional center with limited but overriding power over units that have no formal relation to one another except through that center. Some theorists of federalism argue, however, that this model falls short of the principles of federalism altogether. Ferran Requejo argues that this model confuses federalism with regional decentralization and/or the application of a principle of subsidiarity. On this basis, he takes issue with the claim that the current constitution of Spain is federalist, for at least two reasons: the distinct national groups of the Basque country, Catalonia, and Galicia have the same rights and powers as other autonomous units (symmetry), and the federal government retains control over many important issues, such as taxation, constitutional reform, and judiciary, with the regions implementing directives from the center with some autonomy.[12]

Daniel Elazar distinguishes what he calls a "matrix" model of federalism from the more typical center–periphery model. The matrix model is more complex than the center–autonomous locale model. It disperses authority and power among units in networks of different relationships.[13]

We can conceive federal systems with both vertical and horizontal relationships in potential federal systems. Any federal system will have some rules and procedures that govern the relation of the units to the federation in a vertical way. A common or central government needs to implement a federal constitution and adjudicate disputes about its meaning and application. Since much of the reason for units to stand in ongoing relationships of negotiation and cooperation concerns promoting efficient and fair economic relations between units, it is usually appropriate for the federal government to regulate a common currency, and to regulate the terms of interunit commerce, including labor markets and labor standards. When groups reside next to or interspersed with one another in a geographic region, finally, they face a common set of environmental conditions which require common regulation. A decentered asymmetrical federalism perhaps need not involve a central authority in any issues beyond these.

For many other issues, units can relate to one another directly without invoking or going through a central federal government. This is what I mean by a "horizontal" dimension to federalism. Self-governing political units have many reasons to relate to one another directly without going through a center: to resolve some conflict between them that does not concern other units, to work out joint ways of addressing shared problems, to facilitate objectives each has whose realization affects some but not all the others, and so on. Some federations might benefit from instituting principles and procedures that make it easier for units to develop horizontal authorities and agreements.[14]

Large contiguous territories versus smaller discontiguous territories

Federated systems, finally, need not assume that the units of self-determination are relatively large, contiguous, bounded territories, as in, for example, the German federation. Small units such as cities, towns, and neighborhoods can count as self-governing units that are nested within federal constitutions which regulate their relationships with one another. Some urban theorists in the United States, for example, advocate forms of metropolitan governance along lines of horizontal federalism between the dozens or hundreds of jurisdictionally distinct municipalities in a metropolitan region. Rather than bring these jurisdictions under a single centralized authority that would override their local decisions, they call for regularized systems of negotiation and cooperation between municipal units.[15] I noted above that the residential patterns of many multiethnic regional contexts involve groups whose members reside in dispersed towns, villages, or neighborhoods surrounded by or next to towns and neighborhoods the majority of whose members identify with different groups. In keeping with these facts, it is possible to conceive a unit jurisdictionally constituting a self-determining people as itself not a contiguous territory, but rather a set of discontiguous locales in between which lie locales that belong to other self-determining jurisdictions.

Application to Palestine/Israel

I suggest that the distinction between self-determination as non-interference and as nondomination, along with institutional possibilities of federalism that follow from it, offers a framework for conceptualizing institutional possibilities for the context of Palestine/Israel. Before I delineate how, let me explain the status of such an account. As the title of this essay indicates, I offer nondomination as a normative ideal for interpreting self-determination. Ideals are not proposals or direct guides for action. The main purpose of normative ideals is to awaken political imagination about alternatives. Such imagining enables us to take a critical distance from existing facts, so that they can be better evaluated. This is all I hope that the account below might do for those thinking and working for justice and peace in Palestine/Israel. What I offer is not a political program or an institutional design; this level of analysis is more abstract than that required by institutional design. Much less can this account be taken as a "peace plan."

The most that I can claim for this application of the ideas laid out in previous sections of this paper is that it may help political actors both inside and outside Palestine/Israel conceptually to sort out alternatives among institutional possibilities. The theoretical distinction between a noninterference and a nondomination model of self-determination suggests that there are three primary ways to conceptualize political institutional change in Palestine/Israel from the current situation of occupation and resistance: (1) two separate sovereign states; (2) a single secular, individualist state for the region; and (3) a federation of self-governing units. While the first two each represent important normative principles, both have problems, I suggest, that derive from their assumption of the paradigm of a unitary state. I will argue that the third alternative serves as a better ideal of self-determination for both Palestinians and Israeli Jews under a paradigm of nondomination.

Two separate sovereign states

The most commonly expressed vision of the future of the region today calls for establishing a Palestinian state in the West Bank and Gaza, and perhaps including East Jerusalem, though positions differ on this latter question. This Palestinian state would exist independently of and alongside the state of Israel, which will return to its pre-1967 borders. Ideally, the territory of each state would have clear borders, and a contiguous territory, so that a citizen of one need not cross the territory of the other in order to reach another part of his or her own state. Some provision would have to be made for a "corridor" between the West Bank and the Gaza strip for this ideal to be approximated in Palestine. Each state would have sole jurisdiction over what goes on within its territory, and the right to tell outsiders not to interfere with its sovereign actions. Israel and the international community would recognize the Palestinian state as sovereign, with the same status as other sovereign states.

I support the establishment of a Palestinian state. Whatever the institutional arrangements that may be most just and desirable in the long term, a necessary step toward those arrangements is that Palestinians in the occupied territories, as well as many of those now in the Palestinian diaspora, should exercise more self-government and have greater legal authority over land and resources. Most articulations of the two-state solution to the conflict between Israel and Palestinians, however, assume a model of self-determination as noninterference, which implies being separate. They tend to assume that each people can have sovereignty over a territory of their own, where they can promote the economic development and cultural expression of their distinct people, and that the conditions of their self-determination can be fulfilled by asserting that outsiders not interfere with their internal business. This image of clearly separate sovereign states relating to one another only as neighbors and through formal bilateral agreements is hard to square, however, with the existing reality that Palestinians and Jews dwell so thoroughly among one another, and that the current terms of their relationships are profoundly unequal.[16]

The two separate sovereign states image of the future of Palestine/Israel does not adequately address the spatial togetherness of the two groups. Palestinians dwell in Israel in towns or neighborhoods adjoining those of Jews; currently hundreds of thousands of Jews live in settlements in the occupied territories. The territories envisioned as belonging to each group, especially to the Palestinians, are not contiguous, and the city of Jerusalem is a contested space claimed by both. Of course, these present facts result from a history of domination and expropriation of Palestinian territory by Israel. Nevertheless, they would be difficult to reverse entirely, and at this stage a partial reversal could leave Palestinians even worse off. Recent announcement of an Israeli policy of "disengagement" from Palestinian territories has prompted cries of outrage because, among other reasons, such an effort at separation by the more privileged party would leave Palestinians imprisoned without opportunities for flourishing, rather than self-determining.

Palestinians and Israelis are similarly affected by the natural environment of the region, its weather, and shortage of water. They are also economically interdependent, but on an unequal basis. Creating a Palestinian state in the West Bank and Gaza, and declaring that state sovereign, which is to say that it exercises a right of self-determination as noninterference, does little to address the deep and unjust inequalities between Israel and the Palestinians. Can a Palestinian state be viable when Israel continues to dominate military and police power over lands adjacent to and separating the Palestinian territories? Given existing inequalities of power and technical know how, how can a Palestinian state alongside Israel be assured of fair access to water? Shouldn't Palestinian workers be able to move freely in the region to go to work, including into Israel? In order that the Palestinian economy develops and the Israeli economy flourishes, don't trade and investment opportunities need to be facilitated on a region-wide basis?

The creation of a Palestinian state, furthermore, does not address the situation and aspirations of Palestinians, who comprise more than one-fifth of Israel's citizens. Unless they would be willing to move to a Palestinian state outside Israel, which polls say most of them are not, having the two states separate simply does not lift the burden of inequality and domination Palestinians currently suffer in Israel. Palestinian citizens of Israel suffer many kinds of discrimination, and have limited freedom of association and cultural expression. Some have had their lands taken by the state and their houses demolished, and others suffer different indignities at the hands of both the state and private organizations. Of course, demands should be made on Israel to respect the rights of all its citizens, and Palestinian citizens are not the only minorities arguably treated unfairly in Israeli society. Because many Palestinian Israelis have or desire personal and political connection with Palestinians now living in the occupied territories, as well as with those living in Jordan, Lebanon, and Syria, Palestinian institutions from which they are entirely separate sit poorly with their aspirations for connection with the Palestinian project of self-determination.[17] In this connection, most articulations of a plan of two separate states do not respond to the aspirations of Palestinians now living outside either territory to return to those territories.

A singular secular state for Palestine/Israel

We can imagine a completely different form of political institution for this region, one that certainly recognizes that the peoples living in the region now live closely among one another in many locales. There might be a single political unit covering the territory that is now Israel along with the territories Israel occupied in 1967, but one belonging to no particular nationality or religious group. This single state would be secular and individualist. All members would have equal and identical rights, and law and social policy would give no recognition to groups.

A secular individualist state in what is now Palestine/Israel has been the dream of many people who care about this conflict since before the founding of Israel. With the establishment of a separate Palestinian state apparently on hold, discussion of a singular secular individualist state has been revived to some extent.[18]

That all members of a polity should have equal civil and political rights is a basic principle of morality and international law, and a secular individualist state is arguably the most direct way to institutionalize that principle. At least at this point in the history of conflict in the region, however, this is a problematic alternative just because it recognizes only individuals and gives no status to peoples. Some Jews, both inside and outside Israel, find this suggestion an anathema because they understand it as the elimination of Israel as a state for the Jewish *people*.[19] Insofar as this alternative gives no specific recognition to groups or to the aspirations of peoples to self-determination, they are right. Peoples, such as the Jewish people and the Palestinian people, have a legitimate claim for a social and political means to govern themselves in their own ways and to enact public expressions of their history and culture as a people. The humanist vision of a secular individualist state conflicts with these goals. Each people has some grounds for their fear of being oppressed as a group with such a nominally neutral state: Jews because they would soon be a minority, and Palestinians because Jews would begin with greater power, wealth and privilege.

Bi-national federalism

The second of the above alternatives denies the claim of a people for institutional self-determination. The first alternative recognizes claims of self-determination, but does so in an exclusionary way that fails to respond to interdependence and relations of domination.

Institutions implementing an understanding of self-determination as nondomination offer a third conceptual alternative. In this application, we envision a distinct political unit or units for the Jewish people and the Palestinian people. Each unit or set of units exercises political, cultural, and local resource autonomy. As I imagine this alternative, it does not involve two and only two units, one Palestinian and one Jewish; rather it imagines a number of smaller and dispersed Palestinian- and Jewish-identified units, as well as some that are identified only by locale. Citizens of each, however, whatever their group affiliations, have equal civil and political rights additionally within a system of shared rule in which the units participate. The purpose of a federated level is to constitute and maintain regular procedures through which units negotiate their ongoing relationships, in order to limit the possibility of some dominating others and to promote the benefits of cooperative action and economies of scale. Over the last 50 years there have also been discussions about federal solutions for conflict in the region, though most of these have presumed meanings of federalism which I have brought into question in the previous section.

In the previous section I put into question the image of federation that assumes its units as large, contiguous territories each of which has the same rights and powers. A federated system of Israeli and Palestinian jurisdictions might be best envisioned also as challenging these assumptions. Some alternative imaginings about Palestine/Israel propose shared rule over Jerusalem, which would constitute a distinct jurisdiction with specific rights and powers not symmetrical to or falling under the jurisdiction of either the Israeli or Palestinian state.[20] One articulation of this idea of a district of Jerusalem envisions a metropolitan federation of local self-governing districts peopled mostly by Jews or Palestinians, and each giving expression to the self-determining desires of those peoples.[21] A more general vision of federation between Palestinian and Jewish units in districts of Palestine/Israel cannot imagine simply a vertical relation between local and federal institutions. Instead, locally self-governing towns or districts coming under Palestinian jurisdiction would need to engage in relations of cooperation and negotiation with neighboring local towns or districts coming under Israeli jurisdiction.[22] Such interspersed federated discontiguous local districts would extend over the breadth of what is now Israel and the occupied territories. Insofar as they might have direct relationships, they would be enacting horizontal federalism of the sort I have discussed above.

Envisioning self-determining units as relatively small, the size of municipalities or metropolitan areas, and horizontally related to other such units, has an additional normative advantage. Units that begin such a relationship understanding themselves as representing distinct peoples might evolve more sense of mutual identification over time because they interact about problems they face together or establish cooperative relations around specific issues or interests. Whereas self-determination understood as state sovereignty and noninterference tends to reinforce closed and essentialized national identities, self-determination as nondomination can be more open to change and fusion, as developed voluntarily by people who live and work in close proximity.

The conception of self-determination as nondomination applies in principle, in my view, to the entire world. It implies that sovereignty as noninterference is not the appropriate principle for any of the world's peoples, and thus implies that the existing states of the world, as well as peoples claiming self-determination but who do not have states, ought to develop more integrated institutions of cooperation at local, regional, and global levels. Self-determination as nondomination can be fully institutionalized in one place only if it is institutionalized in others.

A scenario of self-determination as nondomination for Jews, Palestinians, and others in Palestine/Israel thus cannot be isolated from an imagined future for the wider Middle East region. The state of Israel that defines itself as a Jewish state currently exercises inexcusable domination of Palestinians both inside Israel and in the occupied territories. When we widen the lens to include the entire Middle Eastern region, however, it is the Jewish people who appear vulnerable to domination by an Arab majority. The fates of all the peoples in the region are necessarily linked by factors such as environmental conditions and economic interaction. Stable institutions of self-determination for both Jews and Palestinians in this region ultimately would seem to require establishing federated institutions of conflict resolution and cooperative action among several of the now existing states in the region together with a reconfigured set of autonomous units in Palestine/Israel.[23] Regional autonomy in such wider federated relationships would have to support the autonomy and prosperity of predominantly Jewish self-governing units alongside predominantly Arab ones.

The question of the right of Palestinians displaced in the process that created Israel to return to their homelands is difficult for any of these three options to face. It is perhaps the least vexing for the singular state alternative. Any institutional arrangement for the future of Palestine/Israel should recognize the Palestinians in Jordan, Syria, Lebanon, and in the occupied territories who were, or whose parents and grandparents were, forced out of their homes. I have no wisdom to offer here about what this should mean in practice. Insofar as a vision of horizontal federalism might and should be extended beyond Palestine/Israel to the entire Middle Eastern region, however (as well as in principle to other parts of the world), self-determination as nondomination might also offer resources to imagine ways that Palestinian refugees can claim their rights of relationship to other dispersed Palestinians.

The primary purpose of this essay has been to explain and defend the moral value of a conception of self-determination as relational autonomy or nondomination, as against the still more accepted principle of self-determination as noninterference. Because of the dense interrelation of Palestinian and Jewish people in the lands of Palestine/Israel, I find this conception particularly apt here for trying to imagine alternative institutional possibilities. Conflicts among peoples all over the world, however, often involve similar spatial and economic interdependence that require imagination of autonomy without separation. Most of these proximities and unequal relations of interdependence also result from histories of unjust domination which should be recognized, but cannot be completely undone. The question is now how to afford peoples who consider themselves distinct self-determination while limiting their ability to dominate others and enabling their ability to cooperate.

The alternative I have imagined for Palestine/Israel is not a political proposal. Political actors involved in the conflict themselves must develop those. Despite the rigidity of some leaders and other political actors both inside and outside the region – and not least the leaders of my government, the United States – there is nevertheless hope for change because both Palestinian and Israeli participants in civil society have been working across the divide to try to offer new possibilities for peace.

Part II

War and Violence

4

Power, Violence, and Legitimacy: A Reading of Hannah Arendt in an Age of Police Brutality and Humanitarian Intervention

In the spring of 1999 I was completing a book on democracy. Its arguments assume a basic commitment to democratic values – the rule of law, liberty, equal respect, and a desire to work out disagreement through discussion. Suddenly I was paralyzed in my work. With NATO bombs raining on Yugoslavia, reflection on the essentially nonviolent values of democracy felt irrelevant at best and arrogantly privileged at worst.

While living in Vienna in 1998 I had followed with horror the escalating attacks by Serbian soldiers on both armed and unarmed Albanian Kosovars, which seemed more immediate there than they had in the United States. Thus, in the early months of 1999, I had hoped that the negotiations including the United States, Western European countries, Russia, and Yugoslavia would succeed in stopping this violence. When European negotiators delivered their final offer and it was rejected by Yugoslavia, for a few days I swallowed the self-righteous rhetoric of United States and European leaders, and I approved of the NATO war.

When it became clear that the war made the Serbian army more able and willing than before to force the flight of hundreds of thousands of Albanian Kosovars, and that NATO had foreseen these consequences without planning a response to them, I was dumbstruck. When it further appeared that NATO's strategy was to target civilians and cripple the economy of an entire country, I was overcome with shame and rage. Obsessed with this war and the fact that it was being waged by 19 of the world's democracies, none of which had consulted with its citizens, I felt impelled to think about violence. But where could I turn to help me think? In this moment of rupture I reopened

one of the only works of recent political theory that reflects specifically on the theme of violence: Hannah Arendt's essay, *On Violence*.[1]

Arendt there notes that political theorists have rarely reflected on
violence as such. While there is a long tradition of theoretical writing
on warfare, most of this theorizes strategy, balance of power, or the
meaning of sovereignty violation, rather than reflecting specifically
on the meaning and use of violence per se. Forty years later, her
observation remains good. Although the last decades of the twentieth century saw acts of violent horror that mock midcentury
pledges of "never again," most contemporary political theorists have
neglected systematic reflection on violence in public affairs.[2] Perhaps
just as remarkable, in the vast recent literature interpreting and
extending Arendt's ideas, there is little focused discussion about her
conceptualization of violence and the logic of its relation to other key
political concepts.[3]

In this essay I focus on Arendt's small text on violence, which distills
and expands some of the insights and positions she developed in other
texts, such as *The Origins of Totalitarianism*, *On Revolution*, and *The
Human Condition*.[4] *On Violence* is a dense and suggestive essay. I find
its positions confusing and that Arendt does not follow through on an
elaboration of some of its important distinctions. Her central and self-
consciously counterintuitive claim is that power and violence are
opposites. I aim to make sense of this contentious claim, and to explain
how it challenges commonly accepted understandings of the relationship of state power and violence. I shall elaborate Arendt's claim that
violence may sometimes be justified, but it cannot be legitimate.
Through this reading of Arendt I will reflect on and evaluate manifes-
tations of official violence which I believe enjoy too much acceptance
in contemporary societies: the use of violent means by police and military intervention that claims to protect human rights. Along with
Martha Minow, I will criticize a view of the state and law which takes
violence as a necessary and normal tool. Minow argues that the nor-
malized use of violence by states contributes more to fueling cycles of
violence than it does to halting them.[5] Arendt's distinction between
power and violence offers material for criticizing official violence and
for an alternative conceptualization of state power.

Prelude: clearing away the mess

Written at the height of the Vietnam War and in the wake of campus protest all over the world, *On Violence* reveals Arendt as the

arrogant conservative many of us wish she were not. Despite her theoretical praise for council democracy, when something like it erupts on campus lawns in her neighborhood, Arendt reacts more like an annoyed professor than a republican citizen. She shares with the student protestors a revulsion of the war in Vietnam; indeed, this is one of her motives for writing the essay. She thinks that the logic of the student movements undermines the spirit of the university, however, especially when students demand to study subjects they deem more "relevant" than the standard curriculum.

Antiwar activists and curriculum reformers, however, apparently are not the people most to be feared. It is the "appearance of the Black Power movement on the campuses" (p. 18) that most disturbs her. Arendt heaps contempt on these students who demand courses in "non-existent subjects" such as women's studies or Black studies, and asserts that this movement has succeeded in forcing universities to admit unqualified students. Arendt thought that universities were going to hell, that student radicals, especially Black student radicals, were responsible for this sorry situation, and that this tragedy was symptomatic of a general loss of public reason.

The interest of Black radicals, she says, is to lower academic standards, and to bring the cries of brute social need to ivied halls, where their din drowns out all deliberation. Influenced by Sartre, Fanon, Mao, Che, and other confused and dangerous revolutionaries, the Black student movement celebrates violence, and in so doing it abandons the nobility of the Civil Rights movement. "To expect people, who have not the slightest notion of what the res publica, the public thing, is, to behave nonviolently and argue rationally in matters of interest is neither realistic nor reasonable" (p. 78). Arendt's attitude toward student radicals and especially toward Black radicals, as expressed in this text, is embarrassing and offensive. As some important recent commentary on Arendt's writing as a public intellectual points out, Arendt had a poor understanding of racism in America and of the movements around her resisting it.[6]

The text has other political flaws. Arendt surely overdraws the distinction between Marx, who for all his commitment to an idea of progress never gave up an understanding of praxis, and twentieth-century Marxism, in the persons of Sartre and Fanon, which she regards as naive, dangerous, corrupted, and mechanistic. In this text as in others, moreover, Arendt insists that the entrance of need onto the public stage of modernity leads to nothing but mischief. Many have argued that she is simply wrong about this, and I agree with them.[7] Arendt's ideas have many such problems and prejudices, but I do not need to repeat the criticisms that others have made so well.

The core conceptualization of violence and power that I wish to elaborate from Arendt's suggestive reflections, however, can be disentangled from these other concerns and set out on its own. Contemporary politics can learn much from doing so.

Violence as rational and instrumental

I find no definition of violence in Arendt's essay. I shall assume that by "violence" we mean acts by human beings that aim physically to cause pain to, wound or kill other human beings, and/or damage or destroy animals and things that hold a significant place in the lives of people. Active threats to wound or kill also fall under a concept of violence.[8] In this essay Arendt reflects not on any and all forms and occasions of violence, but on violence in public affairs, those actions and events where individuals and groups express aggression, hate, disagreement, and conflict concerning issues of government and rules, coexistence and exclusion, etc., in violent ways. In this essay Arendt aims to overturn several misconceptions about such political violence. Before dwelling on the most important of those, namely Arendt's claim that violence is confused conceptually with power, I shall briefly review another mistake political theorists make about violence, according to Arendt.

One reason that few philosophers choose to theorize about violence, Arendt suggests, may be that they believe that violence is irrational and unpredictable. On this understanding, violence is pervasive but senseless. It ruptures routine, breaks and destroys people and things, but because of its unpredictability and irrationality there is little that theory can say about it. This statement is partly true and partly false. Violence is unpredictable in the same way that action is unpredictable, but it is not usually irrational.

A key characteristic of violence, says Arendt, is its reliance on instruments, the instruments of destruction. Violence is more or less fierce in proportion to the ability of its instruments to inflict damage and destruction on people and things. Not only does violence usually involve the use of instruments, the technical development and number of which magnify destructive effects, but the wounds and killing wrought in acts of violence are usually themselves instrumental. Wanton acts of violence are less common than calculated, deliberate, planned, and carefully executed violent strategems aimed at specific objectives. In that sense most acts of violence are rational. They are, however, also unpredictable for the same reason that action itself is unpredictable.

In *The Human Condition*, Arendt develops her particular concept of action, and distinguishes it from labor and work.[9] Human activity counts as action insofar as it consists in initiative, in bringing something uniquely new into the world. An action is not predetermined from antecedent conditions. Consequently, action is subject to interpretation. The agent has purposes of his or her own construction, which have their place in a narrative of his or her character and plans. Unlike labor or production, for Arendt, action is essentially social because it takes place in relation to others' plans and meanings. For this reason not only is an action unpredictable, a rupture of routine, but so is the reaction of others to an action. Action is an expression of natality, beginning, not only because it ruptures routine, but also because the response of others makes its consequences unpredictable. To the extent that people engage in violence as means to enact their purposes, violence is also unpredictable, a rupture in the course of events.

Violence appears as the most salient unpredictable phenomenon in human affairs only because modern theory tries to conceptualize politics within a science which can render its events predictable. Efforts to turn the study of politics into a science, according to Arendt, are as old as Plato. In their modern form, these efforts construct public affairs and the course of history as subject to regularities. Arendt mentions two models of history and politics as in principle predictable: an organic model and a production model. The organic model treats history and social change as like biological processes. The seeds of the present are in the past; societies and regimes grow, reach maturity, and eventually decay and die. Under the pens of thinkers such as Nietzsche and Sorel, Arendt suggests, violence becomes as inevitable in history as death is in nature. Violence can even become a positive aspect of politics in this framework, because it prunes away the dead wood and generates new growth.

The production model, on the other hand, imagines political events as under the control of a planner guiding them to their intended end. Many revolutionaries of both right and left act as though politics can realize a social plan. Those who try to reduce politics to bureaucratic administration display a similar image of public affairs as ideally under the control of rational plans and well-honed instruments which properly trained people can use to bring about predictable consequences. This productive model can also give a neutral or positive place to violence in history; to produce something out of raw material it is necessary to do violence to its initial form.

Perhaps noticing the instrumental character of violence accounts for its being inserted into a production model of politics. Both the production model and the organic model of politics and history, however, deny the specificity of human affairs as action. They endeavor to dissolve the novelty of human actions into instances of general trends and tendencies. Violence is closer to action than production, insofar as it constitutes a rupture in predictable routines, insofar as it relates subjects to one another, and insofar as the performer cannot predict its consequences because he or she cannot predict how others will react. While violence is connected to the realm of action in these ways, Arendt's main claim in this essay is that violence should be distinguished from power, understood as the capacity for collective action.

Confusion of violence with power

Perhaps another reason that political theorists reflect so little on violence as such, Arendt suggests, is that they assume that violence is already subsumed under their subject matter when they theorize political power. Theorists and political actors typically confuse violence with power. They either take power to be based on the capacity for violence, or they conceptualize violence as an extension of power. Arendt's main task in this essay is to distinguish these two concepts. I shall elaborate the meaning of her distinction, and argue that it has important normative implications.

Political philosophy should be careful to distinguish several apparently close concepts: power, force, strength, authority, and violence. Force is a strictly physical concept, the energy that moves and resists inertia, what imposes constraints or breaks through them. Strength counts as the ability both to exert and to resist force. A body is strong insofar as it can overcome the resistance of another, or insofar as it resists the force that aims to act upon, move, or transform it. A person is strong just insofar as he or she moves against the resistance of things and persons. Strength is indivisible and resides only in one body. Use of strength to exert force, though, can be magnified through instruments. By acquiring instrumental means of exerting force for the sake of destruction and the threat of destruction, individuals or groups often can induce the compliance of others with their commands or wishes. Violence relies on force and strength, and magnifies them with instruments.

Arendt insists, however, that power is conceptually and practically entirely different from violence. Power consists in collective action. Power is the ability of persons jointly to constitute their manner of living together, the way they organize their rules and institutions through reciprocal self-understanding of what the rules are and how they foster cooperation. Thus, power relies not on bodies and instruments that exert force, but primarily on speech – the interpretation of meaning, the articulation of new ideas, the dynamics of persuasion, the linking of understanding and action. Power establishes and maintains institutions, that is, regulated and settled means of cooperating to bring about collective ends. It has its basis and continuance in the consent and support of those who abide by, live according to, and interpret rules and institutions to bring about new collective ends. Those who engage in collective action must communicate and cooperate, discuss their problems, and jointly make plans. Insofar as successful institutions mobilize the cooperation of a large number of people in their operations, who understand the meaning and goals of the institutions, know the rules, and in general endorse their operations, they embody power.

Power is distinct from strength in that it exists between people rather than in them. Power is a feature of action and interaction insofar as people understand one another's words and deeds and coordinate with one another to achieve mutually understood ends. Thus, power involves some kind of agreement, whether in word or action. Those who participate in the collective action that founds and maintains institutions and the enactment of their ends must know what they are doing and engage with one another to coordinate their actions.

With these distinctions, Arendt stands opposed to a major tendency in modern political theory. She holds that the confusion of violence with power stems from a common understanding of state power as the exercise of sovereign domination. Political power, on this view, is nothing other than the rule of some over others, the exercise of command and successful obedience. While Max Weber is hardly alone in this view, his theory of the state may have exerted the most influence over contemporary thinking. For Weber the state has the monopoly over the legitimate use of violence. In this paradigm, state and law are founded on the capacity for violence: the state and its legal system is simply the vehicle that a hegemonic group creates for itself to further its purposes, maintain itself in power, and rule over the rest.[10]

Arendt agrees that if in fact political power, government, means simply that state officials of whatever sort – kings, lords, presidents, cabinet ministers, generals – exercise dominion over the actions of others in a territory, then power and violence are sensibly associated. There is no doubt that many rulers have relied on killing or torture and their threats to induce compliance with their wills and goals from subjects, and that they often succeed. "If the essence of power is the effectiveness of command, then there is no greater power than that which grows out of the barrel of a gun" (p. 37).

Arendt argues, however, that the success and stability of even despotic regimes over a long term depends on eliciting the voluntary cooperation of at least a large mass of subjects with rules and institutions that enact their living together and their common projects, that is on power understood as collective action. Even government understood as sovereign dominion depends for its success on a regularity of mutually understood, cooperative activities, and in this respect on the consent of those ruled.

Historically, such consent and support were often tied to beliefs in the authority of the rulers. Government as sovereignty has rested on the use of violence far less than on belief systems which have anointed certain individuals or groups with the right to the service and obedience of others. Ideologies of authority construct the ground of right in values and personages that transcend politics and mundane narrative time. Authoritarian hierarchical systems of government derive their power to a great extent from the commitment of subjects to these beliefs in the transcendent ground of the right to rule.[11] Thus, Arendt suggests in *On Violence* that we should also distinguish the concept of authority from power. Authority is the quality of receiving unquestioned recognition and obedience as appeal to a transcendent origin from which the ruler's right derives. Power, on the other hand, in the sense of collective action, depends on persuading one another in the here and now to cooperate.

Modernity erodes authority, according to Arendt; the disenchantment of the world means it becomes more difficult for rulers to succeed in eliciting obedience by appealing to unquestioned transcendent foundations. The egalitarian and democratic impulses of modernity reject belief in the divine right of kings or the superior wisdom of philosopher princes that gives them the right of command. Moderns attempt to install science as a new kind of authority, and efforts to base a political hierarchy on expertism continue to be partially successful. The order of experts is not stable, however, because it rests on no timeless and otherworldly cosmology. Under these circumstances, rulers who aim to exercise dominion over subjects must depend even more than before on the collective action of those ruled and their commitment to prevailing institutions and practices.

This fact becomes most apparent if and when people withdraw their consent, when people begin to act collectively toward different ends than those the rulers intend or desire. Rulers are helpless before such a shift in power. If they have the means of violence at their disposal – which usually means depending on the power of organized armies – they can attempt to impose their will on a disobedient public through force. The ruler can bomb neighborhoods, eliminate opponents, and keep a threatening watch over people to limit their ability to communicate and cooperate. Violence and the threat of violence can in this way destroy power, but never create or sustain it. Since power depends on collective action, it rests on the freedom of a plurality of distinct individuals aiming to foster their institutions. The tyrant who rules through violence is relatively impotent. While he may prevent action and resistance, and may be able to enforce service of his needs and desires, he can accomplish nothing worldly.

Of course, history is cluttered with regimes structured by relations of ruler and subject, and these often rely on the threat of violence to compel obedience to the ruler's will when actions threaten to undermine or resist that will. But such regimes of domination are weak just insofar as they must depend on compulsion in this way. They are powerful only if at least a large segment of the people they govern cooperate through consent and collective will, sustaining the institutions in which they live together, express their meanings, and enact their collective goals.

Thus, Arendt contrasts power and violence. "Power and violence are opposites; where one rules absolutely, the other is absent. Violence appears where power is in jeopardy, but left to its own course it ends in power's disappearance. This implies that it is not correct to think of the opposite of violence as nonviolence; to speak of non-violent power is already redundant. Violence can destroy power; it is ultimately incapable of creating it" (p. 56).[12]

Though violence and power are opposites in this conceptual and phenomenological sense, Arendt says that they often occur together. Although governments often rely on the use and threat of violence, systems of government that rest on command and obedience must also rely on the collective action of subjects – power – for their effectiveness. While movements to resist or overturn such regimes must mobilize mass power of collective organization to succeed, they often also use means of violence to aid their objectives. That epitome of violence, war, is also an example of power. A disciplined army depends on the solidarity of its soldiers, their willingness to work together and protect each other under stress.

Power and violence are opposites, but they often occur together. This sounds contradictory.[13] By interpreting Arendt's distinction between violence and power not only as conceptual, but also as normative, we can make sense of this statement. While violence and power in fact often occur together, they need not, and they ought not, at least not often and not very much. The interpretation of governance that identifies it with sovereign dominion is problematic because it conceives political power as necessarily oppressive, and living under government as necessarily a denial of freedom. There is another interpretation of government that does not assume the inevitability of a relation of command and obedience, and the necessary connection with violence these seem to entail. Arendt uses a Greek word for this alternative: isonomy. Jeffrey Isaac describes isonomy as "a concept of power and law whose essence did not rely on the command-obedience relation and which did not identify power and rule or law and command."[14] Isonomy names a process of governance as self-government, where the citizens have equal status and must rely on one another equally for developing collective goals and carrying them out. Just insofar as government in this form depends on speech and persuasion, it precludes violence and violence is its opposite. Government ought to be the exercise of power as the expression and result of people coming together, assessing their problems and collective goals, discussing together how to deal with them, and persuading one another to adopt rules and policies, then each self-consciously acting to effect them.

Arendt finds occasional historical bursts of sheer collective action and publicity, when a plurality of people through their mutual understanding and collective promising enact a public as the space of the appearance of singular and plural deeds and as the expressions of their freedom. People govern themselves by means of rules they formulate, understand and trust one another to follow, as a condition of their own cooperative action. They enact collective projects that originate from their public deliberations upon their institutions, problems, and desires. In this fragile space of power there are no rulers to be obeyed, though there are often leaders and great persuaders.

> What makes a man a political being is his faculty of action; it enables him to get together with his peers, to act in concert, and to reach out for goals and enterprises that would never enter his mind, let alone the desires of his heart, had he not been given this gift – to embark on something new (p. 82).

Such a statement about the meaning of political action – power in Arendt's sense – seems so abstract as to be vacuous. When people act in concert with their peers, what are they doing? What are these goals and enterprises that would otherwise never enter their minds, that are original ruptures in the passage of events, that exhibit this mysterious quality of natality? The question becomes even more acute when one takes account of Arendt's insistence that action is wholly distinct from labor and work, distinct from activities of producing what will meet needs and consuming those products, on the one hand, and from the fashioning of those works that not only build social surroundings, and serve as instruments of living and doing, but also stand as lasting monuments to a people and culture, on the other hand. If collective action neither serves the goals of building cathedrals nor producing food, then what are its goals and enterprises?

Some commentators have complained that Arendt's strong distinction between the social and the political is both unacceptably conservative and renders the concept of political power empty. Arendt decries what she perceives as a modern propensity for the public sphere and law increasingly to be dominated by discussion of how to alleviate social problems – poverty, unequal distribution of wealth, discrimination, urban blight and development, water and transportation planning, the organization of health care, and so on.[15] This deep distrust of an interest in bringing social issues into the light of public discussion partly explains her antipathy to the Black Power movement.

In the essay we are considering, Arendt's vitriolic remarks about bureaucracy are tied to this insistence that the political should not be tainted by the social. Attention to the social elevates the meeting of needs to the primary purpose of government, purges government of politics, and thereby levels it to the lowest common denominator. Bureaucracy attempts to harness people's energies into a kind of machine in which the administration of things will meet needs. The goal of bureaucracy is to implement rules and procedures that determine routines that workers and clients can follow, rendering themselves fungible, to achieve production, distribution, and service delivery objectives as efficiently as possible. The purpose of bureaucracy, that is to say, is to reduce as much as possible any need for action in Arendt's sense. "In a fully developed bureaucracy there is nobody left with whom one can argue, to whom one can present grievances, on whom the pressures of power can be exerted. Bureaucracy is the form of government in which everybody is deprived of political freedom, of the power to act; for the rule by Nobody is not no-rule, and where all are equally powerless we have a tyranny without a tyrant" (p. 81).

The bureaucratic principle is the opposite of power and collective action. Whereas people acting collectively are mindful of their goals and deliberate about the best means to achieve them, in the logic of bureaucracy the means are related to the ends not through opinion and deliberation, but through regulated routine, where distinct activities are efficiently organized. The whole point of bureaucratic logic is that participants should not have to think about how to achieve coordinated ends. Bureaucracies create hierarchies of command and obedience that are supposed to make the operation of routines more efficient. Just to the extent that people become disempowered, however, the bureaucracy becomes less able to fulfill its role of the administration of things and the meeting of needs. Its parts fail to coordinate; the system becomes irrational, or it becomes corrupt – its command mechanisms come to serve private gain rather than the achievement of collectively agreed upon ends. Thus even the effective pursuit of public administration depends on power in Arendt's sense – that people act collectively in a self-conscious way that involves deliberation, persuasion, and following through the collective will with implementation.

As I understand Arendt's concepts, the successful achievement of any socially organized ends depends on power. Collective action is awesome and monumental, but difficult to achieve and sustain. Military campaigns, imperial rule of extensive territory, the establishment of an effective health care service, the organization of a mass resistance movement that brings down a dictatorial regime, the conduct of constitutional dialogue over a period of years, these all require and manifest power in Arendt's sense. There seems to me to be no reason to exclude matters having to do with meeting needs, production, and service provision from the scope of activities to which such power can and should be brought to bear. It is not only bureaucratically organized meeting of needs that carries dangers of the dissipation or corruption of power; they all do. Power only exists as long as it is actively sustained by the plural participants in the endeavor who self-consciously coordinate with one another. If they withdraw their commitment or ease their communication, or if acts of violence break up their relationships, only a shell will be left.

Power, and the political, then, I interpret as an aspect of any social institution or collective activity, including some of those that enact sovereign dominion or repressive domination. Institutions cannot be effective for long unless they have occasions when participants set their collective goals, discuss what institutions, rules, and practices would best coordinate their actions to achieve those goals, and make commitments to one another to carry out their responsibilities in the system of cooperation.

Power is thus necessary for government, but it is also fragile. People easily and often lose this sense of public promise, and disperse into the impotent privacy of a concern for their own survival or pleasure. To the extent that governing institutions remain, they freeze into routinized bureaucracies, become cronyist semiprivate operations, or elicit conformity through terror. The use of violence in public affairs is normatively questionable not only because killing and causing suffering are prima facie wrong. Violence is also morally problematic because its use, especially if routine, widespread, or massive, endangers power. "Violence appears where power is in jeopardy, but left to its own course it ends in power's disappearance" (p. 56). When rulers or those who most benefit from a given order of things find that they or their goals lose popular support, they often try to restore their power through the use of violence. Such actions may well reduce resistance but they do not restore power. Violence not only harms individuals, but it makes their lives difficult to carry on as before. When either rulers or resisters adopt the use of violence as a regular means of trying to elicit the cooperation of others, they tend to produce the opposite effect: flight, retreat into privacy, preemptive strikes, distrust of all by all. The use of violence in politics is problematic, moreover, because its consequences so easily and often escalate beyond the specific intentions its uses have. Violent acts tend to produce violent responses that radiate beyond the original acts.

Arendt's concept of power is abstract and incomplete. Although she discusses people's movements and revolutions as well as the activities of governments, her theory tends to ignore structural social relations, and their manner of channeling power to the systematic advantage of some and the disadvantage of others. Her conceptual distinction between power and violence, however, which I have interpreted as having normative significance as well, opens important possibilities for rethinking the relations of power and freedom.

Legitimacy and justification

Thus far in this essay I have reviewed Arendt's discussion of several confusions about violence and politics to which Arendt believes many theorists have been prone: that violence is irrational or inevitable, and most importantly, that violence is the basis of power. In the following passage she signals another common confusion which she traces to this confusion of violence and power:

> Power needs no justification, being inherent in the very existence of political communities; what it does need is legitimacy. . . . Power springs up whenever people get together to act in concert, but it

derives its legitimacy from the initial getting together rather than from any action that then may follow. Legitimacy, when challenged, bases itself on appeal to the past, while justification relates to an end that lies in the future. Violence can be justifiable, but it never will be legitimate. Its justification loses in plausibility the farther its intended end recedes into the future (p. 52).

Like so much else in this text, Arendt's claims here are provocative and suggestive, but she does not elaborate them further. In this section I will try to follow through on this distinction between legitimacy and justification. Making sense of these claims is key for the arguments about official violence that I will make in the next section. Power does not need justification, but does require legitimacy; violence calls for justification, but it can never be legitimate. What does this mean?

Both legitimacy and justification are concepts of moral reasoning. Both concern ways of giving reasons for an action or structure. In the passage quoted, Arendt offers only one hint about the difference in these forms of giving an account: legitimation appeals to the past, while justification appeals to the future in relation to the act.

To find more texts that will help unlock this mystery one can turn to *On Revolution*. There Arendt draws a connection between power, in the sense of original collective action, and the activity of founding new institutions which can preserve that power and give it embodiment in law.

> Power comes into being only if and when men join themselves together for the purpose of action, and it will disappear when, for whatever reason, they disperse and desert one another. Hence, binding and promising, combining and covenanting are the means by which power is kept in existence. . . . Just as promises and agreements deal with the future and provide stability in the ocean of future uncertainty where the unpredictable may break in from all sides, so the constituting, founding, and world-building capacities of men concern always not so much ourselves and our own time on earth as our "successors" and "posteriorities."[16]

Power consists in collective action, people coming together and supporting one another to do deeds and accomplish goals the like of which "would never enter his mind, let alone the desires of his heart, had he not been given this gift" (*On Violence*, p. 82). Power is often fleeting, however; it springs out of relations between people who accomplish something, and then dissipates. For power to be a force in politics, it needs to be institutionalized, and this is what foundings accomplish. In founding a constitution the empowered collective gives itself relative permanence, a permanence guaranteed through covenants. In the moment of founding participants in a public mutually promise to abide by principles that guide institutions, to organize and give their energy to the implementation of the institutions, and to be loyal to the institutions and to one another through them. The mutuality of promise-making is important for Arendt. She cites the spirit of American revolutionaries who, she says, found legitimate power only in the reciprocity and mutuality of promises made between equals, as distinct from the spurious power of kings and aristocrats, which was not founded on mutual promising.

Arguments that government actions, policies, laws, or representatives are legitimate, then, are backward looking because they refer to founding promises. To say that these leaders or policies are legitimate is to make the argument that they are in conformity with, a present embodiment of, the principles and promises that institutionalize the public's power. Making such an argument, I suggest, requires more than the recital of a history or the citation of founding documents. An argument for the legitimacy of present officials, actions, or laws, I suggest, involves a renewal of the power that came into play in the original process, which itself reaffirms the promises, a new commitment of the collective's participants to one another in terms of mutuality and reciprocity. To argue that a government or policy or action is legitimate in these ways does not itself imply that they are just, right, or good. To the extent that institutionalizing power involves mutual promising, however, there is an implicit commitment to the justice or rightness of principles to guide future action, at least as concerning relations with one another.

With this notion of legitimation we can notice another important difference between Weber and Arendt. Despite his identification of the state with sovereign dominion that rests on monopoly over the means of violence, Weber agrees with Arendt that the naked imposition of domination by continual force and violence is an unsteady basis for ruling. State power is most stable according to Weber when it carries legitimacy. Weber's concept of legitimacy, however, is positivistic. Rulers have legitimacy for him just insofar as their subjects accept some rationalization of their ruling position. This could be a religious story about their divine right, or it could be a story about their aristocratic natures, or about how their greater intelligence or skill make them suited for leadership. Or it could be a story about how people have agreed to establish a constitution. As I understand Weber, the content of the story does not matter as much as that it functions to elicit consent from subjects.[17]

In the passage I quoted from *On Revolution*, Arendt distinguishes mutual promise and covenant that gives power legitimacy from simple consent. I take it that consent is only the absence of opposition and resistance, a willingness on the part of subjects to go along with the rules and decrees, and such consent usually has some basis in belief. Each subject consents alone, however, in relation to the state. Covenants to which accounts of the legitimacy of political officials and actions appeal, on the other hand, are public; indeed, they are the effects and institutionalizations of publics that emerge from collective action.

As I understand Arendt's distinction, justification is a less complex affair than legitimation. First, only an action whose moral value is in question requires justification. This is why Arendt says that power needs no justification. The default position for power is that it is valuable; acting in concert enables a unique and wonderful kind of freedom that human beings experience in no other way. The default position for violence, on the other hand, is that it is a disvalue. Violence destroys, and it is not very violent unless it destroys valuable things – human lives or things meaningful to human lives and action.

Thus, any act of violence calls for justification, an account of why it is morally acceptable. When Arendt claims that such an account is always forward looking, she refers to the instrumental character of violence. A justification of violence can only appeal to the good it brings about, its consequences. Justification of violence cannot be retrospective in the ways that are arguments about legitimacy, because violence is always a rupture that breaks through the continuity of the present with the past. Arendt claims that the plausibility of a justification for violence declines the further its intended good consequence recedes into the future.

Arendt does not offer criteria for what justifies violence in politics. A thorough account would require more space than I have in this essay. The argument I will make next about official violence, however, presupposes some understanding of the limits of the justification of violence. I will assume that most acts of violence cannot be morally justified; they are in the service of wrongful efforts on the part of some people to dominate and coerce others into doing what they want, or to remove the resistance of others. A narrow range of violent actions may be justified, however, according to such considerations as the following: whether they are likely to prevent serious harm, under circumstances where other preventive measures are not available; and whether they are constrained in their consequences, that is, do not have harmful consequences that reach beyond their immediate effect, whether intended or unintended. Few real-world acts of violence satisfy these conditions, I suggest, especially in the context of politics and public affairs.

There is a final aspect to the distinction between the legitimacy of power and the justification of violence that I interpret from Arendt's hints. Whereas arguments about the legitimacy of one act or policy can often appeal to previous arguments about legitimacy, arguments justifying violence cannot appeal as such to precedent. As I said above, there is a kind of default character to legitimacy that justifications of violence do not share. If it can be shown that a government is legitimate, then the presumption follows that its acts and policies are legitimate. The legitimacy of one law or policy helps reinforce the legitimacy of others. This is appropriate if legitimacy corresponds to a web of institutionalized power expressing the mutual commitments of a public. Because any act of violence is a rupture that endangers that potential or actual commitment and mutuality, however, each act of violence must be justified on its own, on a case by case basis, not by appeal to similar acts from the past, but by argument about its particular unique circumstances and consequences. While there may be very general moral principles and criteria that can be used in such arguments, no institution or authority can produce a set of rules that morally legitimate acts of violence in advance.

Official violence

I will now apply this interpretation of the opposition of power and violence to a particular class of violent acts: those perpetrated by agents of the state as a means to achieve their mission of law enforcement. Martha Minow suggests that government's "uses of violence – in response to crime, disorder, homeless people, and international affairs – also contributes to a pervasive message that violence is acceptable, necessary, and even admirable."[18] She argues that if we wish to prevent violence in spaces as different as living rooms and open fields, we must question the widespread assumption that states ought to use violence to achieve their legitimate ends. I think that Arendt's distinction between violence and power, along with my elaboration of her distinction between legitimacy and justification, can help in this project.

The two differing interpretations of state power that I have reviewed – the Weberian and the Arendtian – yield two radically different understandings of official violence. A Weberian interpretation finds the threat and use of violence to be an essential and normal

component of the actions of legitimate state officials in carrying out
their duties. The critical view of violence that I find in Arendt, on the
other hand, along with her theory of power as collective action, imply
that official violence is always questionable, and thus requires justification. Official violence often fails this justificatory test.

I examine official violence in two forms: police violence in domestic law enforcement and the use of military force by one or more
states against another state or states with the aim of responding to
violations of human rights or the threat of such violations. A Weberian interpretation of state power or sovereignty, I argue, has difficulty
making sense of a concept of police brutality; Arendt's theory offers
the conceptual means to do so. International "police actions" that
claim to enforce international human rights law, or so-called humanitarian intervention, can be theorized on analogy with domestic law
enforcement criteria. If one accepts Arendt's distinction between violence and power, I shall argue, then acts of so-called humanitarian
intervention become questionable.

Police brutality

Arendt herself thematizes police brutality in her essay. She embeds
her impassioned criticism of this mode of official violence in an
arrogant interpretation of the student radicalism and Black community activism. Recall that she heaps contempt on students who
demand courses in "nonexistent subjects" such as women's studies
or Black studies, and asserts that these movements have succeeded
in forcing universities to admit unqualified students by threatening
violence.

Given these deep prejudices against student radicalism, it is especially interesting that she reserves the worst condemnation for official violence – for the impotent bigness of the United States and the
Soviet Union amassing their weapons of mass destruction, and for
the police who respond to protestors with gas, batons, and guns. Police
brutality against essentially nonviolent demonstrations is responsible
for radicalizing the student movement. Violent and massive police
attacks on protestors at the Democratic Party convention in Chicago
in 1968 were a sign of the utter impotence of both the Chicago city
administration, its police force, and the members of the ruling
Establishment of the country. When officials have lost power – that
is, when they no longer have the support and cooperation of masses
of people – they rarely resist the temptation to substitute violence for
power. Almost inevitably, however, the resort to violence further

undermines power, and violence becomes a senseless and irrational end in itself.

In one of her appendices Arendt hypothesizes that police brutality is linked to police inefficiency. To the extent that the police force is unable to prevent crimes or solve those committed, they resort to acts of naked violence against people in the streets. Whether or not her claimed correlations are correct, she expresses a judgment few juries in the US today share: it is not the prerogative of police officers to brutalize citizens when attempting to perform their duties. Arendt worries about a Black racism that responds with violent rage to "ill-designed integration policies whose consequences their authors can easily escape" (p. 77). She seems to fear a ragged horde rising up from the privacy of its poverty to obliterate what little is left of a civilized public sphere. She judges more horrible, however, the prospect of a white racist backlash in which "the climate of opinion in the country might deteriorate to the point where a majority of its citizens would be willing to pay the price of the invisible terror of a police state for law and order in the streets" (p. 77). Such words make an eerie echo in this age where prison-building is a growth industry, sweeping homeless people from the streets with fire hoses has become common, and the number of executions has quadrupled in ten years.

In the late 1990s the United States Justice Department, not exactly a promoter of nonviolence and quiet reason in law enforcement, nevertheless found that some of the routine behavior of police departments in cities such Pittsburgh, PA, was so egregious in its violation of the rights of citizens that it ordered and supervised changes. In Chicago, front-page headlines reported at least a dozen questionable police shootings of citizens in the year 2000. Other citizen complaints are too numerous to report; local protests against police brutality are nearly as regular as church services, but I sense little outrage among most of my neighbors. The streets of Cincinnati recently erupted with anger at what many African-Americans perceived as systematic police abuse. In November 1999 in Seattle, we saw a police riot reminiscent of the Chicago of 1968 that Arendt condemns, but this was mild compared to the actions of police in Genoa in April 2001. Today, it seems to me, perhaps even more than at the time Arendt wrote these words, we have "a kind of police backlash, quite brutal and highly visible." This is something that political philosophers do not generally discuss.

On those rare occasions when police are put on trial for their acts of violence against citizens, juries usually absolve them of guilt. Even in cases where unarmed people have been shot dead by several police officers, they and their advocates have been able to convince juries that their actions fall within their proper line of duty and that their role gives them discretion to use violence when they interpret a situation as requiring it to do their job. Arendt is probably right to suggest that one explanation for why such police violence is so little questioned is that many people believe that it will be used primarily to contain a minority that does not include them. I suggest that an additional explanation for a relatively widespread willingness to condone or excuse official violence results from the ideology of state power that understands it as founded in violence.

The idea that the state is nothing but monopoly on the legitimate use of violence slides easily for many people into the idea that the use of violence by legitimate agents of a legitimate state is itself legitimate. On this account, since the power of the state is ultimately grounded in control over the means of violence, the use of violence by agents of the state is simply an extension and expression of their power. It matters for this account that the state is legitimate, that it brings about and enforces a rule of law, that its agents obtain their offices through proper procedures, and so on. Given a legitimate state whose officials are trying to enforce the law, however, many people think that the maintenance of such "law and order" requires a "show of force." Some might go further: law enforcement officials and other state agents ought to display their willingness to employ the means of violence in order to ensure obedience to the law, and they are most convincing in this display if they actually use violence on a regular basis.

Such an understanding of state power does have a concept of the abuse of power by police. When police use their power in ways that promote their personal gain, when they are corrupt or themselves criminal, they grossly abuse their power. A conception of state power which sees it as grounded in or inherently connected to violence, however, has great difficulty forming a concept of police brutality under circumstances when police believe they are properly doing their job. As long as the official is acting "in the line of duty" and claims that the violent acts are normal or necessary, it seems that many people find them morally acceptable.

As I have discussed above, on the alternative conceptualization suggested by Arendt, the power of states consists in ways they institutionalize the ability for collective action. State institutions can organize decision-making and executive bodies that mobilize to solve collective problems and then the energy to solve them. They actualize this potential only to the extent that people work in them with one another to bring about those results through consciously coordinated action. When state institutions fail to create and implement solutions to collective problems or enact collective visions, which is often, they lack power, and no amount of violence will compensate for that lack. Indeed, the use of violence against those who fail to join the effort is more likely to weaken the ability of the collective to act than to enhance it.

This does not mean that powerful state institutions cannot and should not sometimes force people to abide by its laws and regulations and contribute to its collective goals. Coercion is an inevitable and proper aspect of legal regulation. The sovereigntist view of state power, however, too quickly equates coercion with the threat of violence. I do not have the space to develop a full argument for the claim here, but I suggest that successful coercion is usually more a result of power than of violence. Where there are settled laws and regulations whose objectives are clear and widely accepted, and which were legislated by means of legitimate procedures, then those who attempt to violate or circumvent the laws suffer various forms of sanction, shaming, and punishment often without any violence at all being brought to bear. Some people who would otherwise not do what these laws require are motivated to obey them because they fear these consequences, but this is not the same as saying that they are motivated by the threat of violence.

Arendt's account of power and violence suggests that the use of official violence is always deeply problematic and always calls for specific justification. It can never be regarded as normal and legitimate, because it cannot appeal to founding first principles that authorize it, and because each act of violence endangers the trust and security on which collective power rests. Some acts of official violence may be justified, but these can only be decided case by case according to restrictive criteria such as those I outlined above: their scope is limited, their effects immediate and contained, and the harm they prevent worse than the one they inflict. Insofar as coercive regulation may rely on the use of physical restraint and force to subdue resisters, it may sometimes be justified. There ought to be the strongest presumption against the infliction of injury, however, let alone killing. My observation of contemporary police practices in the United States today, as well as many other places, leads me to conclude that both many police officers and citizens consider such acts a normal and acceptable extension of state power. Every specific act of official violence, however, needs as much justification as acts of violence committed by others, and nothing can legitimate them in advance.

Martha Minow is right to worry that the state's embrace of violence in such systems as police training for assaulting, shooting, and brutalizing suspects may contribute to a general societal approval of violence. She points to a few cities in the United States that have embraced community policing as an alternative model by which to structure the entire practice of policing, where "the use of state power does not model the violence it is intended to prevent."[19] Community policing is a decades old concept in the United States, of course; its concepts and practices in most cities, however, are confined only to a few neighborhoods or programs, alongside and in the context of more general models of policing that rely on threat and use of violence as normal. This balance should at least be reversed, with threats of violence infrequent and contained within a context of organized citizen cooperation and watchfulness.

So-called humanitarian intervention

The last two decades have seen swift support for the conviction that human rights principles should override the claim by states that sovereignty gives them absolute right to regulate what goes on in their territories in whatever way they choose. There is increasing support in the world for the principle that, especially when there are serious and extensive violations of human rights by a state, or when a state is unable to protect its citizens from massive violence, outside agents not only have a right but a duty to intervene to try to protect lives and well-being. I endorse this general direction of international law that limits state sovereignty for the sake of promoting human rights. Nevertheless, I find disturbing that some international actors appear to assume that such commitments to human rights themselves legitimate some states making war on others. Arendt's distinctions between power and violence, and particularly her argument that violence may sometimes be justified but never legitimate, are useful, I suggest, for reflecting on moral issues of so-called humanitarian intervention. I shall argue that these issues about the morally appropriate use of violence parallel those concerning domestic police action.

The judgment has become widespread that the sovereignty of states which seriously violate human rights can be overridden by outsiders who seek to prevent or sanction such violation. International law concerning human rights requires transparency and enforcement, and only state institutions have the powers these requirements imply. In the absence of global state institutions today, single states or coalitions of states recently have taken it upon themselves to act as global police, invading other states or bombing them from above, claiming to do so for the purposes of enforcing human rights. The assumption seems to be strong that it is morally permissible and may be morally required for states to engage in military action against states that violate human rights.

A relatively new development in this evolving human rights regime consists in efforts to legitimate such interventions. Especially in the last decade, some of the world's strongest military powers and alliances have engaged in nondefensive military actions for which they have first sought and claimed to have received legal or quasi-legal authorization. Western powers sought and received the approval of the United Nations Security Council before they launched their war against Iraq in 1991. While the NATO war against Yugoslavia did not have the authorization of the United Nations, NATO claimed that it was legitimate because of the process of discussion and decision-making that took place among the leaders of its 19 members, as well as among a few states outside the alliance. In such processes, world military forces attempt to legitimate their actions when they appeal to international principles they claim have or ought to have the force of law, and when they can point to procedures of international discussion and decision-making that they claim authorize their actions. The opinion seems to be taking hold of powerful international leaders and many of the general public, moreover, that the use of violence against "rogue" states is acceptable and normal, and needs little or no justification beyond a consensus that the state is a law breaker.

If Arendt's account of violence and power is right, however, such an immediate and massive resort to violence as a tool of international law enforcement may be a sign of impotence more than power. I believe that this evolving situation where some states and perhaps also the United Nations speak and act as though they are legitimate agents empowered to do what they judge necessary to enforce the law may be at least as dangerous to peace and international stability as is international anarchy. There appears to be little international imagination for alternative methods of motivating or compelling compliance with human rights norms, and almost no international will to install competent institutions that could enact more settled discussion and cooperation among peoples of the world. When war, indeed devastating war, is almost the first resort of international police powers, and when states engage in what they believe is righteous violence, it opens gulfs of distrust.

On Arendt's account, the use of violence in international relations can be no more legitimate than in domestic life. While international violence, like domestic violence, may sometimes be justified, there too justification must be in terms of its consequences and not by appeal to any supposedly authorizing covenants or principles. Especially when air war and the use of indiscriminate weapons such as land mines are the preferred military means, the claim that such violence is justified is usually difficult to sustain in Arendt's terms: the destruction is too massive, the consequences too long term and unpredictable, too many lives are risked and lost, especially those of civilians. In this era when weapons of mass destruction continue to proliferate, their use against a state on one occasion stimulates their defensive accumulation by others. At the beginning of her essay Arendt declares that these frightful instruments of war have rendered such action irrational. "The technical development of implements of violence has now reached the point where no political goal could conceivably correspond to their destructive potential or justify their actual use in armed conflict. Hence, warfare – from time immemorial the final merciless arbiter in international disputes – has lost much of its effectiveness and nearly all its glamour" (p. 3).

So I will return to my beginning, the NATO war against Yugoslavia. There are significant similarities between this war and incidents of police brutality. NATO claimed that its actions were aimed at stopping the perpetration of crimes by a rogue state. That state had committed crimes against humanity, and NATO claimed to be acting as a legal agent for humanity itself, rather than acting to further its own specific treaty interests or the specific interests of its member nations. NATO officials spoke and acted as if this police-for-the-world role authorized it to use any and all military force in whatever way and for as long as necessary to achieve its objective, the military defeat of Yugoslavia and the capitulation of its President to the terms NATO set for the return of the Kosovar Albanians and the establishment of a government in which they would exercise self-government.

The Independent International Commission on Kosovo concluded in its report that the NATO war was not legal, because it did not have UN authorization. They argued, however, that the war was legitimate. Given the harms coming to Albanian Kosovars, the fact that NATO is multinational, had procedures of deliberation, and had the capacity for military intervention, the Commission agreed with the claim that NATO in this case was acting for humanity to respond to humanitarian crisis. One of their major recommendations for the future of international relations is that institutions and procedures be put in place which can put the legal authorization of humanitarian wars on a firmer footing.[20]

I have argued above that it is a mistake to think that the fact that the state authorizes police to enforce the law itself licenses police to be violent. Use of violent means by police must be independently justified not by appeal to prior authorization, but by showing that the consequences of the violent acts will prevent more harm than they produce. The same holds, I contend, for international relations. I hope that the world is moving toward a condition where there are stronger transnational institutions with the ability legally to authorize multinational and global organizations to police the behavior of states toward the people within their territories as well as toward other states. It is dangerous to assume, however, that stronger institutions of international law themselves can and should authorize the use of violence. Just as in the domestic case, violence must be justified by arguing that it is the only means available to do good, that it does more good than harm, and that it is effective without having undesirable long-term consequences. By such reasoning, I submit that the NATO war was not justified.

Despite its conclusion that the war was legitimate, the Independent Commission also offers much evidence that the war did not achieve its objectives of saving the lives and society of the Albanian Kosovars, and that in general it wreaked more destruction than it prevented. Before March 1999, Serbian forces had employed terror to drive many Albanians in Kosovo away from their homes, but after European protection monitors were pulled out in advance of the NATO bombing campaign, the forced removal and killing of civilians by Serb forces hugely increased. While the report lays first responsibility for the death and suffering inflicted on the removed Kosovars at the feet of the leaders of the Republic of Yugoslavia, they find nevertheless that the NATO campaign aided and abetted the "ethnic cleansing" operation. Not only did the Western "humanitarian" war contribute to suffering on a mass scale, but neither the NATO states nor the United States were at all prepared to respond to the masses of people flooding overburdened border states.

After the war most of the refugees returned to Kosovo, but it is hard to say that they went home. The bombing virtually destroyed the country. Around 120,000 houses in Kosovo were destroyed or damaged by the war, and 250 schools needed repair. Roads were in ruins, bridges destroyed, telephone lines down, and there was no electricity. Thousands of unexploded cluster bombs lay in fields and alleys, and are still killing people. Both the uranium dioxide released into the atmosphere by some of the shells and the toxic leaks caused by some of the bombs have made Kosovo an environmental disaster.

The war not only destroyed economic and environmental infrastructure, but institutions as well. At war's end, there was no functioning health care system, judiciary, or banking system. To the extent that any local governments remained, most were unable to police the streets or perform even the most basic municipal services.

The moral calculation of the consequences of the NATO war must count harm to Serbs as well as to Albanians. Because NATO was unable seriously to weaken the Serbian military with its air war, it took the war to the cities of the north, where endangering civilians was unavoidable; about 500 civilians were killed in Serbia, and at least 820 wounded by NATO sorties. Many more suffered as a result of the virtual elimination of electricity, telecommunications, and industrial capacity of the country.

The war's aftermath so far does not give hope that its long-term consequences are positive. The forces occupying Kosovo under the official mandate of the United Nations could not prevent the killing of hundreds of Serbs from Kosovo, and the expulsion of most of the rest. Since June 1999, Albanian Kosovars have not exercised the self-government they desired, but have effectively been ruled by an international organization. Ethnic conflict and distrust in the region has not abated and is probably worse as a consequence of the war.[21]

On the account of violence that I have derived from Arendt, war cannot be legitimated, as NATO tried to do, but it may perhaps be justified. Such justification comes only by appeal to consequences, I have argued, and those consequences must take all persons affected equally into account. Despite its allegedly noble purposes, then, I think we must conclude that the NATO war was wrong. Theorists, political leaders, and citizens should be careful not to confuse violence with power, even when exercised by legitimate agents of the state or international law. In an age of brutality, we should be very suspicious of the use of violence, and do far more to build institutions that organize the power of collective action without violence.

5

Envisioning a Global Rule of Law
(with Daniele Archibugi)

The attacks on the World Trade Center and the Pentagon in September 2001 can appear within two different frames of interpretation. The first sees them as attacks on the United States as a state and its people. The second views them as crimes against humanity. The difference in interpretation is not technical, but political, and each implies different strategies of reaction. Shortly after the attack some public leaders, such as Mary Robinson, then Director of the United Nations Commission on Human Rights, recommended that the United States and the rest of the world adopt the second interpretation. It seemed that there might be some open discussion of how to interpret the attacks as an event in international affairs, and what sort of response was called for. In a few weeks, however, the United States solidified its interpretation as an attack on a state for which the appropriate response would be war on another state or states.

In this essay we question this statist response to the terrorist attacks, and offer some vision of how the United States and other global actors might have conceived and can still conceive of their possibilities for action under a cosmopolitan vision of political responsibility. We argue that a different response to these attacks, based on the rule of law and international cooperation, could have been equally effective to combat terrorism in the long run, and, in our view, could have also opened the way to a more just and stable world order.

We wish to thank Marc Herold, Mathias Koenig-Archibugi, Duncan Snidal, Michael Walzer, and Alexander Wendt for their criticism and suggestions. Thanks to Anne Harrington and David Newstone for research assistance.

The statist interpretation

The Bush Administration framed the attacks as an act of war on America, for which military retaliation was judged to be the appropriate response. This framework meant finding a state or states to engage in war, and the US chose Afghanistan on the grounds that the Taliban government harbored and supported Al Qaeda. It singled out Iraq, Syria, Somalia, and other countries as additional states toward which military action may be taken, and in March 2003 launched a war against Iraq that has led to indefinite occupation. The Bush Administration continues to insist that its actions in Iraq are part of its world-wide war on terror.

The construction of a response to the attacks and the prevention of terrorist acts as a state-to-state military conflict, however, has been difficult to sustain. Even within a traditional state-centered world politics, the fact that the government of Afghanistan allowed Al Qaeda leaders to run camps in its territory provides an uncertain justification for making war on the state. Aware of that shakiness, the United States shifted its reasons for the war against the Taliban from a rationale of self-defense to a humanitarian defense of freeing the Afghan people, especially its women, from oppression. We find this rationale cynical and opportunistic, since neither Bush nor the Clinton Administration had previously articulated any concern with the plight of the Afghan people. Although the United States continues to have a military presence in Afghanistan, and has contributed some material aid to rebuilding institutions there, the adventure in Iraq has taken center stage, for the most part leaving the Afghani people, men and women, less safe, poorer, and more dependent on opium trade than they were before the US war.

Responding to the terrorist attacks through the conduct of a war against a "state" neither fits the case nor is it likely to be effective in making a safer world. Although the war has destroyed some Al Qaeda bases and the US has captured some members of that group, the Bush Administration-appointed commission to investigate the terrorist attacks determined that there is no direct connection between the casualties of that war and the 19 suicidal attackers of September 11.[1] Widely circulating estimates of civilian deaths in Afghanistan give a minimum of 1,000 and some as many as 3,700, and hundreds are likely to die from unexploded bombs.[2] It is still unknown the number of soldiers and armed men who have been killed but some of the information, among it the massacre of hundreds of the Taliban prisoners in the prison of Mazar-i-Sharif, has raised serious concern about the legality in which the war operations have been conducted.[3] The establishment of the detention camp in Guantanamo, to which hundreds of captured men were sent and officially deemed outside the scope of the Geneva Convention's rules for prisoners of war, is unprecedented and an affront to human rights. The policy of operating outside the rule of law there seems to have enabled the establishment of secret detention camps and horrible methods of interrogation by the United States in several other parts of the world. There is little reason to think that the war against Afghanistan has deterred other would-be terrorists around the world. Afghanistan is very unstable, even four years after the major military action.

Although the United States did not act alone in prosecuting the war, it called the shots. The US decided with whom to cooperate and assigned the role of other actors. It is difficult not to interpret US policy in recent years as an effort to consolidate even more firmly its position as sovereign of the world. While many Americans no doubt think that this is a good thing, we believe that the existence of a single world military power that aims to enforce its will both is an anathema to democratic culture and impedes efforts to promote peace.

In the 1990s, the US has used its military force in the Persian Gulf, Somalia, Panama, the Balkans, and many other places. In every case, the US interventions had victims, but few were Americans. The apparently endless wars in Afghanistan and Iraq have brought more American deaths; more than 250 soldiers have died in Afghanistan, and more than 2,100 in Iraq as of December 2005. The magnitude of US military and economic power and the willingness of the United States to wield it asymmetrically and with only the thinnest veneer of multilateralism elicits hostile reactions all over the world, even from people thought to be allies. A survey conducted by the Pew Research Center and the *International Herald Tribune* in December 2001 found that most of the non-Americans among the 275 political and business leaders polled believe that the United States wrongly uses its power and that some of its policies are responsible for growing global disparities in well-being.[4] In response to such hegemony, it seems to us imperative that leaders and citizens all over the world should envision a global rule of law and should try to shame and pressure the United States to act more in conformity with such a vision.

An alternative vision

Aspirations to a global society governed by fair rules should be counted among the casualties of September 11. The fall of the Berlin

Wall brought with it hope of constituting a world order founded on
international legality and with strengthened institutions of international cooperation. Recent debates and demonstrations about the
policies and procedures of international trade and financial organizations have assumed the emergence of more global-level governance. Some international law theorists argue that networks of global
governance have evolved over a number of regulatory issues in the
last twenty years. These do not nor will they form anything like a
global state, but operate with functional jurisdiction.[5] The question is
whether global regulatory regimes will represent solely the interests
of the world's most powerful actors or can include the voices and
interests of the global majority in transparent and accountable
institutions.

We base a vision of an alternative response to terrorism on these
aspirations for just and democratic global governance. Hitherto, discussions of an international rule of law and global regulatory systems
have paid less attention to the prevention and investigation of crimes
and their prosecution in an international system, than to matters such
as international trade, investment, or environmental protection. We
propose two premises for reasoning about what an alternative
response to the terrorist attacks of September 11 might have been
and still can be. First, the situation should be conceptualized in
people-to-people, rather than state-to-state, terms.[6] The attackers
were not representatives of a state, but members of private organizations, and those whom they killed were, for the most part, private
individuals from at least 70 different countries. Thus, second, the
events should be conceptualized as crimes, not acts of war, to which
the proper response is criminal investigation and prosecution within
a rule of law, and legally mandated measures for preventing and
deterring similar crimes.

For this reason, we disagree with those who think that the concept
of "just war" can be applied to the US military reaction to the attacks
of September 2001.[7] Most prominently, Jean Elshtain argues that
traditional Catholic doctrine of just war applies to the new conditions of international terrorism. She accepts that the war against
Afghanistan was a just response of self-defense to the attacks of September 11, and also endorses the war against Iraq on similar grounds
that the United States is currently faced with threat from Islamic fun-
damentalism. She scoffs at the notion that the world could mobilize
an alternative response in the form of international law enforcement,
claiming, we believe incorrectly, that states are the only effective
actors in international relations, and that this fact will be true for the
foreseeable future.[8]

Democratic states do not usually, and ought never, respond arbitrarily and with military power to terrorist attacks committed inside their borders. Spain in response to threats from the Basque separatist group ETA, Italy in dealing with the Red Brigades, the United States in response to the bombing in Oklahoma City, all mobilized the instruments of law and police power. More recently, Spain's reaction to the terrorist attack in Madrid in 2004 has been to mobilize international criminal investigation, not to make war-like noises against Morocco. Stepping out of legal bounds, as did the Spanish government for a while when it authorized some state agents to use extrajudicial methods to combat terrorism, seems to have the effect of increasing the risk of attack. The enemies of peace point to illegal actions by states to justify their own illegal actions.

The world ought to respond to international terrorist organizations, we suggest, according to the same principles of the rule of law that these governments use in responding to domestic terrorist organizations. Responding to acts and threats of terrorism and to transnational terrorist networks under a global rule of law need not imply being "softer" on terrorists than using a state-to-state response led by a hegemonic state. On the contrary, a genuinely global cooperative law enforcement response would be more effective in identifying and apprehending culprits, as well as preventing future attacks, while at the same time harming fewer people and destroying fewer goods, than was the war against Afghanistan.[9]

We offer five principles to guide international policy to respond to threats and problems of violence. They each point to ideals and institutions of global cooperation that do not now exist. In that sense we intend them as visionary. At the same time, we believe that all five principles can serve to guide action now in the following way. As they consider options for how to respond to threats of terrorism, political actors and citizens can and should ask which courses of action have the potential to help realize the ideals the principles express, and which actions are more likely to move the world away from them.

Legitimize and strengthen international institutions

Actions and policies that treat terrorism and threats of terrorism as involving all the world's peoples within a rule of law should utilize international organizations and legal instruments. The United Nations system is most important here. Although there are many flaws in its design and operations, which should be changed, the United Nations is the only transnational institution with representation of nearly all the world's peoples. Institutions, policies, and conventions of the United Nations, moreover, cover many of the most urgent world problems.

Currently, the UN is in an impossible position. On the one hand, it is called on the scene to restore peace, build governments and infrastructure, aid refugees, conduct health campaigns, and pursue many other activities, in dozens of regions of the world simultaneously. On the other hand, member states routinely deny the UN the means for carrying out such missions, not only by failing to provide funds, but also by limiting its authority. When the UN's efforts prove inadequate to solve problems, as often happens, world leaders regularly heap abuse on the organization for being unresponsive and inept. The United States and other world powers cannot continue to dump the consequences of its wars and economic decisions on the United Nations while at the same time encouraging people to disdain the organization.

The present organization of the UN Security Council, with its five permanent members reflecting global politics in 1945, needs serious reform. That Security Council, however, passed three resolutions after the attacks of September 11 (Resolutions no. 1368, Sept 12, 2001; no. 1373, Sept 28, 2001; and no. 1377, Nov 12, 2001), which call for transnational cooperation among all member states to deter and investigate terrorist and other transnational criminal activity. If government leaders allied with social movements, the US could be pressed to enter more genuinely multilateral efforts to combat transnational criminal networks, efforts that gave more decision-making participation to the less-developed world. The tragic paralysis of the international community in response to the worst killing in Palestine and Israel in two decades signals even more urgently the need to strengthen and reform the United Nations as a peace-making institution.

Coordinate law enforcement and intelligence gathering institutions across the world

Since September 2001, the United States Congress has conducted an inquiry into how two of the most sophisticated investigative and intelligence organizations in the world, the CIA and the FBI, could have been caught so unawares by a crime of such huge proportions. We suggest that one explanation is the state-centeredness of both agencies, along with the investigative and intelligence gathering agencies of most states. Simultaneous with increased transnational organization and movement of capital, labor, technology, and culture is the transnational organization and movement of crime. Intelligence and law enforcement institutions, however, lag terribly behind this reality. Intelligence continues to be principally an instrument of individual states against their enemies; in a spy culture the agencies of one state engage in secret activities in relation to other states, explicitly not trusting one another. Domestic law enforcement agencies, furthermore, each have their own systems that make communication and cooperation across borders difficult. The September attacks should serve as a siren call for reversing these structures of intelligence and law enforcement, to enable greater cooperation among agencies to protect *citizens* of the world, not states.

The United States appears to take a unilateral approach to international terrorist investigation and prosecution, however, undermining the bases of cooperation with other countries. The recent revelations that CIA operatives kidnapped an Egyptian cleric within the sovereign territory of Italy apparently without the knowledge or cooperation of Italian officials is just one example of this US breach of cooperative spirit in violation of international agreements.

There are some international instruments on which to build for the purpose of strengthening international law enforcement cooperation. INTERPOL, the international police organization with 179 member nations, has worked against terrorism, drug trafficking, money laundering, white collar crime, computer crime, counterfeit money, organized crime, and traffic in women and children for decades. Even though its budget is minuscule compared to the task, it maintains extensive databases of known and suspected terrorists and criminals. It organizes data on counterfeit passports and stolen credit card accounts that can be useful to law enforcement agents in nearly any country. Yet state-based intelligence agencies infrequently work with the organization to access its data in their work.[10]

At its millennium meeting in November 2000, the UN General Assembly adopted the Convention Against Transnational Organized Crime, which 140 countries, including the United States, have already signed. This convention requires states to strengthen domestic laws aimed to control organized crime, and encourages states to enhance systems of transnational cooperation in legal expertise, extradition, and criminal investigation. It specifically calls for providing technical assistance to less-developed countries to upgrade their capacities for dealing with organized crime. Although at the moment this convention may be little more than a piece of paper, like some other UN-negotiated treaties and conventions, it can be used by political leaders and social movements to demand institutions and resources that put its principles into action. The United States, along with many other states, can act to advance international cooperation in law enforcement, both domestic and transnational, as well as to create and strengthen global law enforcement agencies. A collective effort to combat terrorism with a greater involvement of the UN will certainly be beneficial to the United States, but this would imply that the United States should commit itself to a greater loyalty towards the organization. As the President of the United Nations Association of the USA has rightly stressed, "to sustain the commitment of UN member states in this new war [against terrorism], and to dispel resistance stemming from resentment of American 'double standards,' Washington needs to affirm what the American public has long acknowledged – the rule of law applies to the great as well as the small."[11]

A greater collaboration against organized political crime implies breaking down the statist distinction between domestic-oriented police and internationally oriented spy agencies. Current policy in the United States and in many Western countries blurs this distinction, however, in just the wrong direction. By allowing the CIA and FBI to cooperate inside the US, the government fosters a more repressive internal state at the same time that it becomes more defensive and suspicious externally. Increased transnational law enforcement cooperation should come with procedures of accountability and transparency in order to protect the rights of individuals.

Increase financial regulation

One of the most efficient ways to strike at terrorist networks, and organized crime more generally, is to hit their money. It is surprising that though Osama bin Laden has been known to head and fund terrorist operations for years, Al Qaeda has had the liberty to move the capital necessary. Why has no one until now succeeded at attacking the finances? We believe the answer lies partly in the fact that world business leaders resist financial regulation. Corporations regularly move their money around the world, for example, in order to avoid paying taxes. Tracking and regulating the movement of funds can dry up their flow to support criminal activities. A war on the free flow of money does not produce "collateral damage," create refugees, or pollute the air. The United States has indeed enhanced its capacity to investigate and regulate money flows. In this area it is obvious that even the most awesome military power of the world must depend on the cooperation of other governments, especially governments that dislike US foreign policy. Such necessary cooperation is difficult to maintain when the same governments or their allies face military threats or covert intelligence operations from the United States.[12]

Use international courts

The United States has put its response to attacks and threat of terrorism in a state-to-state framework only for as long as it suits its goals. By refusing to treat those captured in the war against Afghanistan as prisoners of war, the US takes the picture out of the statist frame. The Bush Administration argues that the prisoners are illegal combatants not covered by international law as stated in the Geneva Convention. At the same time, it has decreed that it will not apply its domestic principles of due process to noncitizen suspects apprehended in the United States or elsewhere. Thus, the US declares before the world that any non-Americans whom it apprehends and claims to connect with terrorism will not be given the protection of the law.[13] This stance is so outrageous that it has fomented dissent even within the Bush Administration and from within its most loyal ally, Britain. In response the Administration has slightly altered its stated position, but not its treatment of prisoners.

When the United States began putting into place its plan for military tribunals for those captured, Vice President Cheney said, "Terrorists don't deserve the same guarantees and safeguards that would be used for an American citizens going through the normal judicial process."[14] This statement reveals that Cheney scorns the most elementary principles of due process: presumably it is up to judicial procedure to determine who is and who not a criminal.

If the September 11 attacks are seen as crimes against humanity rather than against only the US, an international tribunal instituted by the United Nations, based on the model of those for the ex-Yugoslavia and Rwanda, with the processing judges coming from Western and Islamic countries, would be appropriate. This would also have the advantage of not appearing as a conflict between America and Islam, but rather between the entire international community and a limited group of criminals. In the end, ad hoc tribunals should be handed over to a permanent International Criminal Court, approved by Treaty in Rome in July 1998 and which was started to be implemented on April 12, 2002, even though the Bush Administration withdrew its support, an unprecedented diplomatic act. "Had the International Criminal Court been in existence," noted the international lawyer Greenwood, "and had the relevant states been parties to its statute, the perpetrators of the 11 September atrocities could have been tried by that Court for crimes against humanity."[15]

We have heard several arguments against using international courts to prosecute persons suspected of performing or materially contributing to terrorist acts. It's too slow, too expensive, and would wrongly give terrorists a forum in which to air their ideas. We find all these reasons disingenuous. It should not be any slower to pursue due process on an international level than at a state level; the speed the United States seeks seems to be at the expense of due process. Like-wise, it should not be much more expensive to pay for an interna-tional trial than a state-level trial if both are fair. Finally, any public court proceeding, at any level, offers opportunities for actors to express their point of view on the alleged crimes; that is what they are for, and that is, of course, why the military tribunals the Bush Administration plans will not be open to public view.

Narrow global inequalities

Since September 2001, many commentators have suggested that the vast disparities in wealth and well-being between northern hemi-spheric societies such as the US, the EU, or Japan, on the one hand, and the Middle East and South Asia, on the other hand, be taken into account in understanding what causes and motivates individuals to join or form terrorist groups. We agree with those who respond that these structural injustices neither justify nor excuse criminal acts. Nor do these circumstances even explain terrorist acts, for there are many poor places that do not provide recruits for international terrorist organizations.

Still, a huge portion of the world's population lives in horrible poverty.[16] We believe, as do many others in both the less developed and more developed parts of the world, that this poverty persists at least partly because of policies of the rich states, private corporations based in those countries, and international organizations in which those states and corporations have disproportionate power. Even those skeptical of this claim, however, should condemn the reluctance of the people and government of the United States, Europe, and Japan to effect significant transfer of capital, technological capacity, and goods to raise the quality of life of the world's poorest people. There is no doubt that such indifference amidst affluence fosters resentment in many corners of the world, and endangers peace and prosperity for many outside the shantytowns. We are encouraged that the debt cancellation movement has finally achieved at least some minimal success with the discussions of debt cancellations for 18 countries at the G8 summit of 2005, and that economists of the stature of Jeffrey Sachs claim that world poverty can be eliminated if only the rich countries put their political will to it. Much, much more needs to be done.

At another tragic moment of history, with the defeat of Fascism at the end of World War II, the US understood that its security and prosperity depended on the rebirth of Europe. To enable this rebirth, the US dedicated a huge amount of resources to the Marshall Plan, to rebuild the infrastructure of devastated European societies. No development aid program since that time has been so large in scale and so effective. That this was done once should give hope that having the will opens the way to invest in poor societies to enable them to flourish. For decades, social movements and governments in the less-developed world have demanded that the powerful economic actors of the world stop exploiting their resources and workers and start programs of real investment in the infrastructure and human beings of poor countries. The developed world remains largely unresponsive to this calamity. Official development assistance of the OECD countries in 2004 was 0.25 percent of their combined GNPs,[17] and private funding is also paltry. In 2004, the United States devoted 0.16 percent of its GNP to development assistance. The many attempts made by global civil society to increase the resources devoted to development have so far not been matched by concrete action.[18]

Even the Bush Administration cannot avoid acknowledging this moral imperative. It could not stay away from the UN-sponsored conference on rebuilding Afghanistan in January 2002, as it walked out on the Conference on Racism in August 2001 and the Climate Change Conference in December. At the January conference the United States pledged a mere $300 million for the first year, and Japan and Europe each pledged $500 million for the first two and one-half years. Since then, the United States has pledged $875 million.[19] Before the earthquake of March 2002, the World Bank estimated that at least $4.9 *billion* was required for the two and a half years to help rebuild Afghanistan at the most minimal level. Even at this moment of crisis, the rich countries of the world remain unbelievably stingy, and the poor people of the world are watching.

The world will not be able to move toward fair, inclusive, and effective global governance without major reallocation of economic, technological, and organizational capacities to reduce existing global disparities in the quality of life and institutional order. For such ends, we need new and strengthened international institutions that better represent the voices and perspectives of all the world's peoples rather than existing international finance and development institutions such as the World Bank, with more ability to promote global redistribution. Without the global equivalent of the Marshall Plan, even the best-designed cooperative efforts to respond to transnational organized crime can only be defensive and intermittent in their effectiveness.

Conclusion

The terrorist attacks of September 11, 2001, were a major challenge for the United States, its European allies, and the rest of the world. Those that have since occurred in Indonesia, Spain, and Britain underline this challenge. In 2001, the Bush Administration and its allies decided to retaliate against a country rather than by punishing individually the culprits. Those who opposed the recourse to war were often asked: What should the US have done? In this chapter we have addressed this question by arguing that there was and is an alternative way to combat terrorism. We do not argue that all culprits would have been taken and processed, we do not believe that the implementation of the policies we have suggested would have been sufficient to destroy transnationally organized networks of killers. Certainly, the wars undertaken have achieved neither of these goals. But we are sure that the number of "collateral casualties" would have been much lower if such an alternative strategy were to have been followed. And, perhaps more importantly, the alternative reaction here recommended would have shown to the peoples of the world that the world's powerful leaders are able to support the rule of law and the instruments of justice also beyond their own borders.

Our suggestions should be conceived for the long term. They derive from a general perspective on world politics that dates from much before the tragic events of September 11. The vision on which we draw considers that it is both possible and necessary to develop global democratic institutions.[20] A major new global threat, such as terrorism on the scale of September 11, should provide the chance for democratic countries of the world to nurture a global rule of law rather than a battle of fundamentalisms.

6

The Logic of Masculinist Protection: Reflections on the Current Security State

"My most important job as your President is to defend the homeland; is to protect American people from further attacks."
George W. Bush, March 29, 2002

"Every man I meet wants to protect me. I can't figure out what from."
Mae West

The American and European women's movement of the late 1970s and early 1980s contained a large segment organizing around issues of weapons, war, and peace. Creative civil disobedience actions wove webs of yarn at entrances to the Pentagon and set up colorful camps on cruise missile sites in England's Greenham Common. Writings of the women's peace movement tried to make theoretical connections between male domination and militarism, between masculine gender and the propensity to settle conflicts with violence, and these echoed some of the voices of the women's peace movement earlier in the twentieth century. By the early 1990s the humor and heroism of the women's peace actions had been all but forgotten.

Organized violence, led both by states and by nonstate actors, has certainly not abated in the meantime, and has taken new and frightening forms.[1] Thus, there are urgent reasons to reopen the question of whether looking at war and security issues through a gendered lens can teach lessons that might advance the projects of peace and democracy. In this essay[2] I analyze some of the security events and legal changes in the United States since fall 2001 by means of an account of a logic of masculinist protection.

Much writing about gender and war aims to explain bellicosity or its absence by considering attributes of men and women.[3] Theories adopting this approach attempt to argue that behavioral propensities of men link them to violence and those of women make them more peaceful, and that these differences help account for the structure of states and international relations. Such attempts to connect violence structures with attributes or behavioral propensities that men or women supposedly share, however, rely on unsupportable generalizations about men and women, and often leap too quickly from an account of the traits of persons to institutional structures and collective action. Here, I take a different approach. I take gender as an element not of explanation, but rather of interpretation, a tool of what might be called ideology critique.[4] Viewing issues of war and security through a gender lens, I suggest, means seeing how a certain logic of gendered meanings and images helps organize the way people interpret events and circumstances, along with their positions and possibilities for action within them, and sometimes provides some rationale for action.

I argue that an exposition of the gendered logic of the masculine role of protector in relation to women and children illuminates the meaning and effective appeal of a security state that wages war abroad and expects obedience and loyalty at home. In this patriarchal logic, the role of the masculine protector puts those protected, paradigmatically women and children, in a subordinate position of dependence and obedience. To the extent that citizens of a democratic state allow their leaders to adopt a stance of protectors toward them, these citizens come to occupy a subordinate status like that of women in the patriarchal household. We are to accept a more authoritarian and paternalistic state power, which gets its support partly from the unity a threat produces and our gratitude for protection. At the same time that it legitimates authoritarian power over citizens internally, the logic of masculinist protection justifies aggressive war outside. I interpret Hobbes as a theorist of authoritarian government grounded in fear of threat and the apparent desire for protection it generates.

Although some feminist theorists of peace and security have noticed the appeal to protection as justification for war-making,[5] they have not elaborated the gendered logic of protection to the extent that I try to do here. These accounts concentrate on international relations, moreover, and do less to carry the analysis to an understanding of the relation of states to citizens internally. My interest in this essay is in this dual face of security forms, those that wage war outside a country and conduct surveillance and detention inside. I notice that democratic values of due process, separation of powers, free assembly, and holding powerful actors accountable come into danger when leaders mobilize fear and present themselves as protectors.

Since the attacks of September 11, 2001, I argue, the relation of the leaders of the United States to its citizens is well illuminated by interpreting it under the logic of masculinist protection. The Bush Administration has mobilized the language of fear and threat to gain support for constricting liberty and dissent inside the United States and waging war outside it. This stronger US security state offers a bargain to its citizens: obey our commands, and support our security actions, and we will ensure your protection. This protection bargain between the state and its citizens is not unique to the United States in this period, but rather often legitimates authoritarian government. I argue that the bargain is dangerous in this case as in most others. The essay concludes with a gendered analysis of the war against Afghanistan of fall 2001. While the Bush Administration initially justified the war as a defensive action necessary to protect Americans, its rhetoric quickly supplemented this legitimation with an appeal to the liberation of Afghan women. I suggest that some of the groundwork for this appeal may have been laid by feminist campaigns concerning the Taliban, which the Bush Administration chose at this moment to exploit. The apparent success of this appeal in justifying the war to many Americans should trouble feminists, I argue, and prompt us to examine whether American or Western feminists sometimes adopt the stance of protector in relation to some women of the world whom we construct as more dependent or subordinate.

Masculinism as protection

Several theorists of gender argue that masculinity and femininity should not be conceptualized with a single logic, but rather that ideas and values of masculinity and femininity, and their relation to one another, take several different and sometimes overlapping forms.[6] In this spirit, I propose to single out a particular logic of masculinism which I believe has not received very much attention in recent feminist theory, that associated with the position of male head of household as a protector of the family, and by extension masculine leaders and risk takers as protectors of a population. Twenty years ago Judith Stiehm called attention to the relevance of a logic of masculinist protection to analysis of war and security issues, and I will draw on some of her ideas.[7] Her analysis more presupposes than it defines the meaning of a masculine role as protector, so this is where I will begin.

The logic of masculinist protection contrasts with a model of masculinity assumed by much feminist theory, of masculinity as self-consciously dominative. On the male domination model, masculine men wish to master women sexually for the sake of their own gratification and to have the pleasures of domination. They bond with other men in comradely male settings which afford them specific benefits from which they exclude women, and they harass women in order to enforce this exclusion and maintain their superiority.[8]

This image of the selfish, aggressive, dominative man who desires sexual capture of women corresponds to much about male-dominated institutions and the behavior of many men within them. For my purposes in this essay, however, it is important to recall another more benign image of masculinity, more associated with ideas of chivalry. In this latter image, real men are neither selfish nor do they seek to enslave or overpower others for the sake of enhancing themselves. Instead, the gallantly masculine man is loving and self-sacrificing, especially in relation to women. He faces the world's difficulties and dangers in order to shield women from harm and allow them to pursue elevating and decorative arts. The role of this courageous, responsible, and virtuous man is that of a protector.

The "good" man is one who keeps vigilant watch over the safety of his family and readily risks himself in the face of threats from the outside in order to protect the subordinate members of his household. The logic of masculinist protection, then, includes the image of the selfish aggressor who wishes to invade the lord's property and sexually conquer his women. These are the "bad" men. Good men can only appear in their goodness if we assume that lurking outside the warm familial walls are aggressors who wish to attack them. The dominative masculinity in this way constitutes protective masculinity as its other. The world out there is heartless and uncivilized, and the movements and motives of the men in it are unpredictable and difficult to discern. The protector must therefore take all precautions against these threats, remain watchful and suspicious, and be ready to fight and sacrifice for the sake of his loved ones.[9] Masculine protection is needed to make a home a haven.

Central to the logic of masculinist protection is the subordinate relation of those in the protected position. In return for male protection, the woman concedes critical distance from decision-making autonomy. When the household lives under a threat, there cannot be divided wills and arguments about who will do what, or what is the best course of action. The head of the household should decide what measures are necessary to secure the people and property, and he gives the orders they must follow if they and their relations are to remain safe. As Judith Stiehm puts it:

> The protector cannot achieve status simply through his accomplishment, then. Because he has dependents he is as socially connected as one who is dependent. He is expected to provide for others. Often a protector tries to get help from and also control the lives of those he protects – in order to "better protect" them.[10]

Feminine subordination, in this logic, does not constitute submission to a violent and overbearing bully. The feminine woman, rather, on this construction, adores her protector, and happily defers to his judgment in return for the promise of security he offers. She looks up to him with gratitude for his manliness and admiration for his willingness to face the dangers of the world for her sake. That he finds her worthy of such risks gives substance to her self. It is only fitting that she should minister to his needs and obey his dictates.

Hobbes is the great theorist of political power founded upon a need and desire for protection. He depicts a state of nature in which people live in small families where each believes some of the others envy them and desire to enlarge themselves by stealing from or conquering them. As a consequence, everyone in this state of nature must live in a state of fear and insecurity, even when not immediately under attack. Each household must live with the knowledge that outsiders might wish to attack them, especially if they appear weak and vulnerable, so each must construct defensive fortresses and be on watch. It is only sensible, moreover, to conduct preemptive strikes against those who might wish to attack, to try to weaken them. But each knows that the others are likely to make defensive raids, which only add to fear and insecurity. In Hobbes's state of nature, some people may be motivated by simple greed and desire for conquest and domination. In this state of nature, everyone has reason to feel insecure, however, not because all have these dominative motives, but because they are uncertain about who does, and understand their own vulnerability.

In her contemporary classic *The Sexual Contract*, Carole Pateman interprets Hobbes along the lines of contemporary feminist accounts of men as selfish aggressors and sexual predators. In the state of nature, roving men take advantage of women encumbered by children, and force them to submit to sexual domination. Sometimes they keep the women around as sexual servants; thus arises marriage. These strong and aggressive men force other men to labor for them

at the point of a sword. On Pateman's account, this is how the patriarchal household forms, through overpowering force.[11]

One can just as well read Hobbes's ideas through the lens of the
apparently more benign masculinity of protection. Here, we can
imagine that men and women get together out of attraction and feel
love for the children they beget. On this construction, families have
their origin in a desire for companionship and caring. In the state of
nature, however, each unit has reason to fear the strangers who might
rob or kill them, each then finds it prudent at times to engage in preemptive strikes, and to adopt a threatening stance toward the outsiders. On this alternative account, then, patriarchal right emerges
from male specialization in security. The patriarch's will rules because
he faces the dangers outside and needs to organize defenses. Female
subordination, in this account, derives from this position of being
protected.

Both Pateman's story of male domination and the one I have
reconstructed depict patriarchal gender relations as having unequal
power. It is important to attend to the difference, however, I
think, because in one relation the hierarchical power is obvious and
in the other it is more masked by virtue and love. Michel Foucault
argues that power conceived and enacted as repressive power, the
desire and ability of an agent to force the other to obey his commands, has receded in importance in modern institutions. Other
forms of power that enlist the desire of those over whom it is exercised better describe many power relations both historically and
today. One such form of power Foucault calls pastoral power. This is
the kind of power that the priest exercises over his parish, and by
extension that many experts in the care of individuals exercise
over those cared for.[12] This power often appears gentle and benevolent both to its wielders and to those under its sway, but it is no less
powerful for that reason. Masculinist protection is more like pastoral
power than dominative power that exploits those it rules for its own
aggrandizement.

The state as protector and subordinate citizenship

The gendered logic of masculinist protection has some relevance to
individual family life even in modern urban America. Every time a
father warns his daughter of the dangerous men he fears will exploit
her and forbids her from "running around" the city, he inhabits the
role of the male protector. Nevertheless, in everyday family life and

other sites of interaction between men and women, the legitimation of female inequality and subordination by appeal to a need for protection has dwindled. My purpose in articulating a logic of masculinist protection is not to argue that it describes private life today, but rather to argue that we learn something about public life, specifically about the relation of a state to its citizens, when state officials successfully mobilize fear. States often justify their expectations of obedience and loyalty, their establishment of surveillance, police, intimidation, detention, and the repression of criticism and dissent, by appeal to their role as protectors of citizens. I find in Hobbes a clever account of authoritarian rule grounded in the assumption of threat and fear as basic to the human condition, and thus a need for protection as the highest good.

Hobbes tells a story about why individuals and families find it necessary to constitute a sovereign, a single power to rule them all. In response to the constant fear under which they live, families may join confederations or protection associations. Such protection associations, however, no matter how large and powerful, do not reduce the reasons for fear and insecurity. As long as the possibility exists that others will form protective associations larger and stronger than their own, the nasty state of war persists. As long as there is a potential for competition among units, and they hold the means to try to force their desires on one another, they must live in fear. Without submission to a common power to which they yield their separate forces, moreover, members of a protective association are liable to turn on one another during times when they need to rely on one another for protection from others.[13] So Hobbes argues that only a Leviathan can assure safety, quell the fear and uncertainty that generates a spiral of danger. All the petty protectors in the state of nature give up their powers of aggression and defense, which they turn over to the sovereign. They make a covenant with one another to live in peace and constitute civil society under the common rule of an absolute authority who makes, interprets, and enforces the laws of the commonwealth for the sake of peace and security of subjects.

Readers of Hobbes sometimes find in the image of Leviathan a mean and selfish tyrant who sucks up the wealth and loyalty of subjects for his own aggrandizement. Democratic values and freedoms would be much easier to assert and preserve in modern politics if the face of authoritarianism were so ugly and easy to recognize. Like the benevolent patriarch, however, Leviathan often wears another aspect, that of the selfless and wise protector, whose actions aim to foster and maintain security. What I call a security state is one whose rulers subordinate citizens to ad hoc surveillance, search, or detention, and which represses criticism of such arbitrary power, justifying such measures as within the prerogative of those authorities whose primary duty is to maintain security and protect the people.

The security state has an external and an internal aspect. It constitutes itself in relation to an enemy outside, an unpredictable aggressor against which the state needs vigilant defense. It organizes political and economic capacities around the accumulation of weapons and the mobilization of a military to respond to this outsider threat. The state's identity is militaristic, and it engages in military action, but with the point of view of the defendant rather than the aggressor. Even when the security regime makes a first strike, it justifies its move as necessary to preempt the threatening aggressor outside. Security states do not justify their wars by appealing to sentiments of greed or desire for conquest; they appeal to their role as protectors.

Internally, the security state must root out the enemy within. There is always the danger than among us are agents who have an interest in disturbing our peace, violating our persons and property, and allowing outsiders to invade our communities and institutions. To protect the state and its citizens, officials must therefore keep a careful watch on everyone, observe and search them to make sure they do not intend evil actions and do not have the means to perform them. The security regime overhears conversations in order to try to discover conspiracies of disaster and disruption, and prevents people from forming crowds or walking the streets after dark. In a security regime there cannot be separation of power or critical accountability of official action to a public. Nor can a security regime allow expression of dissent.

Once again, Hobbes explains why not. It is necessary that the sovereign be one. The commonwealth can secure peace only if it unites the plurality of its members into one will. Even if the sovereign consists in an assembly of officials and not only one ruler, it must be united in will and purpose. It is the mutual covenant that each man makes to all the others to give over his right of governing his own affairs to the sovereign, on condition that all others do the same, that gives the sovereign both its power and unit of will.[14] Sovereign authority, then, must be absolute, and it cannot be divided. The sovereign decides what is necessary to protect the commonwealth and its members. The sovereign decides what actions or opinions constitute a danger to peace, and properly suppresses them.

> The condition of man in this life shall never be without inconveniences;
> but there happeneth in no commonwealth any greater inconvenience,

but what proceeds from the subject's disobedience and breach of these covenants from which the commonwealth hath its being, and whosoever, thinking sovereign power too great, will seek to make it less, must subject himself to the power that can limit it, that is to say, to a greater.[15]

Through the logic of protection the state demotes members of a democracy to dependants. State officials adopt the stance of masculine protector, telling us to entrust our lives to them, not to question their decisions about what will keep us safe. Their protector position puts the citizens and residents who depend on their strength and vigilance in the position of women and children under the charge of the male protector.[16] Most regimes that suspend certain rights and legal procedures declare a state of emergency. They claim that special measures of unity and obedience are required in order to ensure protection from unusual danger. Because they take the risks and organize the agency of the state, it is their prerogative to determine the objectives of protective action and their means. In a security state there is no room for separate and shared powers, nor for questioning and criticizing the protector's decisions and orders. Good citizenship in a security regime consists in cooperative obedience for the sake of the safety of all.

The authoritarian security paradigm, I have argued, takes a form analogous to the masculine protector toward his wife and the other members of his patriarchal household. In this structure, I have suggested, masculine superiority flows not from acts of repressive domination, but from the willingness to risk and sacrifice for the sake of the others.[17] For her part, the subordinate female in this structure neither resents nor resists the man's dominance, but rather she admires it, and is grateful for its promise of protection.

Patriotism has an analogous emotive function in the constitution of the security state. Under threat from outsiders, all of us, authorities and citizens, imagine ourselves a single body enclosed on and loving itself. We affirm our oneness with our fellow citizens and together affirm our single will behind the will of the leaders who have vowed to protect us. It is not merely that dissent is dangerous; worse yet, it is ungrateful. Subordinate citizenship does not merely acquiesce to limitation on freedom in exchange for a promise of security; the consent is active, as solidarity with the others uniting behind and in grateful love of country.

The United States as a security state

A security state is what every state would have to be if Hobbes were right that human relations are always on the verge of disorder and violence, if only an authoritarian government that brooks no division of power or dissent can keep the peace, and if maintaining peace and security is unambiguously the highest value. Democratic theory and practice, however, question each of these Hobbesian assumptions. Democrats agree that a major purpose of government is to keep peace and promote public safety, but we deny that unquestioning obedience to a unified sovereign is the only means to achieve this, and we question that values of freedom and autonomy must be traded against the value of security. In a nonideal world of would-be aggressors, and states having imperfect procedural justice, transparency, accountability, and lax rights enforcement, every state exhibits features of a security state to some extent. It seems to me, however, that in recent months the United States has slipped too far down the authoritarian continuum. The logic of masculinist protection, I suggest, provides a framework for understanding how government leaders who expand arbitrary power and restrict democratic freedom believe they are doing the right thing, and why citizens accept their actions. It also helps explain this state's righteous rationale for aggressive war.

A marauding gang of outsiders attacked buildings in New York and Washington with living bombs, killing thousands in barely an instant, and terrifying large numbers of people in the country. Our government responded with a security alert, at home and abroad. Many were frightened, and the heads of state stepped up to offer us protection. Less than a week after the attacks, the Bush Administration announced the creation of an Office of Homeland Security to centralize its protection efforts. "Our nation has been put on notice: we are not immune from attack. We will take defensive measures against terrorism to protect Americans."[18]

The events of September 11, 2001, are certainly a turning point for American politics, the relation of the government to its citizens and to the rest of the world. Americans learned that "oceans no longer matter when it comes to making us safe,"[19] that we are just as vulnerable as persons elsewhere who have long lived with the awareness that some people have motive and means to kill and wound randomly. More than a year later, it appears that little has changed, either in the fear some Americans have of another attack or in the material ability of law enforcement to predict or prevent one.[20] Much has changed in the letter and application of the law in the United States, however, and in the environment of democracy. The Bush Administration has repeatedly appealed to the primacy of its role as protector of innocent citizens and liberator of women and children to justify consolidating and centralizing executive power at home and dominative war abroad.

It is arguable that before September 11 airports and other public places in the United States were too lax in their security screening protocol. I welcome more thorough security procedures; this essay is not an argument against public officials taking measures to try to keep people safe. The key questions are how much power should officials have, how much freedom should citizens have, how fair are the procedures, how well do they follow due process, and how easily can citizens review official policies and actions to hold them accountable. With respect to these questions there have been very large and damaging changes in the United States since fall, 2001, although a direction toward some of them had been enacted by legislation and judicial action in the years before.

The US security state has expanded the prerogative of the executive and eroded the power of the legislative or judicial branches to review executive decisions or to be independent sources of decision-making. In the week after the September 11 attacks, for example, Congress passed a resolution effectively waiving its constitutionally mandated power to deliberate and decide on whether the state shall go to war. Months later, again with virtually no debate, Congress approved the largest increase in the military budget in twenty years. Since the war on terrorism has no declared ending, the executive may have been granted permanent legal discretion to do what it wants with US military personnel and equipment, at current taxpayer expense of nearly $400 billion per year.

Drafted quickly and passed with almost no debate, the USA Patriot Act signed on October 26, 2001, severely reduces the power of courts to review and limit executive actions to keep organizations under surveillance, limit their activities, search and seize, or detain individuals. Under its provisions, individuals and organizations have had their records investigated, or their assets seized, or their activities and correspondence monitored. Citizen access to government files and records that took so much struggle to achieve in the 1970s has been severely reduced, with no fanfare and thus no protest. Thousands of people have been detained, interrogated, or jailed at the discretion of law enforcement or immigration officials, and hundreds remain in jails without being charged with any crime. Few are allowed access to lawyers. Many foreign residents have been deported or threatened with deportation, sometimes without time to arrange their lives. Laws with similar purposes have been passed in other supposedly liberal democratic states, such as the United Kingdom and Australia.

The American executive has taken other steps to enlarge and centralize its power and put itself above the law. In November, 2002, Congress approved the creation of a Department of Homeland Security, which merges twenty-two existing federal agencies. The Bush Administration has flaunted principles of a rule of law at the international level by holding captured citizens of many countries prisoner and declaring its prerogative to bring any or all of them before secret tribunals.

These and other legal and policy changes have far-reaching implications. The most ordinary and fundamental expectations of due process have been undermined when search and surveillance do not require court approval, when persons can be jailed without charge, and when there is no regularity or predictability to the process a person in custody will undergo. The basic American principle of the separation of power has been suspended, with no reversal in sight. Legislatures and judiciaries at federal and more local levels have been stripped of some formal powers and decline to use much of what they have left to question, criticize, or block executive action. Most citizens apparently register approval for the increased policing and war-making powers, and the ability for those who do not to organize, criticize publicly, and protest in public streets and squares has been seriously curtailed, not only by fear of peer and employer disapproval, but directly by official repression and intimidation.

How can citizens and their representatives in a democracy allow such rapid challenge to their political principles and institutions, with so little discussion and protest? The process of limiting civil liberties, due process, and deliberation about war has itself been deeply undemocratic, a bold assertion of dictatorial power. One part of the answer lies in a conviction that most people believe that *their* rights and freedoms will not be threatened. Aliens will be subject to surveillance and deportation, and these enemies who have infiltrated deserve to be routed out by any means, and we can leave it to the discretion of police officers, immigration officials, and military personnel to determine who they are. Already, many of those whose records have been seized or who have been detained without charge are US citizens, however, and the new legislation and guidelines do not make any citizen immune. Well, then, many of us tell ourselves, the ones whose privacy is invaded or freedoms are limited by government action must be doing something wrong and deserve what they get. Since I am not doing anything wrong, I am protected. The move from a relatively free society to one over which the state exercises authoritarian domination often occurs just by means of this logic; citizens do not realize how easily they may find themselves under suspicion by authorities over whose decisions there is no public scrutiny. The principle of trial by a jury of peers in which the accused is presumed innocent is an important protection any person has from false charge and arbitrary power. The slippery slope from the fearsome outsiders, to the aliens within, to the bad fellow citizens is likely to end at my brother's front door.

The deeper explanation for why people who live in what promotes itself as one of the most enlightened democracies in history so easily allow and even support the erosion of basic rights lies in the mobilization of fear. John Keane challenges the opinion that democracies privatize fear. On the contrary, he claims, contemporary commercial communications media in democratic societies often exploit and incite fear. Although freedom of speech and press make possible such public accumulation of fear, the process threatens to shut down civic freedom.

> Fear is indeed a thief. It robs subjects of their capacity to act with or against others. It leaves them shaken, sometimes permanently traumatized. And when large numbers fall under the dark clouds of fear, no sun shines on civil society. Fear saps its energies and tears and twists at the institutions of political representation. Fear eats the soul of democracy.[21]

Public leaders invoke fear, then they promise to keep those living under them safe. Because we are afraid, and our fears are stirred by what we see on television or read in the newspaper, we are grateful to the leaders and officers who say they will shoulder the risk in order to protect us. The logic of masculinist protection works to elevate the protector to a position of superior authority and demote the rest of us to a position of grateful dependency. Ideals of democratic equality and accountability go by the wayside in the process. Although some researchers claim to have noticed a shift in the acceptability of women occupying positions of authority since fall, 2001,[22] in the contemporary United States, the position of protector and the position of those protected does not correspond to that of men and women. A few of the most security minded leaders are women, and many of those who accept the promise of protection are men. What matters, I believe, is the gendered meaning of the positions and the association of familial caring they carry for people. It also matters that this relationship carries an implicit deal: forego freedom, due process, and the right to hold leaders accountable, and in return we will make sure that you are safe.

Is it a good deal?

I discussed earlier how the logic of masculinist protection constitutes the "good" men who protect their women and children by relation to other "bad" men liable to attack. In this logic, virtuous masculinity depends on its constitutive relation to the presumption of evil others. Feminists have much analyzed a correlate dichotomy between the "good" woman and the "bad" woman. Simply put, a "good" woman stands under the male protection of a father or husband, submits to his judgment about what is necessary for her protection, and remains loyal to him. A "bad" woman is one unlucky enough not to have a man willing to protect her, or who refuses such protection by claiming the right to run her own life. In either case, the woman without a male protector is fair game for any man to dominate. There is a bargain implicit in the masculinity protector role: either submit to my governance or all the bad men out there are liable to approach you, and I will not try to stop them.

I have argued so far that the position of citizens and residents under a security state entails a similar bargain. There are bad people out there who might want to attack us. The state pledges to protect us, but tells us that we should submit to its rule and decisions without questioning, criticizing, or demanding independent review of the decisions. Some of the measures in place to protect us entail limitation on our freedom, and especially the limitation of the freedom of particular classes of people. The deal is: you must trade some liberty and autonomy for the sake of the protection we offer. Is it a good deal?

Some years ago, Susan Rae Peterson likened the state's relation to women under a system of male domination to a protection racket. The gangland crowd offers protection from other gangs to individuals, their families, and businesses, for a fee. If anyone declines their services, the gangsters teach them a brutal lesson, and by example teach a lesson to others who might wish to go their own way. Thus, those who wish to break free of the racketeer's protection discover that they are most in danger from him. Insofar as state laws and policies assume or reinforce the view that a "good" woman should move under the guidance of a man, Peterson argued, the state functions as a protection racket. It threatens or allows men to threaten those women who wish to be independent of the individualized protection of husbands or boyfriends. Not only do the protectors withhold protection from the women who claim autonomy, but they may become attackers.[23]

The security state functions as a similar protection racket for those who live under it. As long as we accept the state's protection, and pay the price it exacts not only in taxpayer dollars, but also in reduction on our freedom and submission to possible surveillance, we are relatively safe. If we try to decline these services, and seek freedom from the position of dependence and obedience in which they put us, we become suspect, and thereby threatened by the very organization that claims to protect us.

Current forms of "homeland security" in the United States look like a protection racket. As long as we are quiet and obedient, we can breathe easy. If we should step out of the bounds of "good" citizens, however, we may find ourselves unprotected and even under attack by the protector state. If we publicly criticize the state's policies, especially the war or foreign policy, we may land on lists of unpatriotic people published to invite our neighbors or employers to sanction us. We may find that we are no longer allowed to assemble in some public places, even when we wish to demonstrate about issues other than war and the security regime, and that we are liable to arrest if we try. When we are able peaceably to protest, government officials nevertheless threaten us with horses and tear gas canisters and cameras taking our pictures. Organizations we support may appear on lists of terrorist organizations at the discretion of bureaucrats, and we won't even know that they are monitoring our email or tapping our phones.

Some citizens become defined as not good citizens simply because of their race or national origin. Although public opinion only recently claimed to disapprove of policy and security practices that use racial or ethnic profiling, now many accept the state's claim that effective protection requires such profiling. Residents who are not citizens, especially those from places defined as sources of danger, lose most of the protection they may have had from attack by neighbors or arbitrary and punitive treatment by state agents.

The United States is by no means unique in enacting such measures and justifying them by appeal to protective emergency, nor is this the first time in the past century when such logic has been apparent. This is not the first time either that citizens have applauded the threatening and surveillance activities of the security regime because they are anxious for protection and believe that such measures will only apply to others – the terrorists, the foreigners, and the disloyal citizens – and not to themselves. We endanger democratic practice, however, when we consent to this bargain. When we fail to question a legal distinction between the good citizen and the bad citizen that affords less legal protection to the latter, and when we allow the rhetoric of fear to label any foreigners as enemies within, increasing numbers of us are liable to find that our attributes or activities put us on the wrong side of the line. If we allow our fear to cow us to submission, we assume the position of subordinates rather than democratic citizens equal to and not above our neighbors, equal to and not beneath our government.

There is little evidence that the way America has chosen to conduct its war on terrorism has, in fact, made us or others in the world any safer. Indeed, it may have put Americans at even greater risk. When United States planes began bombing Afghanistan in October, 2001, officials publicly admitted that the action put Americans inside and outside the country at greater risk from retaliating attackers. It is plausible to suggest that the stances of increased belligerence between India and Pakistan that emerged in summer, 2002, result in part from US military actions, and it seems that the government of Israel has been emboldened by the US example to conduct its own brutal war on terrorism. The Bush Administration has buried the Cold War doctrine of deterrence and announced its willingness to make preemptive strikes against what it decides are terrorist threats. There is no reason to think that the war against Iraq has made Americans any safer from terrorist attack, and some reason to think that it has increased this risk. The claimed desire to protect by means of guns generates a spiral of danger and uncertainty.[24]

The logic of masculinity protection positions leaders, along with some other officials such as soldiers and firefighters, as protectors, and the rest of us in the subordinate position of dependent, protected people. Justifications for the suspension of due process or partial abrogation of privacy rights and civil liberties, as well as condemnation of dissent, rest on an implicit deal: that these are necessary trade-offs for effective protection. The legitimacy of this deal is questionable, however, not only because it may not be effective in protecting us, but also because it cheapens and endangers democracy. Subordinate citizenship is not compatible with democracy. The relation of leaders to citizens under democratic norms ought to be one of equality, not in the sense of equal power, but in the sense that citizens have an equal right and responsibility with leaders to make policy judgments, and thus that leaders entrusted with special powers should be held accountable to citizens. Institutions of due process, public procedure and record, organized opposition and criticism, public review, both enact and recognize such equal citizenship. Trading them for protection puts us at the mercy of the protectors.

War and feminism

The logic of masculinist protection, I have argued, helps account for the rationale leaders give for deepening a security state and its acceptance by those living under their rule. There are two faces to the security state, one facing outward to defend against enemies and the other facing inward to keep those under protection under necessary control. So far I have concentrated on describing recent legislative and executive actions of the United States government in terms of the inward looking face. Now I shall turn to the outward looking face, the United States as war maker.

In fall, 2001, the US led a bombing campaign against Afghanistan. Even though that state had not taken aggressive action against the United States, the US justified the war as a defensive reaction to the attacks of September 11. Perhaps because the claim that the state of Afghanistan actively supported Al Qaeda was weak, the US quickly repackaged the war as a case of humanitarian intervention to liberate the Afghan people. The logic of masculinist protection appears in the claimed relationship of the United States to people outside the West, particularly in Islamic countries, ruled by brutal dictatorships. The United States will fight and sacrifice to save them. The Bush Administration tried to use a similar discourse to justify the war against Iraq. The United States defends not only itself in this scenario, but the freedom of all the world, for whom the weapons Iraq might have had are a threat. By saving ourselves we also save the Iraqi people from domination. So the United States is the protector of the world. Through this logic the American people and others who choose to identify with the actions of the United States can put themselves into the role of the protector even as the state restricts our freedom for our own good.

Packaging the war against Afghanistan as a humanitarian war to protect the Afghani people from domination was particularly effective because the Bush Administration and journalists focused on women. The women of Afghanistan constituted the ultimate victims, putting the US in the position of ultimate protector. Use of the rhetoric of women's rights by the Bush Administration during and after the war against Afghanistan should make feminists very uncomfortable. I wonder whether some seeds for such cynical appeals to the need to save women might not have been sown by some recent American and European feminist discourse and practice that positioned itself as protector of oppressed women in Asia and Africa.

On November 17, 2001, Laura Bush became the first First Lady to give the President's Saturday morning radio address, which was devoted to condemning what she called the Taliban's war on women and justifying the US war as an effort to free Afghan women. Since the overthrow of the Taliban regime, the Bush Administration has repeatedly invoked women's liberation to justify the war. In his 2002 State of the Union address, for example, George W. Bush said, "The last time we met in this chamber the mothers and daughters of Afghanistan were captives in their own homes, forbidden from working or going to school. Today women are free, and are part of Afghanistan's new government."[25] On International Women's Day Laura Bush again spoke to the UN Commission on the Status of Women, linking the terrorist attacks with the oppression of women, and thus, by implication, the war on terrorism with the liberation of women.

> The terrorist attacks of September 11 galvanized the international community. Many of us have drawn valuable lessons from the tragedies. People around the world are looking closely at the roles women play in their societies. Afghanistan under the Taliban gave the world a sobering example of a country where women were denied their rights and their place in society. Today, the world is helping Afghan women return to the lives they once knew. Women were once important contributors to Afghan society, and they had the right to vote as early as the 1920s. . . . This is a time of rebuilding – of unprecedented opportunity – thanks to efforts led by the United Nations, the United States, the new Afghan government, and our allies around the world.[26]

Years before the attacks of September 2001, American feminists mounted a campaign directed at saving the women of Afghanistan from the Taliban. Although they lobbied the Clinton Administration to put pressure on the Taliban government regarding women's rights, neither Clinton nor Bush evinced any concern for the situation of women under the Taliban before the war. Appeal to women's rights was thus a cynical attempt to gain support for the war among the citizens of the United States and other liberal countries. Some feminists jumped onto the war bandwagon. Shortly after the war began, for example, Eleanor Smeal, leader of the Feminist Majority, chatted cordially with US generals. "They went off about the role of women in this effort and how imperative it was that women were now in every level of the Air Force and Navy," said Smeal, who found herself cheered by the idea of women flying F16s. "It's a different kind of war," she says, echoing the President's assessment of Operation Enduring Freedom.[27]

Certainly, the Taliban should have been condemned for its policies, as should all the world's governments that perpetrate or allow systematic and discriminatory harms to and subordination of women. The Taliban stood with only a few other governments of the world in the degree of legally enforced restriction of women's freedom and horrible punishments. Even before the war it seemed to me, and still seems to me, that feminist focus on women under the Taliban constructed these women as exoticized others and paradigmatic victims in need of salvation by Western feminists, and conveniently deflected attention from perhaps more intractable and mundane problems of gender-based violence, domination, and poverty in many other parts of the world, including the enlightened West. What is wrong with this stance, if it has existed, is that it fails to consider the women as equals, and it does not have principled ways of distancing itself from paternalist militarism.

The stance of the male protector, I have argued, is one of loving self-sacrifice, with those in the feminine position as the objects of love and guardianship. Chivalrous forms of masculinism express and enact concern for the well-being of women, but they do so within a structure of superiority and subordination. The male protector confronts evil aggressors in the name of the right and the good, while those under his protection submit to his order and serve as handmaids to his efforts. Colonialist ideologies have often expressed a similar logic. The knights of civilization aim to bring enlightened understanding to the further regions of the world still living in cruel and irrational traditions that keep them from developing the economic and political structures that will bring them a good life. The suppression of women in these societies is a symptom of such backwardness. Troops will be needed to bring order and guard fledgling institutions, and foreign aid workers to feed, cure, and educate, but all this is only a period of tutelage that will end when the subject people demonstrate their ability to gain their own livelihood and run their own affairs. Many people living in Asian, African, and Latin American societies believe that not only US military hegemony but also international trade and financial institutions, and many Western-based nongovernmental development agencies, position them in this way as feminized or infantilized women and children under the protection and guidance of the wise and active father.

In its rhetoric and practice, according to some scholars, the British feminist movement of the late nineteenth and early twentieth centuries aligned itself with the universal humanitarian civilizing mission invoked as the justification for the British Empire. Feminists endorsed male imperial leaders' assessment of the status of women in other nations as a measure of their level of moral development. Such interest in the status of women was useful to feminists in pointing out the hypocrisy of denying women's rights in the center as one fought for them in the periphery. Providing services for Indian women and other oppressed women in the empire also offered opportunities for the employment of middle-class professional women.[28]

Some contemporary feminists have worried that Western feminism today has had some tendency to express and act in similar ways in relation to non-Western women. In a well-known essay Chandra Mohanty, for example, claims that Western feminists too often use an objectified general category of Third World women, who are represented as passive and victimized by their unenlightened cultures and political regimes.[29] Uma Narayan claims that much feminist discussion of the situation of women in Asian and African societies, or women in Asian immigrant communities in Western societies, "replicates problematic aspects of Western representations of Third World nations and communities, aspects that have their roots in the history of colonization."[30]

Assuming these criticisms of some of the discourse, attitudes, and actions of Western feminists have some validity, the stance they identify helps account for the ease with which feminist rhetoric can be taken up by today's imperialist power and used for its own ends. It also helps account for the support of some feminists for the war against Afghanistan. Sometimes feminists may identify with the stance of the masculine protector in relation to vulnerable and victimized women. The protector–protected relation is no more egalitarian, however, when between women than between men and women.

According to some recent reports, the lives of women in Afghanistan have changed little since before the war, except that some of them have lost their homes, their relatives, and what little livelihood they had.[31] The oppression of most of them remains embedded in social structure, custom, and a culture of warlord anarchism. I would not argue that humanitarian reasons can never justify going to war against a state. Such protectionist grounds for military intervention, however, I think must be limited to situations of genocide or impending genocide and where the war actually makes rescue possible.[32] Even if the United States government is sincere in its conviction that its military efforts are intended to save the world from evil, its political and military hegemony materially harms many poor and defenseless people of the world, and places most of the world in a position of subordination that nurtures resentment.

Democratic global citizenship

The contemporary security state in the United States, like many security states, has two faces, one looking outward and the other inward. Each aspect reinforces the other. Both threaten democratic values, in the institutions and practices of the United States, as well as globally. Citizens and residents who accept the security state because they fear attack allow themselves to be positioned as women and children in relation to the paternal protector leaders. At the same time, to the extent that we identify with a rhetoric of war for the sake of saving the victims of tyranny, we put ourselves in a position superior to those we construct as in need of our aid. Whether looking outward or inward, adopting a more democratic ethos entails rejecting the inequality inherent in the protector–protected logic.

When leaders promulgate fear and promise to keep us safe, they conjure up childish fantasies and desires. We are vulnerable beings, and we want very much to be made safe by a being superior in power to all that might threaten us. Democratic citizens, however, should resist leaders' attempts to play father over us. We should insist that government does its job to promote security without issuing guarantees it cannot redeem or requiring subordination from the people it promises to protect.

Democratic citizenship should first involve admitting that no state can make any of us completely safe, and that leaders who promise that are themselves suspect. The world is full of risks. Prudence dictates that we assess risks, get information about their sources, and try to minimize them, and we rightly expect our government to do much of this for us. In a democracy, citizens should not have to trade this public responsibility for submission to surveillance, arbitrary decision, and the stifling of criticism.

In making this claim I am extending recent feminist arguments against a model of citizenship that requires each citizen to be independent and self-sufficient in order to be equal and fully autonomous. Feminist theorists of care and welfare have argued that the rights and dignity of individuals should not be diminished just because they need help and support to enable them to carry out their chosen project.[33] Persons who need care or other forms of social support ought not to be forced into a position of subordination and obedience in relation to those who provide care and support; not only should they retain the rights of full citizens to choose their own way of life and hold authorities accountable, but they ought to be able to criticize the way in which support comes to them. This feminist argument rejects the assumption behind a notion of self-sufficient citizenship that a need for social support or care is more exceptional than normal. On the contrary, the well-being of all persons can be enhanced by the care and support of others, and in modern societies some of this generalized care and support ought to be organized and guaranteed through state institutions. The organization of reasonable measures to protect people from harm and make people confident that they can move and act relatively safely is another form of social support. Citizens should not have to trade their liberty of movement or right to protest and to hold leaders accountable in return for such security.

Democratic citizenship thus means ultimately rejecting the hierarchy of protector and protected. In the article I cited above, Judith Stiehm argues that rejection of this hierarchy implies installing a position of defender in place of that of both the protector and the protected. A society of defenders is "a society composed of citizens equally liable to experience violence and equally responsible for exercising society's violence."[34] Modern democracies, including American democracy, are founded partly on the principle that citizens should be able to defend themselves if they are also to defend the republic from tyranny. In the twenty-first century, in a world of organized and less organized military institutions and weapons capable of unimaginable destruction, it is hard to know what it might mean for world citizens to exercise collective self-defense. It certainly does not mean that every individual should amass his or her own weapons cache. Nor does it mean whole groups and nations engaging in arms races. The distinction between defender and protector invokes an ideal of equality in the work of defense, and today this may have at least as much to do with political processes that limit weapons and their use as well as wielding arms.

The United States claims to use its arms to do this, much as a policeman does in domestic life. In a democratic relationship, however, the policeman-protector comes under the collective authority of the people whose neighborhood he patrols. Democratic citizenship at a global level, then, would constitute a relationship of respect and political equality among the world's peoples where none of us think that we stand in the position of the paternal authority who knows what is good for the still developing others. To the extent that global law enforcement is necessary, it is only legitimate if the world's peoples together have formulated the rules and actions of such enforcement.

7

Decentering the Project of Global Democracy

In an important statement co-signed by Jacques Derrida and published in the *Frankfurter Allgemeine Zeitung* on May 31, 2003, Jürgen Habermas calls upon European states and citizens to forge a common European foreign policy to balance the hegemonic power of the United States.[1] Europeans should forge a common political identity to stand up to this hegemonic power, but an identity that is open toward ideas of cosmopolitan democracy. I am grateful to these civic minded philosophers for issuing such a call to public responsibility at this historical moment when the United States and the United Kingdom seem ready to occupy Iraq indefinitely and the US threatens other states. I welcome the call for Europe to be more independent of the United States in assessing its own interests and the interests of the world, and I agree that a united and different stance from Europe might temper the arrogance of US foreign policy. I wonder, however, just how cosmopolitan is the stance taken in the statement. From the point of view of the rest of the world, and especially from the point of view of the states and people in the global South, the philosophers' appeal may look more like a recentering of Europe than the invocation of an inclusive global democracy.

Habermas begins by citing February 15, 2003, as a historic day which may "go down in history as a sign for the birth of a European public sphere" (p. 4). On that day, he notes, millions rallied to oppose war in Iraq, in cities across Europe, including London, Rome, Madrid, Barcelona, Berlin, and Paris. It is the coordinated simultaneity of these demonstrations, Habermas suggests, that harbingers a European public sphere.

But this interpretation distorts the historical facts. On that same weekend there were mass demonstrations on every other continent as well – in Sydney, Tokyo, Seoul, Manila, Vancouver, Toronto, Mexico City, Tegucigalpa, São Paulo, Lagos, Johannesburg, Nairobi, Tel Aviv, Cairo, Istanbul, Warsaw, Moscow, and hundreds of other cities, including many in the US. According to people with whom I have spoken, the worldwide coordination of these demonstrations was planned at the third meeting of the World Social Forum in Porto Alegre in January 2003. The worldwide coordination of these demonstrations thus may signal the emergence of a *global* public sphere, of which European publics are wings, but whose heart may lie in the southern hemisphere.

The philosophers' appeal suggests that Europe has a special obligation at this historical moment to promote peace and justice through international law, against a US policy that flaunts such internationalism. Europe must be the "locomotive" propelling the citizens of the world on their journey toward cosmopolitan democracy. Using the international institutions of the United Nations, economic summits such as G8 meetings, and the World Trade Organization, the International Monetary Fund, and the World Bank, the core states of Europe "should exert [their] influence in shaping the design for a coming global domestic policy" (p. 6).

Certainly, Europe should exert its influence, especially against efforts of the United States to bypass or sever the thin threads of international connection that international policies have spun in the last half-century. The image that I derive from this injunction to use public fora of the UN, WTO, IMF, and economic summits, however, conjures meetings of advanced industrial states of the northern hemisphere in political contestation with one another. In this image, most of the world's people watch the North American and European rivals debating; a few other countries temporarily enter the discussion on one side or the other. From the point of view of most of the world's people, that is, Europe's confrontation with the United States may look like sibling rivalry. If the hegemony of the United States should be confronted and resisted, and it should, why not enlist the efforts of the peoples of Africa, Asia, and Latin America, as well as Europe, from the beginning?

In order for Europe to carry out its global mission as engine of the cosmopolitan train, Habermas says that Europeans must forge a stronger sense of European identity that transcends the parochialism of national identity. Many of the institutions and values that originated in Europe, such as Christianity, capitalism, science, democracy, and human rights, he says, have proliferated beyond Europe. A

European identity for today can be culled from the distinctively reflexive way that European societies have responded to the problems generated by modernity, nationalism, and capitalist expansion. In the welfare state Europeans have developed a solution to the inequalities generated by capitalism, and European states have managed to maintain the standards of welfare in the face of strong globalizing economic pressures to change. Europeans also have already begun to put the aggressive dangers of nationalism behind them by instituting the European Union. These successes can and should serve as exemplars to the world.

A European identity, however, cannot exist unless there are others from whom it is differentiated. The call to embrace a particularist European identity, then, means constructing a new distinction between insiders and outsiders. Habermas's main concern is to distinguish a European from an American identity. "For us, a president who opens his daily business with open prayer, and associates his significant decisions with a divine mission, is hard to imagine." Others, in the East and South, stand in the shadows, perhaps, huddled at the edges of this playground where the big boys call each other names. And what of the other within? Is a European identity expansive enough to include the millions of children of Asian and African descent whose parents and grandparents have migrated to the metropole? Like many Americans, many Europeans have reacted to recent global conflicts by distancing themselves from those they identify as foreigners. Surely, invoking a European identity inhibits tolerance within and solidarity with those far away. Here, I fear that Habermas may reinscribe the logic of the nation-state for Europe, rather than transcend it.

In *The Invention of the Americas*,[2] Enrique Dussel retells the story of modernity as based on the European colonial project. Having spent centuries fighting the Muslims and driving them eastward, and having discovered the treasures, power, and technical innovation of the empires in far Asia, Europe found itself on the edges of the world. The European imagination invented America, Dussel argues, as a means of putting itself back at the center. Doesn't the philosophers' appeal look like an attempt to recenter Europe? Europe will stand between the power of the United States and the interests of an inclusive global order, tempering the former and offering leadership for the latter. I agree that the hegemony of the United States should be confronted and resisted, and recent months have shown that European people and states united in that resistance have the potential to bring more balance to power. Europe cannot and should not engage in such confrontation, however, *on behalf* of the rest of the peoples of the world, but *with* them.

The appeal for a European foreign policy ends by referring to a relationship between European countries and the global South: it recalls Europe's imperial past. A hundred years ago the great European nations experienced the "bloom" of imperial power. Since then their power has declined and Europeans have experienced the "loss" of empire. This experience of decline, Habermas says, has allowed Europeans to become reflexive. "They could learn from the perspective of the defeated to perceive themselves in the dubious role of victors who are called to account for the violence of a forcible and uprooting process of modernization."

In this reflection I hear Habermas invite his audience in their imaginations to adopt the perspective of formerly colonized others, and learn to look at Europe and Europeans from that perspective. Certainly, engaging in such an exercise is better than being self-absorbed, as one might assert is the United States and are many Americans. But wouldn't it be better to have real discussions with people and states of the South and East on the sort of equal basis that might tell Europeans (and Americans) things they may not wish to hear about their biases and duties? Where is the forum that Europe has entered to be held accountable?

Referring to colonialism and imperialism as an "uprooting process of modernization" makes it sound like colonialism is an unfortunate by-product of the otherwise universalistic and enlightened project Europe led to establish the principles of human rights, rule of law, and expanded productivity. Colonialism was not just a vicious process of modernization, but a system of slavery and labor exploitation. What are the signs that European people and states have responded to a call for accountability with gestures of contrition and reparation?

As an American, I and others like me have distinct responsibilities to resist the US government's unilateral policies and push for positive change. Citizens of European states have their own responsibilities toward their states and in the policies of the European Union. Rather than reposition Europe as a central player in global politics, however, the progressive project ought to be, in the phrase of Dipesh Chakrabarty, to *provincialize* Europe (as well as the United States).[3] Peoples from all parts of the globe, and especially from those parts whose people are most excluded and dominated by American- and European-led capital processes, ought to sit on terms of equality that recognize the particularity of each to work on solutions to global problems.

The fora at which Habermas proposes that Europe might exert its influence against the current dangerous unilateralist thrust of US foreign policy all tend to privilege the global North and dominate the global South. The structure of the United Nations Security Council privileges the five permanent members. The constitutions of the International Monetary Fund and the World Bank give more power and influence to wealthy countries than poor ones. Many peoples of the southern hemisphere suffer the consequences of crushing debt and microeconomic coercion imposed by some of these international institutions, in the name of fiscal responsibility and the stabilization of currency markets. Shouldn't the project of cosmopolitan democracy raise the question of the reform or abolition of these institutions?

Global inequalities are not merely a legacy of colonialism, but result from ongoing structural processes that daily widen the gap between those with nothing and those living in privileged affluence. While even the poorest country has rich people, and affluent countries have poor people, most of the those who can assume affluent comfort as a way of life dwell in North America and Europe. Without question, European countries do better than the United States in providing meaningful transfers to redress these inequalities. Even Europe's generosity in this regard is pitifully low, however, and along with that of the United States has been declining since 1990.

The privileges of wealth, social order, consumer comfort, well-developed infrastructure, strong capacity to finance government activity, and solidaristic culture make European states and citizens well positioned to take leadership in the project of strengthening international law and peaceful conflict resolution, and instituting mechanisms of global redistribution. Certainly, they should exert influence to pressure, shame, and encourage the United States and its citizens to join in this project. We are taking no steps toward cosmopolitan democracy, however, if the many other peoples of the world do not have influential seats at a table that holds the powerful accountable to the poor and affords real influence to less affluent regions. The weekend of February 15, 2003, signaled a global public sphere that existed before then and has persisted. Many European and North American participants in global civil society look to activists from Brazil or Kenya or India or Sri Lanka for insight and leadership. A democratic European foreign policy would listen across an empty center to those and other southern voices in a circle of equality.

8

Reflections on Hegemony and Global Democracy

The world did not need the war against Iraq to understand that the United States stands alone among states in the magnitude of its military might. The blatant manner in which the United States flaunted that power in the face of fierce opposition from global civil society and nearly all states, however, demonstrates that the United States will use its power in ways that it judges right, without the approval or consent of other agents.

US economic power is not so bold and singular. Although US-based corporate interests dominate world economic decision-making, these are allied with the corporate interests of a small number of rich countries of the world, who gather several times a year under different banners to make global economic policy – the World Economic Forum, World Bank and IMF meetings, the G8 Summit.

As the military power of the United States and the economic hegemony of makers of the Washington consensus have become more consolidated and less apologetic, popular opposition to them has also grown. For three years, a World Social Forum has attracted tens of thousands of activists and advocates to Brazil to say no to the policies of the global economic rulers. More than one hundred million people poured into streets all over the world in February 2003, many of them to support their own governments' active resistance to US determination to wage war against Iraq.[1]

At this historic moment we live under world dictatorship; some call it Empire, and some of them pronounce the word with a positive tone. In saying this I do not mean to claim that democracy has vanished from the domestic political processes of many states. Rather, I mean that the United States as a world military power, and allied with important corporate and international economic powers, functions as an authoritarian ruler over major international affairs. A dictatorship is a regime willing and able to exert its will without consulting with or answering to those affected by its decisions and actions. The global hegemonic power behaves as a dictator in that sense. Recent admission by the United States that it may not be able or willing to restore basic security and services to Iraq by itself tempers to a small extent this autocratic rule. Because the United States continues to insist on cooperation from other states on terms it sets, however, the hegemonic situation remains at least that of aspiring dictatorship.

At the same time, however, the global grass roots social movements I have referred to rally around the slogan "Another world is possible!" What is the other world? Why is it important to envision it? Is it possible? These are the big questions I will address in this short essay. My reflections are largely conceptual and normative, though also speak to action in a few ways.

First, I will review reasons for why global military and economic hegemony is both wrong and dangerous. Then I will develop some conceptual elements of a vision of global democracy that enables rather than overrides local and regional self-determination. Third, I connect arguments for global redistribution and economic empowerment to this vision of global democracy. In concluding, I will face the paradox that arises for any movement to resist tyranny: how can transformation toward democracy occur when we live under powerful autocratic rulers?

What's wrong with hegemony? The argument for global democracy

The United States claims to use its power to promote long-term international security, human rights, internal democracy, and economic development. Many people both inside and outside the United States challenge the credibility of these claims, and I agree that there is reason to doubt them. For the sake of clarifying principles, however, let us assume that they are sincere claims. Suppose it is true that the hegemonic military power has the global common good at heart, and that it aims to right wrongs and transform states and international relations to make them more peaceful and just. Suppose the ruling economic powers have only the common good of the people of the world in view. If the intended ends of the use of dominative power are sincerely sought and good in themselves, what can be the objection to such hegemonic power?

In principle, this is the same question as whether there are reasons to object to a benevolent dictator ruling a single state. We can look to many sources for philosophical arguments against autocratic rule even when it aims at justice. I will draw on two suggested by John Locke and supplement them with one of my own.

The role of human rights principles in international and domestic political discourse today is much like that of natural law in medieval and early modern Western societies. Human rights principles are fundamental moral standards of right and good whose meaning and validity do not depend on particular institutions. In his *Second Treatise of Government*, John Locke constructs a state of nature governed by natural law. Each actor in the state of nature has the rational capacity to know the laws of nature. Just the fact that each actor has the right to interpret and execute the law of nature according to his own lights, Locke argues, is likely to generate unacceptable levels of conflict and disagreement, which can be remedied only by the institution of a government whose law objectively binds them all. When an agent has only his own reason to consult about whether the law of nature has been broken and what is the proper response to infraction, Locke argues, he is liable both to be biased in favor of his own interests and to punish others excessively.[2] Having only his own point of view as a guide, that is, a moral agent in the state of nature does not have adequate means to distinguish his own good from the general good, his own interest from what is objectively right. The moral agent can sincerely wish to interpret and enforce the law of nature, but has no way of limiting the influence of particularist biases in his interpretation of the law.[3] Locke also argues that we are all fallible in our reasoning and ability to know and take account of relevant facts. Consequently, the lone moral agent who wishes to apply the law of nature correctly has no check against error and no way to become aware of such errors.

One response to this problem in the history of philosophy is to theorize a distinction between two points of view for reasoning: an impartial general point of view and a particular point of view. I do not have space here to review philosophical criticisms of ideas of a view from nowhere, or a general will that stands apart from all partiality.[4] As I understand one line of these critiques, the problem is that a putative general standpoint remains monological. The problem we are trying to solve is that the agent's point of view of reasoning is not limited by another point of view to reveal its biases and errors. Postulating a single general standpoint simply pushes this problem to another level. Only a process of dialogic interaction among agents reasoning about what is right can produce a distinction in the awareness of each between his or her own particular needs, interests, and perspectives and a more general understanding of what regulatory principles take account of the needs, interests, and perspectives of everyone.[5]

A dialogic theory of democracy, most often called deliberative democracy but also called discursive or communicative democracy, applies such dialogic ethics to political philosophy. In *Inclusion and Democracy*, I contribute to this general theoretical approach the particular argument that, under conditions of structural social inequality, inclusion of all members of a polity in a democratic discussion means more than equal formal rights to participate. Since structural inequalities give political advantage to those groups that also have social and economic advantage, an inclusive deliberative process must take special measures to ensure that needs, interests, and perspectives of relatively marginalized people gain voice and influence in the deliberative process. The argument for compensatory representation for economically and socially weaker individuals and groups is not simply one of fairness in the distribution of political influence, although it is that. Only the voicing of all social perspectives on issues and proposals, I argue, can produce the sort of public objectivity that distinguishes partial and particular interests and judgments from those that can claim objectivity.[6]

Carried to the level of global politics, this argument implies that human rights can be consistently and permanently defended only if there is an inclusive global system of deliberation and decision-making that decides when they are in danger and how they should be protected. The increased density of interaction and interdependence in the world has made the opportunity and need for more global-level regulation of security, human rights, trade regulation, development policy, and other global issues. Global governance can have moral legitimacy only if such regulatory processes are formed through the interaction of multiple perspectives drawing on the experience and interests of all the world's people.

Self-determination as nondomination

Some people resist calls for global democracy because they want to retain national sovereignty. Without respect for the self-determination and autonomy of peoples in a pluralist system of states, it might be said, the smaller and weaker peoples would be entirely swamped and forced to assimilate to an allegedly cosmopolitan system that would only enhance the economic and political power of today's strong global powers. Rather than conceiving and trying to enact a system of global democracy, it would be better to strengthen national sovereignty against the forces of military and economic domination by outsiders.[7]

At least two reasons speak against such a project to retrench Westphalian sovereignty. The degree of interdependence among the world's people has proceeded far enough that few states can effectively cushion their internal affairs from the effects of actions and policies performed by outside states and organizations.[8] The legitimacy of traditional nation-state sovereignty, moreover, has come into question by minority social movements who claim to be unjustly dominated by states. A pluralistic conception of global democracy with a properly formulated principle of self-determination at its center, I suggest, better responds to both current problems of transnational and subnational domination.

The most common understanding of the meaning of a principle of self-determination today continues to equate self-determination with sovereignty. Understood as sovereignty, a principle of self-determination means noninterference. The self-determining entity has a closely bounded sphere over which it can and should have exclusive control, and with which outsiders should refrain from interfering. This interpretation of self-determination allows for some of the autonomous entities to exploit or gain power in relation to others so long as they do not directly interfere with their regulatory right over their internal jurisdiction.[9] A hands-off, noninterference understanding of self-determination, moreover, leaves autonomous entities without claims to aid and support if the processes of interaction among them deprives them of the resources to sustain their own well-being. Understanding self-determination as sovereignty, finally, fails to protect individuals or groups against the possibility that the state or other persons in the jurisdiction will wrongly dominate them.

In previous writing, I have argued for a conceptualization of self-determination that draws on feminist analyses of relational autonomy and Philip Pettit's republican concept of nondomination.[10] A concept of relational autonomy recognizes that the agency and capabilities of any individual or group is relationally constituted. No agent is an island with a strict division between an inside over which he or she has sole control and an outside which he or she neither influences nor is influenced by. This is even more true of social collectives – groups and peoples. Groups or peoples who consider themselves distinct from others by virtue of location, environment, history, cultural practices, or goals of action are embedded in fluid relations with other groups which generate mutual obligations and potential for conflict and domination. In such relations, autonomy can have real meaning as the ability of groups to make and carry out their own decisions about how they will organize their collective action, with a prima facie obligation on the part of others not to interfere in these actions.

Such autonomy must be conditional, however, on recognizing the relations in which the group stands with others, and that its actions may affect them adversely. Where relations between autonomous agents come into conflict, or where they generate shared problems, or where they enable the emergence of inequalities that make some vulnerable to domination by others, self-determination calls for autonomous units joining a common process of adjudication, negotiation, and collective problem-solving.

Institutionalizing self-determination as nondomination

How does the concept of self-determination as nondomination contribute to a vision of global democracy? While here I can address this question only briefly and in a very general way, I find that there is much theoretical imagination being devoted to this project. Both local self-determination and global political equality among peoples, and global-level collective problem-solving can best be enacted by means of a system of local and regional units with considerable autonomy to organize their own collective lives and actions, nested within a set of global-level regulatory regimes in whose procedures and decisions they all participate. The relation of global regulatory and negotiating schemes to regional and local political organization should not be a simple hierarchy of law imposed from a center on the locales. Instead, global institutions could provide for a discussion about common problems and procedures for horizontal relationships between locally and regionally autonomous units to adjudicate conflict, negotiate agreements, and work out cooperative projects. Global procedures and regulatory institutions themselves are polyarchic, in this model, with different centers for different global issues, such as security, finance and investment, environment, health, and welfare. The function of global-level procedures and regulatory institutions is to protect autonomous units from vulnerability to domination by others, to protect individuals inside units from severe rights violations, and to develop cooperative programs for addressing problems shared by autonomous units. While many of these autonomous units are territorially defined, enactment of a principle of self-determination also should allow for units of autonomous decision-making whose members do not all reside in a single territory occupied only or primarily by them.[11]

A vision of global democracy with relational autonomy at its center involves multiple levels of decision-making in which representatives of those bound by decisions take part. It should involve systems of both upward and downward accountability – local units having to explain their actions to outsiders and to global-level review processes, and global decisions having to answer to locales. As already mentioned, however, administrative interaction and negotiation ought to move horizontally as well as vertically. In order for this level of cooperation to occur and vulnerability to domination of some units by others or lower levels by upper levels to be prevented, relational autonomy requires a process where every unit has control over basic resources necessary to that autonomy. Thus, another major function of global-level institutions of regulation and cooperation is to monitor such resource allocation and reallocate when necessary to support local autonomy.

Models of global and regional governance along these lines have been variously called cosmopolitan democracy,[12] diverse federalism,[13] directly deliberative polyarchy,[14] multisited federalism,[15] decentered decentralization,[16] accountable autonomy,[17] and differentiated solidarity.[18] These theories apply similar principles of institutional design to nested relationships among locales in a metropolitan region and/or between different locales across the world. In this sort of vision there can remain a place for that level of governance we know as states, which retain the most developed enforcement capacities. As enforcers and administrators, states can be conceived of as mediators between the local and group-differentiated and the global. As such, they are powerful actors, but they are not sovereign as traditionally understood.

Economic empowerment

No discussion of global democracy can ignore the vast inequalities between the global affluent and the global poor, which the existing system of hegemonic global capital produces and reproduces. Billions of people in the world, the majority of them in less-developed countries of the southern hemisphere, suffer in desperate poverty. The societies in which many of these live have little infrastructure to produce the goods and services their people need or the governance capacity to produce order and coordinated action. Not only does this situation produce and perpetuate misery, but it effectively excludes many peoples of the world from the possibility of participating in global governance schemes in a meaningful way, even if and to the extent such governance might exist. Most countries are nominal members of the World Trade Organization, for example, which differs from the International Monetary Fund and the World Bank in affording each member country an equally weighted vote. Many countries lack the resources, however, to send representatives to meetings or provide them with staff adequate to do the research and make the arguments that could give them effective voice in deliberations. More generally, existing global inequalities make many peoples and states vulnerable to domination and exploitation by corporate, governmental, and international actors. Local self-determination has little meaning, moreover, if relationally autonomous units do not have significant control over some resources needed to make a decent life for their members and to realize some of their collective goals. A project of global democratization requires some moves toward global justice.

An explosion of recent philosophical writing debates the question: do obligations of justice extend beyond the boundaries of a single nation-state? While some philosophers continue to maintain that they do not,[19] this position's plausibility is waning.[20] Arguments that there are transnational obligations of justice cannot appeal simply to the facts of need. The neediness of masses of people and vulnerabilities into which this puts them can at best back moral responsibilities of beneficence. Under this view, agents who can relieve the neediness of distant others ought to do so, other things being equal, but they do not strictly have obligations to do so. In this charity view of the moral claims of needy others on those with more resources, it is up to the donor to decide the level of gift and under what conditions it shall be given. To the extent that there exists transnational aid in the world today, it largely takes this form of beneficence, whether given by governments, private associations, or individuals. Because this structure puts recipients in the position of supplicants who must gratefully abide by whatever conditions donors put on their gifts, it may reinforce relations of global domination more than undermine them.

The best argument for a global scope to obligations of justice appeals to connection as well as need. People in different parts of the world are connected to one another in diverse and overlapping networks of social cooperation. Processes of transnational trade, investment, migration, communication, and cultural exchange have produced globalized schemes of social cooperation, and the existing basic structures of this social cooperation are unjust to the extent that they greatly benefit a few while rendering many others poor and vulnerable to domination and exploitation.[21]

If the basic structures of transnational social cooperation produce and reproduce injustice between peoples, then these structures should be changed. Reflections on methods of producing structural change, however, go beyond my time and capacity for this essay. I will mention two proposals for global redistribution that could, if acted on, have structural effects: demand for debt cancellation and the establishment of global tax.

There are at least two arguments for canceling the debts that many of the world's poorest countries owe to international institutions, states, and private banks. The initial process of lending and borrowing in the 1950s and 1960s relied on a faulty economic theory of development "take off" and entailed many irresponsible lending decisions.[22] More important, perhaps, the scale of debt that has accrued in the intervening decades is so massive that entire national economies are distorted in their efforts to service the debt. If it is just and legitimate to propose that debt be canceled so that the Iraqi people can rebuild their society, then the case is even more compelling for many less resourced and more debt-burdened countries of the world.[23]

Persons as different as grass-roots activists from the barrios of Mexico and Nobel Prize winning economists who have walked the halls of Washington recently have called for systems of global taxation. The Tobin Tax is the most popular proposal, which would put a small surcharge on financial transactions. Besides generating revenue for the operation of stronger global regulatory institutions and redistribution, according to some of its advocates a financial transaction tax would have the effect of slowing the movement of capital, thus keeping it under more local control.[24] Philosophical, economic, and social movement literatures offer other creative ideas for global taxation systems, such as Thomas Pogge's idea of a global resource dividend.[25]

Is another world possible?

Ideas and arguments about what global democracy and global justice require are more well developed than are ideas about what the people and organizations of the world can do to get them. The reason for optimism on this point lies in the growth and imagination of transnational social movements, especially including people and associations for the southern hemisphere who vocally oppose the existing structures of military and economic hegemony. For three years tens of thousands of these people have gathered at a World Social Forum, and anticorporate globalization demonstrations have been visible and vocal at nearly every major meeting of global elites in the last five years.[26]

These transnational social movements, however, are largely discussion oriented, immediate, and oppositional. Some activists argue that these movements should on principle refrain from formulating and trying to achieve specific programmatic objectives for institutional change. I understand the importance of retaining an outsider, critical voice, and I appreciate the value of broadly inclusive discussion that might be cut off by trying to agree on objectives for action. Nevertheless, some organizations and institutions should propose institutional and policy alternatives for making global governance more democratic and just.

If we currently live under a global dictatorship, it seems impossible to imagine such alternatives. Hegemony is the only game around. Seeing no alternative, most people become resigned to it and states suck up to its power, hoping to save themselves from bombs and maybe receive some trickle-down benefits. Resignation and cynical support are the life blood of any dictatorship, however, whether in a petty principality or in the world. The only way to weaken a dictator is to withdraw cooperation with him. The only means of moving from hegemony to democracy, then, is for states, private organizations, and individuals to try to organize with one another to resist the efforts of the United States and the international financial and corporate powers with which it is allied to run world affairs their way. A few movements to do this are underway, and there are other proposals on various tables.

While perhaps still too small to have serious redistributive effects on earnings, fair trade consumer movements directly link consumer choice to benefits for primary producers. Increasing numbers of organizations, both in the United States and elsewhere, to take another example, aim to defund the World Bank by boycotting the bonds on which the bulk of its funding depends.

At a level of state coordination, some writers argue that an important way to confront American-dominated military and economic interests can be to elevate the Euro currency in transnational trading. From the point of view of many of the less powerful peoples of the world, of course, this could simply mean trading one scary dictator for another, somewhat less scary one. More positively, perhaps, some writers propose that the European Union is well positioned to implement a financial transactions tax or some other tax for purposes of funding global governance and redistribution, and that if it did other states might join.

There is, finally, the possibility of working on and through the United Nations as well as creating new global institutions. Since the United States and the United Kingdom waged their war against Iraq in direct confrontation with the UN Security Council, many people from all parts of the political spectrum have concluded that the UN has become even more irrelevant to the workings of global politics than it was before.

Yet aspirations to democratize governance of the world and discharge obligations of global justice clearly require some kind of global institutions that in principle include or represent everyone in the world. Today the United Nations, and in particular the General Assembly, is the only institution which comes close to including all the world's peoples, albeit in a small and highly imperfect way. There is much truth in the suggestion of some that the United Nations often seems to function as a tool and legitimizer of the goals of US military and economic interests. Events of spring 2003 show, however, that the United Nations can be a stage for global debate and political conflict. For two decades global social movements have used official issue-oriented meetings of the UN as occasions to make policy demands on states and international organizations and to envision more radical alternatives. As I finish writing this essay, the Bush Administration is trying to get UN approval for a multilateral force in Iraq under US command, and France is asserting its resistance to this proposal. If domestic civil societies only exist in relation to states, then perhaps the global civil society so celebrated by many activists stands in relation to the official international organization of the United Nations.

Ultimately, the existing United Nations must be reformed or transformed to serve any purpose conducive to democracy and justice. The current composition of the Security Council is unfair and outdated. The Bretton Woods institutions should be abolished and the world should make a new start on global finance regulation. Local self-determination in the context of global coordination would be furthered, moreover, by the establishment of a People's Assembly alongside the General Assembly.[27] In the long run, the best way to rein in unilateral US military force, moreover, is to bring into being transnational military forces with greater authority and capacity than UN forces have yet been given.[28] The fact of global hegemony should not discourage us from working toward these ends, but rather ought to persuade us that we have no choice but to do so.

Part III

Global Justice

9

Responsibility, Social Connection, and Global Labor Justice

In this essay I clarify the status of claims about global justice and injustice that are increasingly voiced and accepted in our world.[1] Such claims present a problem for political philosophy because until recently most philosophical approaches to justice assumed that obligations of justice hold only between those living under a common constitution within a single political community. I will argue that obligations of justice arise between persons by virtue of the social processes that connect them; political institutions are the response to these obligations rather than their basis. I develop an account of some such social processes as structural, and argue that some harms come to people as a result of structural social injustice. Claims that obligations of justice extend globally for some issues, then, are grounded in the fact that some structural social processes connect people across the world without regard to political boundaries.

The second and more central project of this essay is to theorize the responsibilities moral agents may be said to have in relation to such global social processes. How ought moral agents, whether individual or institutional, conceptualize their responsibilities in relation to global injustice? I propose a model of responsibility from social connection as an interpretation of obligations of justice arising from structural social processes. I use the example of justice in transnational processes of the production, distribution, and marketing of clothing to illustrate operations of structural social processes that extend widely across regions of the world.[2]

The social connection model of responsibility says that all agents who contribute by their actions to the structural processes that produce injustice have responsibilities to work to remedy these injustices. I distinguish this model from a more standard model of responsibility, which I call a liability model. I specify five features of the social connection model of responsibility that distinguish it from the liability model: it does not isolate perpetrators; it judges background conditions of action; it is more forward looking than backward looking; its responsibility is essentially shared; and it can be discharged only through collective action. The final section of the paper begins to articulate parameters of reasoning that agents can use for thinking about their own action in relation to structural injustice.

Global connections and obligations of justice

A widely accepted philosophical view continues to hold that the scope of obligations of justice is defined by membership in a common political community. On this account, people have obligations of justice only to other people with whom they live together under a common constitution, or whom they recognize as belonging to the same nation as themselves. In all of his writing on justice, for example, Rawls assumes that the scope of those who have obligations of justice to one another is a single, relatively closed society.[3] The members of each such society are mutually bound by obligations of justice they do not have to outsiders. This is not to say that insiders have no moral obligations to outsiders. There are some moral obligations that human beings have to one another as humans; these are cosmopolitan obligations or obligations to respect human rights. In *The Law of Peoples* Rawls reiterates that principles of justice as fairness mutually oblige members of distinct societies to one another, yet do not apply to the moral relationships among people between societies across the globe. The law of peoples is broader and thinner than justice as fairness.[4]

David Miller also conceives principles of justice as having in their scope only relations among those persons who dwell together within the same nation-state. Obligations to organize coercive institutions to ensure distributive fairness according to need, desert, and equal respect obtain only between persons who belong together in the same nation-state and who live under a single political constitution.[5] Miller worries that a globalizing world is making state sovereignty more porous and liable to being affected by and affecting persons and circumstances outside these nation-state borders. He concludes from this undeniable fact not that principles of justice should follow these globalizing trends, but rather that social justice itself may be a historically specific idea and set of practices whose time is passed.[6]

As I understand the logic of this position, it holds that obligations of justice presuppose the existence of shared political institutions. It is incoherent to say that relationships between people are unjust or just, on this interpretation, in the absence of shared institutions for adjudicating such claims or regulating their relations. Some more general and less stringent obligations obtain between persons across political jurisdictions just because they are human. But these are not obligations of justice.

A contrary position about moral obligation I will call cosmopolitan–utilitarian. On this view, nation-state membership or any other sort of particularist relationship among persons is irrelevant to assessing the nature, depth, or scope of obligations they have to one another. Moral agents have identical obligations to all human beings, and this perhaps includes other creatures. There is a moral imperative to minimize suffering, wherever it occurs. Every agent is obliged to do what he or she can to minimize suffering everywhere, right up to the point where he or she begins to suffer. Political membership of either the agent or the sufferers is relevant only instrumentally as providing efficient means of discharging obligations and distributing particular tasks. Much about global relationships, however, can override this issue of convenience. Peter Singer and Peter Unger are two prominent examples of theorists who hold this view.[7]

I think that each of these accounts is wanting. Critics of the cosmopolitan–utilitarian position argue that it is too demanding.[8] It flies in the face of moral intuition, moreover, to suggest that all moral agents have exactly the same duties to all other agents and no special obligations to some subset of persons with whom an agent has special relationship. While the basic moral respect owed to all persons grounds the cosmopolitan obligations that Immanuel Kant calls hospitality,[9] obligations of justice require more and are based on more than common humanity.

Critics of the position that limits the scope of obligations of justice to common political membership, on the other hand, are right to argue that it is arbitrary to consider nation-state membership as a source of obligations of justice. Political communities have evolved in contingent and arbitrary ways more connected to power than moral right. People often stand in dense relationships with others prior to, apart from, or outside political communities. These relationships may be such that their actions affect one another in ways that tend to produce conflict. Or they cooperate with numbers of others in ongoing practices and institutions that meet some shared objectives. In such social relations, we expect fair terms of conflict resolution and cooperation. Thus, against the cosmopolitan–utilitarian position, I believe that some account needs to be offered of the nature of social relationships that ground claims that people have obligations of justice to one another. It is not enough to say that the others are human.

The nation-state position, however, makes prior what is posterior from a moral point of view. Ontologically and morally speaking, though not necessarily temporally, social connection is prior to political institutions. This is the great insight of social contract theory. The social connections of civil society may well exist without political institutions to govern them. A society consists in connected or mutually influencing institutions and practices through which people enact their projects and seek their happiness, and in doing so affect the conditions under which others act, often profoundly. A social contract theory like that of John Locke argues that the need and desire for political institutions arises because socially connected persons with multiple and sometimes conflicting institutional commitments recognize that their relationships are liable to conflict and inequalities of power that can lead to mistrust, violence, exploitation, and domination. The moral status of political institutions arises from the obligations of justice generated by social connection, as some of the instruments through which these obligations can be discharged.

In his landmark work *Political Theory and International Relations*, Charles Beitz challenged Rawls's assumption that the scope of obligations of justice extends only between members of a single political community by arguing that there exists an international *society* even in the absence of a comprehensive political constitution to regulate it. Ongoing economic processes of production, investment, and trade connect people in diverse regions of the world, and these relationships are often unequal in power and material resources. People move across borders, and institutions of expression and communication are increasingly global in their reach. The activities of many religious, artistic, scientific, legal, and service-providing institutions and networks extend to many parts of the world without too much regard for nation-state membership and boundaries. Beitz concludes that principles of justice such as those Rawls argues for apply globally because there are dense global social and economic relationships.[10] A need for political institutions sufficiently wide in scope and strong to regulate these relationships to insure their fairness follows from the global scope of obligations of justice, rather than grounding the obligations.

Onora O'Neill argues somewhat differently to a similar conclusion. The scope of an agent's moral obligation extends to all those whom the agent assumes in conducting her or his activity. Each of us pursues our interests and goals within the frame of specific institutions and practices, and within which we know others do the same. Our actions are partly based on the actions of others, insofar as we depend on them to carry out certain tasks, and/or insofar as our general knowledge of what other people are doing enables us to formulate expectations and predictions about events and institutional outcomes that affects us or condition our actions. In today's world of globalized markets, interdependent states, rapid and dense communication, the scope of the actors we implicitly assume in many of our actions is often global. The social relations that connect us to others are not restricted to nation-state borders. Our actions are conditioned by and contribute to institutions that affect distant others, and their actions contribute to the operation of institutions that affect us. Because our actions assume these others as condition for our own actions, O'Neill argues, we have made practical moral commitments to them by virtue of our actions. That is, even when we are not conscious of or actively deny a moral relationship to these other people, to the extent that our actions depend on the assumption that distant others are doing certain things, we have obligations of justice in relation to them.

It is not possible to trace how each person's actions produce specific effects on others because there are too many mediating actions and events. Nevertheless, we have obligations to those who condition and enable our own actions, as they do on us. There is an asymmetry in these obligations, however, O'Neill argues, insofar as some people are rendered more vulnerable to coercion, domination, or deprivation by the institutional relations. While everyone in the system of structural and institutional relations stands in circumstances of justice that give them obligations with respect to all the others, those institutionally and materially situated to be able to do more to affect the conditions of vulnerability have greater obligations.[11]

I interpret both Beitz and O'Neill, along with other theorists of global justice such as Thomas Pogge,[12] as describing transnational social *structures* and the injustices they may generate as structural injustice. Alan Buchanan similarly argues that there exists a global basic structure that generates obligations of justice between people across national boundaries.[13] Before I conceptualize structural injustice and introduce the concept of responsibility that corresponds to it, however, let me elaborate a particular example of claims about injustice as involving transnational social connection, namely the antisweatshop movement.

Example of global injustice: sweatshops

Although I believe that the social connection model of responsibility applies to every case of structural injustice, whether local or global, relationships in the global apparel industry offer a perspicuous example through which I will explain the logic of the social connection model of responsibility. A vocal and multilayered antisweatshop movement, moreover, has in recent years pressed claims on a variety of agents to take responsibility for sweatshop conditions.

Antisweatshop activists have made claims on institutions that purchase clothing in bulk, such as city governments,[14] or which market clothing with their name on them, such as universities,[15] to take responsibility for the poor conditions under which these garments are produced, often in factories on the other side of the world. Social movement activists have also passed out leaflets in front of brand name apparel stores such as Gap or Nike or Disney, or more generic clothing retailers such as Target and Wal-Mart, detailing that much of the clothing sold in those stores is made under sweatshop conditions, and calling upon consumers to take responsibility for those conditions.

Not a few institutions and individuals find absurd the idea that consumers and retailers bear responsibility for working conditions in far away factories, often in other countries. Not unreasonably, they say that even if the workers producing items they buy suffer wrongful exploitation and injustice, we here have nothing to do with it. It is, rather, the owners and managers of the factories who are to blame. Despite the apparent reasonableness of this dissociation, the claims of the antisweatshop movement seem to have struck a chord with many individuals and institutions. I think that to understand why we need a conception of responsibility different from a standard notion of blame or liability.

What, then, are "sweatshops?" Much of the clothing, shoes, and other small consumer items whose production is labor intensive are produced in relatively small manufacturing centers in less developed countries, which operate at the bottom of a chain of specification, distribution, and marketing that often involves hundreds of distinct companies. Research on the global apparel industry has brought to light that sweatshops abound in North America and Europe.[16] The vast majority of sweatshops, however, operate in less developed countries. In 2000, 85 percent of US consumption of footwear, and 50 percent of apparel, was imported.[17]

Conditions in such manufacturing facilities vary, of course, but the following are typical. The vast majority of workers are female, and often as young as 13 or 14. They are often treated in dominative and abusive ways by bosses, and sexual harassment is common. Typically, they work 10- to 16-hour days in peak seasons; if the manufacturer is behind on order the workers may be forced to work through the night. They have few bathroom breaks or other opportunities for rest during their long working day. Sick leave or vacation time are generally unavailable; a worker too ill to work is often fired. Violations of the most basic health and safety standards are normal. Factories are often excessively hot, with no ventilation, insufficient lighting, excessive noise, little fire equipment, blocked exits, poor sanitation, unhygienic canteens and bathrooms, and no access to clean drinking water. Typically, workers in these facilities have no freedom to organize unions to bargain collectively with employers. Workers who complain and try to organize are typically threatened, fired, blacklisted, beaten, and even killed. Local governments often actively or passively support such antiunion activity.[18]

There should be little doubt that conditions such as these violate basic human rights. Many international agreements and conventions prohibit violence and intimidation in the workplace as elsewhere, and stipulate that workers not labor under conditions that threaten their basic health and physical safety. The meaning of such rights, moreover, ought to vary little with local culture or level of industrial development. Exhaustion and the need to pee are cross-cultural experiences. The right to assemble and organize ought to be recognized everywhere, and it is everywhere wrong to intimidate and beat people who try to exercise this right. To say these are rights is to say precisely that there is no valid moral argument for trading them off against profits, or policies designed to foster economic growth, or the earnings of the workers. If many workers endure these violations without complaint because they desperately need those earnings, this is a measure of the coercive pressures of their circumstances rather than of their consent.

But what of their earnings? Economists argue that wage levels for the same kind of work appropriately vary with the local cost of living and labor market conditions, and they are right. Those who argue that the standard of living for workers in sweatshops is often higher than in the countryside from which many of them have moved may be correct. The wage levels of workers in the apparel industry is nevertheless often far below the legal minimum wage.[19] Employers too often renege, moreover, in paying even these meager wages.[20] The workers generally have no recourse when employers underpay them, because they often have no formal employment contracts, and the employers keep poor or no records of the hours employees have worked. It may be true that under normal market conditions a rise in wages for some workers will mean loss of jobs for others; where the wages of a massive number of workers are below subsistence level, as they often are, this is more an argument against accepting normal market conditions than against paying living wages.

Thus far I have cited typical conditions for garment workers in factories. A significant portion of the people who put garments together, however, work from their homes. Employers often prefer putting out to homeworkers because there they do not have to pay for facilities and overheads and they are not legally responsible for working conditions. Workers, especially women workers, often prefer home work to factory work even when it pays less, because they can avoid long and potentially harassing travels to work, can stay with their children, and save face for their husbands who can pretend that their wives are not working.[21] Homeworkers are often the poorest paid, however, and work the longest self-imposed hours. The children or old people with whom the worker wants to stay home, moreover, are often enlisted to help with the work.[22]

The subject of this essay is responsibility in relation to injustice. The structure of the global apparel industry diffuses responsibility for sweatshop conditions. Big-name retailers in North America or Europe rarely themselves own and operate factories in which clothes made to their order are manufactured. Instead, there is a complex chain of production and distribution involving dozens or thousands of contractually distinct entities that bring the clothes manufactured in one place to the store in which people buy them. In this system, each of the layers in the chain believes itself operating close to the margin in a highly competitive environment, and usually is under heavy pressure to meet orders at low cost by firms higher up the chain. The firms higher up the chain, however, often have no legal responsibility for the policies and operations of the other firms below with which they contract.

Facilities where garments and other items are manufactured are typically small. Their activities are difficult to regulate or monitor because their operations frequently shut down in one place and open up in another. The export processing zone policies of many developing countries encourage investment in such firms and generally turn a blind eye to the extent to which they comply with local labor law.

Kimberly Elliott and Richard Freeman present the structure of one US retailer, J. C. Penney, with its subcontracting relations in one developing country, the Philippines. J. C. Penney purchases finished goods through a US importer, Renzo. Renzo conveys J. C. Penney's specifications to Robillard Resources, a Philippino exporter, who contracts with a Philippino clothing contractor that organizes a production chain that includes numerous subcontracting factories. These subcontractors in turn not only organize and supervise factory production of apparel parts, but also organize a system of putting out to workers in their homes.[23] According to Elliott and Freeman, J. C. Penney alone contracts with over 2,000 suppliers in more than 80 countries. Nordstrom has over 50,000 contractors and subcontractors, and Disney licenses products in over 30,000 factories around the world.

Another aspect of the structure of this industry relevant for issues of assigning responsibility has to do with the way that the positions of employer and employee are often blurred in this system. In some factories production line leaders act as subcontracting agents for homeworkers, with the permission and assistance of management. Line workers and home workers rarely receive written contracts; they are encouraged to think of themselves as "self-employed."[24]

In this complex system of production and distribution, the workers who make garments are at the bottom of the chain. The wages they earn generally amount to a small portion of the retail price of an item, often under 6 percent.[25] Each layer of subcontracting that runs between the manufacturer and the store in which the consumer buys items adds to the cost of items. Major logo retailers usually make handsome profits from this system; as one moves down the chain of production and distribution, firms operate in more competitive environments. Small subcontractors in developing countries frequently operate at just the edge of solvency.

Antisweatshop activists argue that the workers at the bottom of this system suffer injustice in the form of domination, coercion, and need deprivation within a global system of vast inequalities. Because of the complexity of the system that brings items from production to sale, and the manner in which it constrains the options of many of the actors within it, this is an example of *structural* injustice. I will now articulate that concept more generally.

Structural injustice[26]

In *A Theory of Justice*, John Rawls says that the subject of justice is the basic structure of society, which concerns "the way in which the major social institutions distribute fundamental rights and duties and determine the division of advantages from social cooperation."[27] Major institutions include, he says, the legal system's definition of basic rights and duties, market relations, the system of property in the means of production, and family organization. To these I would add the basic kinds of positions in the social division of labor.

Rawls says little more about what the concept of structure refers to, however. Social theorists use the term in many ways, and I will not review them here.[28] As I understand the concept, structures denote the confluence of institutional rules and interactive routines, the mobilization of resources, as well as the built environment. These constitute the historical givens in relation to which individuals act, and which are relatively stable over time. Social structures serve as background conditions for individual actions by presenting actors with options; they provide "channels" that both enable and constrain.[29]

I will build up an account of structure and structural processes using elements derived from several theorists. Peter Blau offers the following definition: "A social structure can be defined as a multidimensional space of differentiated social positions among which a population is distributed. The social associations of people provide both the criterion for distinguishing social positions and the connections among them that make them elements of a single social structure."[30] Blau exploits the spatial metaphor implied by the concept of structure. Individual people occupy varying *positions* in the social space, and their positions stand in determinate relation to other positions. Although Pierre Bourdieu uses very different language and concepts for theorizing social structures, he too begins from a spatial metaphor. He conceives structures as "fields" on which individuals stand in varying positions in relation to one another, offering possibilities for interpretation and action.[31]

The structure consists in the connections among the positions and their relationships, and the way the attributes of positions internally constitute one another through those relationships. Young, unskilled migrants from the countryside to the city or from one country to another stand in a certain structural class position in relation to the small entrepreneurs who employ them for apparel manufacture. The entrepreneurs in turn stand in structural positions in relation to investors in large exporting firms and executives in the multinationals whose logos the clothes sport. The workers and potential workers also occupy particular gendered positions in relations to their employers; their positions may also be structured by racial or ethnic differences that render them vulnerable to exclusion or discrimination. These differing structural positions offer differing and unequal opportunities and potential benefits to their occupants, and their relations are such that constrained opportunities and minimal benefits for some often correlate with wider opportunities and greater benefits for others.

It is misleading, however, to reify the metaphor of structure, to think of social structures as entities independent of social actors, lying passively around them easing or inhibiting their movement. On the contrary, social structures exist only in the action and interaction of persons; they exist not as states, but as processes. Anthony Giddens calls this process structuration. He defines social structures in terms of "rules and resources, recursively implicated in the reproduction of social systems."[32] In the idea of the duality of structure, Giddens theorizes how people act on the basis of their knowledge of preexisting structures and in so acting reproduce those structures. We do so because we act according to rules and expectations and because our relationally constituted positions make or do not make certain resources available to us.

Much about the dynamics of the apparel industry, for example, presupposes practices of fashion. Consumers, especially affluent consumers in the North with disposable income, often want to be stylish, and look to friends and media stars to determine what stylish means and whether it is changing. They often "need" new clothes even when those they own are in fine shape. Major retailers both follow the trends and try to manipulate them. Ideas of what is fashionable, as well as conventions of clothes marketed for four or five different "seasons" during the year, drive much about the size of orders and the speed with which they are expected to be delivered, which constrain manufacturers and lead them to overwork workers. Most of these people act as though fashion is some kind of natural force, when in fact its constraints are produced by the ideas that people have about it and the actions they take presuming those ideas.

Defining structures in terms of the rules and resources brought to actions and interactions, however, makes the emergence of structures sound too much like the product of individual and intentional action. The concept of social structure must also include conditions under which actors act, a collective outcome of action which is often impressed onto the physical environment. Jean-Paul Sartre calls this aspect of social structuration the *practico-inert*.[33] Most of the conditions under which people act are sociohistorical: they are the products of previous actions, usually products of many coordinated and uncoordinated but mutually influencing actions. Those collective actions have left determinate effects on the physical and cultural environment which condition future action in specific ways. The gradual consolidation of land holdings by large firms has left many peasants with poor or no land from which they can eke out subsistence. So, many of them move in search of work, erecting shanty towns at the edge of cities. The export processing zones many governments have established where some of these migrants find work are consequences of a history of structural adjustment programs that many indebted governments have been pressured to implement by international financial institutions. The background conditions of the lives of these young workers today are structural consequences of decisions and aggregated economic processes beginning more than three decades ago.

This leads us to a final aspect of the concept of social structure. The actions and interactions of differently positioned persons drawing on the rules and resources the structures offer take place not only on the basis of past actions whose collective effects mark the physical conditions of action. They also often have future effects beyond the immediate purposes and intentions of the actors. Structured social action and interaction often have collective results that no one intends and which may even be counter to the best intentions of the actors. Sartre calls such effects counter-finalities.[34] When a large number of investors make a speculative run on currencies in anticipation of their devaluation, for example, they often unintentionally but predictably produce a financial crisis which throws some people out of work and ruins the fortunes of others.[35]

Structural injustice exists when social processes put large categories of persons under a systematic threat of domination or deprivation of the means to develop and exercise their capacities, at the same time as they enable others to dominate or have a wide range of opportunities for developing and exercising capacities. Structural injustice is a kind of moral wrong distinct from the wrongful action of an individual agent or the willfully repressive policies of a state. Structural injustice occurs as a consequence of many individuals and institutions acting in pursuit of their particular goals and interests, within given institutional rules and accepted norms. All the persons who participate by their actions in the ongoing schemes of cooperation that constitute these structures are responsible for them, in the sense that they are part of the process that causes them. They are not responsible, however, in the sense of having directed the process or intended its outcomes.

Persons stand in systematically different and unequal social positions due to the way institutions operate together. Rather than being a static condition, these factors that constrain and enable individual possibilities are ongoing processes in which many actors participate. These constraints and enablements occur not only by means of institutional rules and norms enforced by sanctions, but by incentive structures that make some courses of action particularly attractive and carry little cost for some, or make other courses of action particularly costly for others. The injustice does not consist in the bare fact that structures constrain actors, for all social structures constrain as well as enable. Rather, the injustice consists in the *way* they constrain and enable, and how these constraints and enablements expand or contract individuals' opportunities. The institutional rules, resources, and practices through which people act do not constitute, in Rawls's phrase, fair terms of cooperation.

When consumers who take flyers in front of Disney stores react to information about sweatshop working conditions with shock or outrage, they are implicitly making a judgment of injustice. They make the judgment that the workers do not merely suffer misfortune, as though a hurricane had carried away their houses, but that the suffering is socially caused. Somebody, we are inclined to say, ought to do something about this. To make the judgment that poor working conditions are unjust implies that somebody *bears responsibility* for their current condition and for their improvement. If the injustice has social structural causes, however, then it would seem that all those who participate in producing and reproducing the structures are implicated in that responsibility. When we say an injustice such as working to exhaustion is structural, we are saying that the workers are not simply victims of mean bosses, though this may be true. Identification of the wrongs that individual actors perpetrate toward them needs to be supplemented with an account of how macrosocial processes encourage such wrongs, why they are widespread and repeated. My question is: how shall we conceptualize responsibility for producing and rectifying structural injustice?

This question presents a puzzle, I suggest, because standard models of responsibility in moral and legal theory do not supply a satisfactory answer. Standard conceptions of legal and moral responsibility appear to require that we trace a direct relationship between the action of an identifiable person or group and a harm. Although structural processes that produce injustice result from the actions of many persons and the policies of many organizations, in most cases it is not possible to trace which specific actions of which specific agents cause which specific parts of the structural processes or their outcomes. In what follows I offer some steps toward a solution to this puzzle by means of a concept of responsibility in relation to injustice that differs from standard models of moral and legal responsibility. A social connection model of responsibility, as I call it, better conceptualizes moral and political issues of responsibility in relation to transnational structural injustice than does what I will call a liability model of responsibility.

Two models of responsibility: liability and social connection

Journalists, religious leaders, social movement activists, and philosophers today sometimes make claims that people in relatively free and affluent countries such as the United States, Canada, or Germany have responsibilities in relation to the harms and deprivations experienced by millions of people in the less developed world. The claims of the antisweatshop movement are one concrete example of such claims which have been relatively successful in getting a hearing and motivating action. To make sense of such claims, I suggest, we need a conception of responsibility different from the most common conception, the liability model. In this section I offer some elements of a conception of responsibility that I argue derives from connection to structural social processes that produce injustice. I explicate this social connection model of responsibility by contrasting it with the liability model.

Liability model

The most common model of assigning responsibility derives from legal reasoning to find guilt or fault for a harm. Under this liability model, one assigns responsibility to particular agents whose actions can be shown as causally connected to the circumstances for which responsibility is sought. This agent can be a collective entity, such as a corporation, but when it is the analysis treats that entity as a single agent for the purposes of assigning responsibility.[36] The actions found causally connected to the circumstances are shown to be voluntary and performed with adequate knowledge of the situation. If candidates for responsibility can successfully show that their action was not voluntary or that they were excusably ignorant, then their responsibility is usually mitigated if not dissolved. When these conditions do exist, however, it is appropriate to blame the agents for the harmful outcomes.[37] A concept of strict liability departs from a fault or blame model in that it holds an agent liable for a harm even if the agent did not intend or was unable to control the outcome, such as when one person's property accidentally causes damage to another person's property.[38] I include such non-blame conceptions of liability together with blame- or fault-based conceptions in one category of responsibility, because they share the conceptual and functional features I detail below.

A liability model of responsibility for human rights violations in apparel factories and subcontracting in the home is certainly appropriate to apply in many situations. When factory owners and managers violate local labor law, for example, as they often do, they ought to be punished.[39] If states in which factories operate fail to find offenders and punish them, as they often do, they ought morally to be blamed for this failure, and the international community should perhaps find ways to apply sanctions to them. Bosses who harass and intimidate workers, managers who put productivity above workers' health, and so on, certainly should be held responsible in a liability sense for wrongful harms these workers suffer.

As I have discussed, however, particular workers in particular facilities in particular places stand within an extensive system of structural social processes that connect the making of garments to those who wear them. Within this system, it is often plausible for the first-line agents of harm to try to mitigate their responsibility by appeal to factors outside their control. They may claim that they have little choice about the wages they pay, and cannot afford to give workers time off, or invest in better ventilation and equipment. They operate in a highly competitive environment, they say, where other operators constantly try to undercut them. They themselves are operating at the edge of solvency and are not exactly making huge profits. They can stay in business only by selling goods at or below the prices of worldwide competitors, and they can do that only by keeping labor and other production costs to a minimum.[40] They are under heavy pressure from the exporters who place orders with them to deliver, and the exporters in turn are under heavy pressure from the big-name companies that have placed orders with them. The factory owners and managers in which the workers toil are small actors with relatively little power in this global system.

A typical justification for state-enforced labor standards appeals to the need to maintain a level playing field among competitors. If there is a human rights floor below which wages and working conditions should not be allowed to fall, the state is the proper agent to guarantee such a floor through regulation. In this way, those employers who wish to be decent to workers need not fear being undersold by less scrupulous employers.

Certainly, the states in which sweatshops operate must be blamed for allowing them to exist. Many state agencies are inept and corrupt, and often enough some of their officials directly profit from the system that exploits their poor compatriots. As the antisweatshop movement uncovers the existence of factories with sweatshop conditions in the United States and other states with supposedly high labor standards and good enforcement processes, it should certainly blame these agencies for not doing their jobs.

There is no excuse for national and state governments in the United States not to enforce labor standards in the apparel industry, or any other industry, and the record here is rather poor.[41] Some governments of less developed countries, however, can say with some justification that they are under severe constraints that prevent them from improving working conditions. Some governments of less developed countries have indirectly encouraged sweatshop practices by constituting special export processing zones whose factories are exempt from taxation and regulation that apply to other enterprises in the country. They have often been advised to establish such zones by international economic experts. These governments will say that they desperately need investment and jobs, and that to get them they must compete with other poor states to promote a "favorable" investment climate, which includes low taxes and minimal regulation. To avoid or play down balance of trade deficits, they need companies that produce for export. They have never had a strong enough public sector properly to monitor and enforce compliance with labor regulations they develop, and it is difficult to create one with their low tax base. Public sector regulating capacity has been reduced further in some cases by policy responses to pressures from international financial institutions such as the International Monetary Fund suggesting that the borrowing states should reduce public spending.

A concept of responsibility as blame or liability is indispensable for a legal system and sense of moral right that respects agents as individuals and expects them to behave in respectful ways toward others. When applying this concept of responsibility, there must be clear rules of evidence, not only for demonstrating the causal connection between this agent and a harm, but also for evaluating the intentions, motives, and consequences of the actions. By proposing a social connection model of responsibility, I do not aim to replace or reject the liability model of responsibility. The above considerations

suggest, however, that where there is structural social injustice a liability model is not sufficient for assigning responsibility. The liability
model relies on a fairly direct interaction between wrongdoer and
wronged party. Where structural social processes constrain and
enable many actors in complex relations, however, those with the
greatest power in the system, or those who derive benefits from its
operations, may well be removed from any interaction with those who
are most harmed in it. While it is usually inappropriate to *blame* those
agents who are connected to but removed from the harm, it is also
inappropriate, I suggest, to allow them (us) to say that they (we) have
nothing to do with it. Thus, I suggest that we need a different conception of responsibility to refer to the obligations that agents who
participate in structural social processes with unjust outcomes have.
I call this a social connection model.

Social connection model

In ordinary language we use the term "responsible" in several ways.
One I have already discussed as paradigmatic of the liability model:
to be responsible is to be guilty or at fault for having caused a harm
and without valid excuses. We also say, however, that people have
certain responsibilities by virtue of their social roles or positions, as
when we say a teacher has specific responsibilities, or we appeal to
our responsibilities as citizens. In this meaning, finding one responsible does not imply finding one at fault or liable for a past wrong, but
rather refers to agents' carrying out activities in a morally appropriate way and aiming for certain outcomes.[42] What I propose as a social
connection model of responsibility draws more on the latter usage of
the term "responsibility" than on the liability usage. It does share with
the liability usage, however, a reference to causes of wrongs, here the
form of structural processes that produce injustice.

The social connection model of responsibility says that individuals
bear responsibility for structural injustice because they contribute by
their actions to the processes that produce unjust outcomes. Our
responsibility derives from belonging together with others in a system
of interdependent processes of cooperation and competition through
which we seek benefits and aim to realize projects. Even though we
cannot trace the outcome, we may regret our own particular actions
in a direct causal chain, and we bear responsibility because we are
part of the process. Within this scheme of social cooperation, each of
us expects justice toward ourselves, and others can legitimately make
claims on us. Responsibility in relation to injustice thus derives not

from living under a common constitution, but rather from participation in the diverse institutional processes that produce structural injustice. In today's world, as I suggested above, many of these structural processes extend beyond nation-state boundaries to include globally dispersed persons. The structure and relationships of the global apparel industry illustrate starkly and concretely such transnational social connections. I shall detail five main features of the social connection model of responsibility by contrasting it with the liability model.

Not isolating   The liability model of responsibility seeks to mark out and isolate those responsible, thereby distinguishing them from others, who by implication are not responsible. Such isolation of the one or ones liable from the others is an important aspect of legal responsibility, both in criminal and in tort law. Social practices of finding guilt or finding fault, or holding strictly liable, focus on particular agents in order to sanction or demand compensation from them and them alone. A system of moral rules and legal accountability should make clear that agents who violate the rule may face accusation as individual agents.

When harms result from the participation of thousands or millions of people in institutions and practices that produce unjust results, however, such an isolating concept of responsibility is inadequate. Where there is structural injustice, finding some people guilty of perpetrating specific wrongful actions does not absolve others whose actions contribute to the outcomes from bearing responsibility. Hired thugs who beat workers in horribly equipped factories are personally guilty of crimes, as are the factory managers who hire them and target particular workers. Finding them guilty, however, does not absolve the multinational corporations from responsibility for the widespread nature of poor working conditions in the factories producing goods they market. Nor does it absolve those of us who purchase the goods from some kind of responsibility to the workers who make them.

Judging background conditions   In a liability concept of responsibility, what counts as a wrong for which we seek a perpetrator and for which he or she might be required to compensate, we generally conceive as a deviation from a baseline. Implicitly, we assume a normal background situation that is morally acceptable, if not ideal. A crime or an actionable harm consists in a morally and often legally unacceptable deviation from this background structure.[43] The liability model considers the process that brought about the harm as a discrete, bounded event that breaks away from the ongoing normal flow.

Punishment, redress, or compensation aims to restore normality or to "make whole" in relation to the baseline circumstance.

A model of responsibility deriving from understanding the mediated connection that agents have to structural injustices, on the other hand, does not evaluate harm that deviates from the normal and acceptable, but rather often brings into question precisely the background conditions that ascriptions of blame or fault assume as normal. When we judge that structural injustice exists, we mean that at least some of the normal and accepted background conditions of action are not morally acceptable. Most of us contribute to a greater or lesser degree to the production and reproduction of structural injustice precisely because we follow the accepted and expected rules and conventions of the communities and institutions in which we act. Usually, we enact these conventions and practices in a habitual way, without explicit reflection and deliberation on what we do, having in the foreground of our consciousness and intention immediate goals we want to achieve and the particular people we need to interact with to achieve them.

We can think of many examples of accepted norms and institutional practices that constitute the background conditions for sweatshops. I have already referred to the fashion system and its seasons as one set of practices which most producers and consumers reinforce to some extent. Executives at major multinational retailers typically devote more attention and money to advertising campaigns to promote the image of the company than to ensuring that the pay and working conditions of the workers who make the clothes they sell are decent. It is normal in this consumer society for companies to devote a large portion of their investment to advertising rather than production. Levels of unemployment in many of the places where sweatshops exist are normally high, and the social processes depriving peasants of the means to make an independent livelihood speedily create more unemployed. One should expect under these circumstances that each superexploitive sweatshop job opening will have multiple applicants, and that the workers in these jobs will normally be compliant and urge their co-workers to be so as well. Today largely taken for granted, each of these aspects of the global apparel system can and should come under critical scrutiny, and questions can be asked about the responsibilities those who act on these assumptions have in relation to the injustice to which they serve as background.

More forward looking than backward looking Assigning responsibility, whether under the liability model or the social connection model, always has both backward looking and forward looking

aspects. The liability model and social connection models of responsibility nevertheless differ in temporal emphasis. On most occasions,
application of the liability model is primarily backward looking. The
social connection model, on the other hand, emphasizes forward
looking issues.

Under the liability model of responsibility, the harm or circumstance for which we seek to hold agents responsible is usually an iso-
latable action or event that has reached a terminus. The robbery has
taken place, or the oil tanker has spewed its contents on the beach.
Usually the purpose of assigning responsibility in terms of blame,
fault, or liability, then, is to seek retribution or compensation for this
past action. To be sure, such backward looking condemnation and
sanction may have a forward looking purpose as well; often it aims
to deter others from similar action in the future, or to identify weak
points in an institutional system that allows or encourages such
blameworthy actions, in order to reform institutions. Once we take
this latter step, however, we may be leaving the liability model
and moving toward the social connection model. The reform project
likely involves responsibility of many people to take actions directed
at those reforms, even though they are not to blame for past
problems.

When conceptualizing responsibility in relation to structural injustice, on the other hand, we are concerned with an ongoing set of
processes that we understand is likely to continue producing harms
unless there are interventions in it. The temporality of assigning and
taking responsibility, then, is more forward looking than backward
looking. Because the particular causal relationship of the actions of
particular individuals or organizations to structural outcomes is often
not possible to trace, there is no point in seeking to exact compensation or redress from only and all those who have contributed to the
outcome, and in proportion to their contribution. The injustices produced through structures have not reached a terminus, but rather are
ongoing. The point is not to blame, punish, or seek redress from those
who did it, but rather to enjoin those who participate by their actions
in the process of collective action to change it.[44]

The antisweatshop movement well illustrates this forward looking
approach. When activists focus on particular factories or on multinationals who contract to manufacture goods under poor factory conditions, they rarely call for shutting down the factory or otherwise
simply punishing the operators.[45] The system of incentives and organizational priorities make it likely that other factories will open in
the place of the one closed. Even when particular perpetrators are
punished, workers continue to suffer structural injustice.

Shared responsibility From the observation that the social connection model differs from the liability model in that it does not isolate those liable in ways that implicitly absolve others, it follows that all those who contribute by their actions to the structural processes producing injustice share responsibility for these harms. Larry May distinguishes shared responsibility from collective responsibility in that the former is a distributed responsibility whereas the latter is not. A collective of persons, such as a corporation, might be said to be responsible for a state of affairs without any of its constituent individuals being determinately responsible for it. Shared responsibility, on the other hand, is a personal responsibility for outcomes or the risks of harmful outcomes, produced by a group of persons. Each is personally responsible for outcomes in a partial way, since he or she alone does not produce the outcomes; the specific part that each plays in producing the outcome cannot be isolated and identified, however, and thus the responsibility is essentially shared.[46]

Discharged only through collective action A final feature of the social connection model that distinguishes it from a liability model of responsibility is that the forward looking responsibility can be discharged only by joining with others in collective action. This feature follows from the essentially shared nature of the responsibility. Thousands or even millions of agents contribute by our actions in particular institutional contexts to the processes that produce unjust outcomes. Our forward looking responsibility consists in changing the institutions and processes so that their outcomes will be less unjust. No one of us can do this on our own. Even if it were possible to do so, a single shopper would not change the working conditions of those toiling in sweatshops by refusing to buy all items he or she had reason to believe were produced under unjust conditions. The structural processes can be altered only if many actors in diverse social positions work together to intervene in them to produce different outcomes.

Responsibility from social connection, then, is ultimately *political* responsibility. Taking responsibility in a forward looking sense under this model involves joining with others to organize collective action to reform the structures. Most fundamentally, what I mean by "politics" here is public communicative engagement with others for the sake of organizing our relationships and coordinating our actions most justly. Discharging my responsibility in relation to sweatshop workers might involve, then, that I try to persuade others that these wrongs are unacceptable and that we collectively can alter social practices and institutional rules and priorities to prevent them. Our working through state institutions is often an effective means of such collective action to change structural processes, but states are not the only tools of effective collective action.[47] In the next section I will discuss and evaluate some of the activities of the antisweatshop movement.

An important corollary of this feature of political responsibility is that many of those properly thought to be victims of harm or injustice may nevertheless share such political responsibility in relation to it. On the liability model of responsibility, blaming those who claim to be victims of injustice usually functions to absolve others of responsibility for their plight. In the social connection model, however, those who can properly be argued to be victims of structural injustice can be called to a responsibility they share with others in the structures in which they engage in actions directed at transforming the structures.

This point certainly applies in antisweatshop activity. Workers themselves have the strongest interest in combating sweatshop conditions. They also have information and relationships with one another useful in order to mobilize productively to try to alter the structures that perpetuate their exploitation. According to some researchers, employer-sponsored monitoring systems that aim to reform sweatshop conditions but fail to involve workers in a meaningful way are often ineffective or actually harm workers.[48] Even when they do not, they tend toward paternalism rather than empowerment of the workers. The workers share responsibility for combating sweatshop conditions, and ought to be organized in order to do so. Especially where freedom to organize is not recognized or not enforced, however, they can discharge their responsibilities only with the support of others, often far away and relatively privileged others, who make public their grievances, put pressure on the agents that would block their unionization, and give them material aid.

I have been arguing that a social connection model of responsibility better corresponds than does a liability model to the intuitions expressed in claims about the responsibilities agents have concerning global justice. The social connection model not only has these philosophical advantages, I suggest, but also has rhetorical advantages in public discussion that aims to motivate people to take responsibility for rectifying social injustice. Claims that some persons participate in producing injustice and ought to stop too often are heard under a liability model of responsibility. The actors addressed hear themselves being blamed for harms. More often than not, agents who believe themselves being blamed react defensively: they look for other agents to blame instead of themselves, or find excuses that mitigate their liability in cases where they admit that their actions do causally contribute to the harm. In situations of structural injustice, it is easy to engage in such blame shifting or excusing discourse, because in fact others are also responsible and there are structural constraints on most of the actors participating in the institutional processes that have unjust outcomes. In many contexts where the issue is how to mobilize collective action for the sake of social change and greater justice, such finger-pointing and blame-switching lead more to resentment and refusal to take responsibility than to a useful basis of action.[49]

When executives of multinational retailers or shoe buyers hear the claims of antisweatshop activists as laying blame on them for the conditions under which the shoes are produced, they rightly become indignant, or scoff at the absurd extremism of the movement. A social connection model of responsibility distinct from and complementary to a liability model allows us to call on one another to take responsibility *together* for sweatshop conditions, without blaming anyone in particular for the structures that encourage their proliferation. This does not necessarily mean that all who share responsibility have an *equal* responsibility. The power to influence the processes that produce unjust outcomes is an important factor distinguishing degrees of responsibility.

Parameters of reasoning

I have proposed a conception of responsibility from social connection to correspond to the intuition that those who participate by their actions in the structural processes producing injustice bear some responsibility for correcting this injustice. In today's world of global interdependencies, many of these structural injustices involve people widely dispersed across the globe, and are by no means limited to processes within a single nation-state.

What I have done so far is only to offer a way of thinking about responsibility in general. One might well object that the conception of responsibility as social connection raises as many questions as it answers. For example, the model says that all who participate by their actions in processes that produce injustice share responsibility for remedy. Does this mean that all participants bear responsibility in the same way and to the same degree? If not, then what are the bases of differentiating kinds and degrees of responsibility? Most of us participate in many structural processes, moreover, that arguably have disadvantaging, harmful, or unjust consequences for others. It is asking too much for most of us to work actively to restructure each and all of the structural injustices for which we arguably share responsibility. How, then, shall we reason about the best ways to use our limited time, resources, and creative energy to respond to structural injustice?

Adequately responding to questions like these would take at least another full essay. Thus, I will only sketch answers here, and illustrate the responses once again through the example of the antisweatshop movement.

Some moral theorists argue that responsibility names a form of obligation distinct from duty. Joel Feinberg, for example, distinguishes between an ethic that focuses on obligation or duty and an ethic that focuses on responsibility. A duty specifies a rule of action or delineates the substance of what actions count as performing the duty. A responsibility, on the other hand, while no less obligatory, is more open as to what counts as carrying it out.[50] A person with responsibilities is obliged to attend to outcomes the responsibilities call for, and to orient her or his actions in ways demonstrably intended to contribute to bringing about those outcomes. Because a person may face many moral demands on her or his actions, and because changes in circumstances are often unpredictable, just how a person goes about discharging her or his responsibilities is a matter of considerable discretion.[51] Given that a combination of responsibilities may be overdemanding, and given that agents have discretion in how they choose to discharge them, it is reasonable to say that it is up to each agent to decide what he or she can and should do under the circumstances, and how he or she should order the moral priorities. Others have the right to question and criticize our decisions and actions, however, especially when we depend on one another to perform effective collective action. Part of what it means to be responsible on the social connection model is to be accountable to others with whom one shares responsibility for what one has decided to do regarding which structural injustices. When an agent is able to give an account of what has been done and why in terms of shared responsibilities for structural injustice, then others usually ought to accept the decision and the way priorities for actions have been set.

These considerations begin an answer to the question I stated above, namely, how should one reason about one's own action with respect to which injustices? In a world with many and deep structural injustices, most of us in principle share more responsibility than we can reasonably be expected to discharge.[52] Thus, we must make choices about where our action can be most useful or which injustices we regard as most urgent. While a theory of responsibility from social connection will not give a list of maxims or imperatives, it should offer some parameters for reasoning to guide such decisions and actions. These in turn address the first question. Different agents plausibly have different kinds of responsibilities in relation to particular issues of justice, and some arguably have a greater degree of responsibility than others.

These differences of kind and degree correlate with an agent's *position* within the structural processes. By virtue of this structural positioning, different agents have different opportunities and capacities, can draw on different kinds and amounts of resources, or face different levels of constraint with respect to processes that can contribute to structural change. I suggest that persons can reason about their action in relation to structural injustice along parameters of *power, privilege, interest,* and *collective ability*.

Power

An agent's position in structural processes usually carries different degrees of potential or actual power or influence over the processes that produce the outcomes. Where individuals and organizations do not have sufficient energy and resources to respond to all structural injustices to which they are connected, they should focus on those where they have more capacity to influence structural processes.

Despite the fact that they are often legally separated from the manufacturing facilities with working conditions and practices that violate human rights, large multinational designers and retailers such as Calvin Klein or J. C. Penney have much greater power in global trade processes than do small manufacturers. The antisweatshop movement thus rightly concentrates its efforts on pressuring these powerful agents actively to work with manufacturers, host governments, unions, and civic organizations to improve wages and factory conditions for the workers and at the same time protect the workers from being laid off.

Because the agents with the greatest power in social structures often have a vested interest in maintaining them as they are, however, external pressure on the powerful is often necessary to move these agents to action, and to prevent them from taking superficial steps rather than making serious changes. Some of the larger exporters, importers, and retailers in the apparel industry, for example, would appear to be able to change the proportion of the price of a pair of shoes that goes to pay workers and improve working conditions, as compared with the proportion that pays for distribution, marketing, advertising, and decorating stores. Changing those proportions, however, may reduce their own profits to some extent. Public disclosure of a company's connection with poor working conditions is not good for business, however, and public reporting of support for change seems to be good for a company's stock price.[53]

Privilege

Where there are structural injustices, these usually produce not only victims of injustice, but persons who acquire relative privilege by virtue of the structures. Most who occupy positions of power with respect to the structures also have privileges that coincide with this power. In most situations of structural injustice, however, there are relatively privileged persons who have relatively little power as individuals or in their institutional positions, at least with respect to the issue of injustice. Middle-class clothing consumers in the global North, for example, stand in a privileged position in the structures of the apparel industry. They benefit from the large selection and affordable prices that the industry offers them. Persons who benefit relatively from structural injustices have special moral responsibilities to contribute to organized efforts to correct them, not because they are to blame, but because they are able to adapt to changed circumstances without suffering serious deprivation. Lower-income clothing consumers, whether in the developing or developed world, may be less able than more affluent consumers to spend more for clothing in order to ensure that the workers who make it are treated fairly.[54]

Interest

Different people and different organizations usually have divergent interests in the maintenance or transformation of structures that produce injustice. Often, those with the greatest interest in reproducing the structures are also those with the greatest power to influence their transformation. Those who are victims of structural injustice often have a greater interest in structural transformation. Earlier, I said that one of the distinctive things about the social connection model of responsibility is that victims of injustice share responsibility with others for cooperating in projects to undermine the injustice. Victims of injustice have the greatest interest in its elimination, and often have unique insights into its social sources and the probable effects of proposals for change.

This point certainly applies in the case of labor conditions in the apparel industry. Actual and potential sweatshop workers are the primary victims of injustice. Analysts of some strategies in the movement to improve conditions for these workers find that they are sometimes ineffectual or paternalistic because the workers' point of view and active participation have not been properly included. Some corporate-sponsored monitoring processes, for example, conduct inspections of factories without talking to workers or only talking to workers on the factory site. Critics argue that workers' experience and complaints must definitely be a part of monitoring processes, but that workers must be interviewed away from the factory sites when owners and managers are not present. Cooperation with local civic organizations whom workers trust is usually necessary to facilitate such interviews.[55]

Other analysts wonder whether the predominance of nongovernmental organizations such as monitoring organizations, education and public accountability organizations, and so on, in the antisweatshop movement weakens the ability of workers to organize unions and allows local governments to continue their lax labor law promulgation and enforcement.[56] Most conclude that NGO activity should work in support of unionization and to pressure for greater government protection of workers' rights to form or choose unions.[57] In this case, as in many other cases of structural injustice, victims of injustice have a responsibility to work together to improve their situation, but they are unlikely to succeed without the help and support of other less vulnerable people who make industry behavior public and pressure agents to change policies or restructure their relationships.[58]

Collective ability

Sometimes, a coincidence of interest, power, and existing organization enables people to act collectively to influence processes more easily regarding one issue of justice than another. That is not always a reason to give priority to that issue, for it may also be that such ease of organization is a sign that the action makes little structural change. Nevertheless, given too many injustices that need remedy, the relative ease with which people can organize collective action to address them can be a useful decision principle.

The decision by some student groups to focus their antisweatshop activism on their colleges and universities illustrates this parameter. The university's function as a large consumer of apparel for their sports teams and also a purveyor through their book stores makes universities a target because their decisions about purchase and marketing have more impact than those of individual consumers. Campus campaigns politicizing such decisions successfully raise awareness of issues of global labor justice even among students and faculty who do not actively support the campaigns. Universities can relatively easily organize with one another to make an impact on the structural processes, as they have done by becoming members of the Fair Labor Association and the Workers Rights Consortium.

Conclusion

Obviously, each of these parameters for reasoning about the ways that individual persons or institutions might meet their responsibilities under a social connection model – power, privilege, interest, and collective ability – needs further elaboration. This sketch should indicate how being positioned differently in the structures that produce injustices suggests different kinds of issues and directions for action by various agents. It also gives more concreteness to the notion that under a social connection model agents share responsibility with others differently situated, with whom they usually must cooperate in order to effect change. As the antisweatshop movement example illustrates, however, such need for cooperation does not mean that agents have no conflicts of interest and no need for struggling with one another. Sharing responsibility partly means that agents challenge one another and call one another to account for what they are doing or not doing. Global social and economic processes bring individuals and institutions into ongoing structural connection with one another across national jurisdictions. Adopting a conception of responsibility that recognizes this connection is an important element to theorizing global justice.

Notes

Chapter 1   Hybrid Democracy: Iroquois Federalism and the Postcolonial Project

1 Nathan Glazer, *We Are All Multiculturalists Now* (Cambridge, MA: Harvard University Press, 1997) p. 40.
2 I am grateful to David Alexander, Robert Goodin, Evan Haefeli, Alison Jaggar, Peter Onuf, and Laurie Ann Whitt for comments on earlier versions of this paper.
3 See Duncan Ivison, "Postcolonialism and Political Theory," in Andrew Vincent, ed., *Political Theory: Tradition and Diversity* (Cambridge: Cambridge University Press, 1997), pp. 154–71.
4 Homi Bhabha, "DisseminNation: Time, Narrative and the Margins of the Modern Nation," in *The Location of Culture* (London: Routledge, 1994), p. 161.
5 Bhabha, "Signs Taken for Wonders: Questions of Ambivalence and Authority under a Tree outside Delhi, May 1817," *The Location of Culture*, p. 112.
6 Ibid. This strategy of reading modern world history as hybrid, where the colonized subjects act upon the colonizers as well as the reverse, should not be confined to histories of the colonized places. Edward Said reads classic European texts as hybrid, internally related to the imperialized Others even as they celebrate European nationalisms; see Said, *Culture and Imperialism* (New York: Random House, 1993).
7 Compare Paul Patton, "Post-structuralism and the Mabo Debate: Difference, Society, and Justice," in Margaret Wilson and Anna Yeatman, eds, *Justice and Identity: Antipodean Practices* (Auckland: Bridget Williams, 1995), pp. 153–71.
8 Jack Weatherford, *Indian Givers: How the Indians of the Americas Transformed the World* (New York: Crown Publishers, 1988). Robert W. Venables, "American Indian Influences on the America of the Founding

Fathers," in Oren Lyons, et al., eds, *Exited in the Land of the Free: Democracy, Indian Nations, and the U.S. Constitution* (Santa Fe, NM: Clear Light Publishers, 1992), pp. 73–124. José Barreiro, ed., *Indian Roots of American Democracy* (Ithaca, NY: Akwe:kon Press, Cornell University, 1988).

9 Donald A. Grinde and Bruce E. Johansen, *Exemplar of Liberty: Native America and the Evolution of Democracy* (Los Angeles: UCLA American Indian Studies and UC Press, 1991).

10 For criticisms of the influence thesis, see Elisabeth Tooker, "The United States Constitution and the Iroquois League," *Ethnohistory*, vol. 35, no. 4, Fall 1988; Philip A. Levy, "Exemplars of Taking Liberties: The Iroquois Influence Thesis and the Problem of Evidence," and Samuel B. Payne, Jr., "The Iroquois League, the Articles of Confederation, and the Constitution," both in *William and Mary Quarterly*, vol. LILI, no. 3, July 1996.

11 See Richard White, *The Middle Ground: Indians, Empires and Republics in the Great Lakes Region, 1650–1815* (Cambridge: Cambridge University Press, 1991); see also Edward Countryman, "Indians, the Colonial Order, and the Social Significance of the American Revolution," *William and Mary Quarterly*, vol. LILI, no. 2, April 1996, pp. 342–62: "If we accept that both slaves and Indians were important components of the colonial formation, neither a the-colonies-were-born-modern perspective nor a the-colonies-were-intrinsically-an-old-order-in-the-European-style perspective does justice to them" (p. 350).

12 H. G. Koenigsberger, "Composite States, Representative Institutions, and the American Revolution," *Historical Research*, 62, 1989, 135–53. See also James Tully, *Strange Multiplicity: Constitutionalism in an Age of Diversity* (Cambridge: Cambridge University Press, 1995), Chapter 3.

13 Countryman, op. cit. See also Rogers M. Smith, *Civic Ideals: Conflicting Visions of Citizenship in U.S History* (New Haven, CT: Yale University Press, 1997), Chapters 5 and 6.

14 Kwasi Wiredu, "Democracy and Consensus in African Traditional Politics: A Plea for a Non-party Polity," and Emmanuel Chukwudi Eze, "Democracy or Consensus? A Response to Wiredu," both in Emmanuel Chukwudi Eze, ed., *Postcolonial African Philosophy: A Critical Reader* (Oxford: Blackwell, 1997); see also the debate led by Wamba-dia-Wamba.

15 Definitions of sovereignty abound, but they vary only subtly. See, for example, Christopher Morris, "Sovereignty is the highest, final, and supreme political and legal authority (and power) within the territorially defined domain of a system of direct rule." *An Essay on the Modern State* (Cambridge: Cambridge University Press, 1998), ms. p. 166. Thomas Pogge distinguishes degrees of sovereignty. For him, sovereignty consists in one agent's having unsupervised and irrevocable authority over another. Given this distinction, I am concerned with absolute sovereignty. I find it a bit puzzling that Pogge includes the condition that the decisions and laws of a sovereign power are *irrevocable*. This seems quite unreasonable, since in practice many states revoke or revise decisions

previously made and no one considers this a challenge to their sovereignty. The condition should rather be put that a sovereign's decisions cannot be revoked or overridden by *another* authority. See Thomas Pogge, "Cosmopolitanism and Sovereignty," *Ethics*, vol. 103, October 1992, pp. 48–75.

16 See Daniel Philpott, "Sovereignty: An Introduction and Brief History," *Journal of International Affairs*, Winter 1995, no. 2, pp. 353–68.

17 See Morris, "Sovereignty is the highest."

18 Charles Beitz, *Political Theory and International Relations* (Princeton, NJ: Princeton University Press, 1979); Onora O'Neill, *Toward Justice and Virtue* (Cambridge: Cambridge University Press, 1996), Chapter 4; Pogge, op. cit. Pogge distinguishes two approaches to social justice, an institutional and an interactional approach. Whereas the interactional approach focuses only on the actions of particular individuals as they affect identifiable persons, the institutional approach theorizes moral responsibility for the fact of others insofar as agents participate in institutions and practices that may or do harm them. An institutional approach as distinct from an interactional approach, he suggests, makes issues of international justice and moral responsibility with respect to distant strangers more visible. I make a similar distinction between a distributive approach to justice and an approach that focuses on the way institutions produce distributions; see Iris Marion Young, *Justice and the Politics of Difference* (Princeton, NJ: Princeton University Press, 1990). Focusing on how structures and institutional relations produce distributive patterns, I suggest, makes a connected international society more visible and the relations of moral responsibilities of distant peoples within it.

19 Beitz, *Political Theory and International Relations*.

20 The work of Samir Amin is classic here; for a recent statement of this sort of argument, see Fernando Henrique Cardoso, "North–South Relations in the Present Context: A New Dependency?" in Martin Carnoy et al., eds, *The New Global Economy in the Information Age* (University Park: Pennsylvania State University Press, 1993), pp. 149–59.

21 Joseph Carens, "Aliens and Citizens: The Case for Open Borders," *Review of Politics*, 49, Spring 1987, pp. 251–73.

22 Will Kymlicka, *Multicultural Citizenship* (Oxford: Oxford University Press, 1995).

23 For one account of different internal challenges to uniformity or universality of the law of sovereign states, see Jacob Levy, "Classifying Cultural Rights," in Ian Shapiro and Will Kymlicka, eds, *Ethnicity and Group Rights* (New York: New York University Press, 1997), pp. 22–68.

24 Hector Diaz Polanco, *Indigenous Peoples in Latin America: The Quest for Self-Determination*, trans, Lucia Rayas (Boulder, CO: Westview Press, 1997), especially Part Two.

25 "From Entitlement to Re-Engagement: An Indigenous Affairs Agenda; *Tino Rangatiratanga* and the Politics of Indigeneity in Aotearoa/New Zealand," Duncan Ivison, Paul Patton, and Will Sanders, eds, *Political*

Theory and the Rights of Indigenous Peoples (Cambridge: Cambridge University Press, 2000).

26 See "Two Concepts of Self-Determination," in this volume.

27 Franke Wilmer, *The Indigenous Voice in World Politics* (Newbury Park, CA: Sage, 1993).

28 John Pocock is no doubt correct to distinguish between confederacy, as intergovernmental relationships held together only by treaties, and federation, a relationship of self-governing entities with a more enduring and general set of procedures guiding their relations. Assuming this distinction, the Iroquois were more of a confederacy than a federation, perhaps, though the Great Law of Peace could be interpreted as a general set of procedures. In any case, as Pocock points out, one of the points of the postcolonial project is to blur the distinction between these. The project aims to construct an understanding of relations between people who now believe they are linked primarily with treaties as a more federated understanding, and to make the relations between peoples within an existing state more like relations between treaty partners.

29 Anna Yeatman's critique of the idea of independence underlying a contractual view of citizenship is important here; see "Beyond Natural Right: The Conditions of Universal Citizenship," in Yeatman, *Postmodern Revisionings of the Political* (New York: Routledge, 1994), pp. 57–79; "Feminism and Citizenship," in Nick Stevenson, ed., *Cultural Citizenship* (London: Sage, 1998). See also Jennifer Nedelsky, "Relational Autonomy," *Yale Journal of Law and Feminism*, vol. 1, no. 1, 1989, pp. 7–36; "Law Boundaries and the Bounded Self," in Robert Post, ed., *Law and the Order of Culture* (Berkeley: University of California Press, 1991).

30 Gerald Frug, *City Making: Building Communities without Building Walls* (Princeton, NJ: Princeton University Press, 1999).

31 David Held, *Democracy and the Global Order* (Cambridge: Polity, 1995), especially Chapters 10 and 12.

32 For a more extended discussion of similar ideas of global democracy, see Iris Marion Young, *Inclusion and Democracy* (Oxford: Oxford University Press, 2000), Chapter 7.

33 See Thomas Pogge, "Creating Super-National Institutions Democratically: Reflections on the European Union's 'Democratic Deficit,'" *Journal of Political Philosophy*, vol. 5, no. 2, June 1997, pp. 163–82.

34 James Tully, *Strange Multiplicity: Constitutionalism in an Age of Diversity* (Cambridge: Cambridge University Press, 1995).

Chapter 2   Two Concepts of Self-Determination

1 Craig Scott, "Indigenous Self-Determination and Decolonization of the International Imagination: A Plea," *Human Rights Quarterly*, vol. 18, 1996, p. 819.

2 I am grateful to David Alexander, Rainer Bauböck, Augie Fleras, Philip Pettit, and Franke Wilmer for helpful comments on an earlier version of this essay.

3 On the state of international law, see Hurst Hannum, "Self-Determination in the Post-Colonial Era," in Donald Clark and Robert Williamson, eds, *Self-Determination: International Perspectives* (New York: St Martin's Press, 1996), pp. 12–44; see also Hannum, *Autonomy, Sovereignty, and Self-Determination: The Accommodation of Conflicting Rights* (Philadelphia: University of Pennsylvania Press, 1990).

4 I develop some of this argument in another paper, "Self-Determination and Global Democracy," in Ian Shapiro and Stephen Macedo, eds, *Designing Democratic Institutions* (New York: New York University Press, 2000); see also I.M. Young, *Inclusion and Democracy* (Oxford: Oxford University Press, 2000), Chapter 7.

5 See Russell Lawrence Barsh, "Indigenous Peoples and the U.N. Commission on Human Rights: A Case of the Immovable Object and the Irresistible Force," *Human Rights Quarterly*, vol. 18, 1996, pp. 782–813.

6 Erica-Irene A. Daes, "The Right of Indigenous Peoples to Self-Determination in the Contemporary World Order," in op. cit. Clark and Williamson, eds, p. 55.

7 Recent discussions affirm that the principle of self-determination does not imply that indigenous peoples wish to or have a right to secede from existing states to form new sovereign states. Much discussion of the meaning of the principle turns on implementation of land rights and self-governance rights within a state. See *Report of the working group established in accordance with Commission on Human Rights resolution 1995/32*, United Nations Economic and Social Council, December 6, 1999.

8 For definitions of sovereignty, see Christopher Morris, *An Essay on the Modern State* (Cambridge: Cambridge University Press, 1998), ms. p. 166; Thomas Pogge, "Cosmopolitanism and Sovereignty," *Ethics*, vol. 103, October 1992, pp. 48–75.

9 See Daniel Philpott, "Sovereignty: An Introduction and Brief History," *Journal of International Affairs*, Winter 1995, no. 2, pp. 353–68.

10 See David Held, *Democracy and the Global Order* (Cambridge: Polity, 1995) Chapters 5 and 6; Ruth Lapidoth, "Sovereignty in Transition," *Journal of International Affairs*, vol. 45, no. 2, Winter 1992, pp. 325–46.

11 See Anna Yeatman, "Beyond Natural Right: The Conditions for Universal Citizenship," in Yeatman, *Postmodern Revisionings of the Political* (New York: Routledge, 1994), pp. 57–79; "Feminism and Citizenship," in Nick Stevenson, ed., *Cultural Citizenship* (London: Sage, 1998); "Relational Individualism," manuscript; see also Jennifer Nedelsky, "Relational Autonomy," *Yale Women's Law Journal*, 1989; "Law, Boundaries, and the Bounded Self," in Robert Post, ed., *Law and the Order of Culture* (Berkeley: University of California Press, 1991); for an application of this feminist revision of autonomy to international relations theory, see Karen Knop, "Re/Statements: Feminism and State Sovereignty in International Law," *Transnational Law and Contemporary Problems*, vol. 3, no. 2, Fall 1993, pp. 293–344; see also Jean Elshtain, "The Sovereign State," *Notre Dame Law Review*, vol. 66, 1991, pp. 1355–84.

12 Philip Pettit, *Republicanism* (Oxford: Oxford University Press, 1997).
13 See Russell Hardin, *One for All* (Chicago: University of Chicago Press, 1995), for a critique of the notion of collective common interests in the context of nationalist politics.
14 For one effort toward this sort of conceptualization in the context of the relation of Maori and Pakeha in New Zealand, see Roger Maaka and Augie Fleras, "Engaging with Indigeneity: Tino Rangatiratanga in Aotearoa," in Duncan Ivison, Paul Patton, and Will Sanders, eds, *Political Theory and the Rights of Indigenous Peoples* (Cambridge: Cambridge University Press, 2000), pp. 89–112.
15 See, for example, Hector Diaz Polanco, *Indigenous Peoples in Latin America: The Quest for Self-Determination*, trans. Lucia Rayas (Boulder, CO: Westview Press, 1997), especially Part Two.
16 See Franke Wilmer, *The Indigenous Voice in World Politics* (London: Sage, 1993).
17 Timothy Egan, "New Prosperity Brings New Conflict to Indian Country," *New York Times*, March 8, 1998, Nation/Metro section. As of February 2000, this dispute remained at a standoff. See "Other Nuclear Waste Facilities Being Considered in Utah," *Salt Lake Tribune*, February 20, 2000.
18 Will Kymlicka, *Multicultural Citizenship* (Oxford: Oxford University Press, 1995); Kymlicka argues that national minorities, including indigenous peoples, ought to have recognized self-government rights, and that such rights limit nation-state sovereignty over them without making them separate sovereign states. Kymlicka does not specify the details of the meaning of self-government in a context of negotiated federated relationships as much as one would like, but it is clear that he has something like this in mind.

Chapter 3   Self-Determination as Nondomination: Ideals Applied to Palestine/Israel

1 I take this phrase from my essay "Together in Difference: Transforming the Logic of Group Political Conflict," first published in Will Kymlicka, ed., *The Rights of Minority Cultures* (Oxford: Oxford University Press, 1995), pp. 155–78. See also *Inclusion and Democracy* (Oxford: Oxford University Press, Chapter 6) for an articulation of a model of local governance among differentiated but not exclusive groups, which there I call "differentiated solidarity." Compare the idea of differentiation in togetherness that Julie Mostov refers to as "soft borders"; Mostov, "Soft Borders and Transnational Citizens," conference on "Identities, Affiliations, and Allegiances," Yale University, October 3–4, 2003.
2 This paper began as a presentation I made at a conference, "Collective Rights of Minorities in Multiethnic States," sponsored by Mada – The Arab Center for Applied Social Science in Nazareth in December 2002;

I thank Nadim Rouhana and Amal Jamal for inviting me to that conference. This version was presented at a conference sponsored by the Center for Comparative Constitutionalism, University of Chicago, "Constitutionalism in the Middle East: Israeli and Palestinian Perspectives," January 23–5, 2004. I am grateful to Howard Adelman, Bashir Bashir, Rainer Bauböck, Neve Gordon, Rashid Khalidi, Amal Jamal, Cass Sunstein, Oren Yoafitel, and anonymous reviewers for *Ethnicities* for comments on earlier drafts.

3 I discuss the claims of indigenous people in more detail and the concept of self-determination that I think best corresponds to this claim in my essay "Two Concepts of Self-determination." See also discussions of indigenous politics in Robert A. Williams, *Linking Arms Together: American Indian Treaty Visions of Law, 1600–1800* (New York: Routledge, 1999); Franke Wilmer, *The Indigenous Voice in World Politics* (New York: Sage, 1993); Paul Keal, *European Conquest and the Rights of Indigenous Peoples: The Moral Backwardness of International Society* (Cambridge: Cambridge University Press, 2003).

4 For an articulate expression of this position, see Yael Tamir, *Liberal Nationalism* (Princeton, NJ: Princeton University Press, 1993).

5 Jacob Levy points out that theorists of multiculturalism and cultural autonomy often bracket the question of land rights; see *The Multiculturalism of Fear* (Oxford: Oxford University Press, 2000), Chapters 6 and 7.

6 Amal Jamal, "Politicizing Indigeneity: On the Morality of Arab Collective Rights in Israel," unpublished ms, Tel Aviv University.

7 I develop this account of self-determination in earlier writing. See "Two Concepts of Self-determination."

8 Susan Moller Okin, *Is Multiculturalism Good for Women?* (Princeton, NJ: Princeton University Press, 1999).

9 I derive the distinction between self-determination as noninterference and as nondomination from Philip Pettit, *Republicanism* (Oxford: Oxford University Press, 1997); Pettit's theory concerns freedom for individuals only; I extend the distinction to conceptualize autonomy for peoples.

10 Daniel J. Elazar, *Exploring Federalism* (Tuscaloosa: University of Alabama Press, 1987), p. 12. For additional conceptual accounts of federalism, see Graham Smith, *Federalism: The Multiethnic Challenge* (London: Longman, 1995); Monserrat Guibernau, *Nations without States: Political Communities in a Global Age* (Cambridge: Polity, 1999).

11 Ferran Requejo, "Political Liberalism and Multinational States: Legitimacy of Plural and Asymmetrical Federalism," in Alain G. Gagnon and James Tully, eds, *Multinational Democracies* (Cambridge: Cambridge University Press, 2001), p. 182.

12 Ibid.

13 Daniel J. Elazar, "Autonomy in a Post-statist World, introduction to Daniel Elazar, ed., *Governing Peoples and Territories* (Philadelphia:

Institute for the Study of Human Issues, 1982); see also *Exploring Federalism*, Chapter 2.

14 Compare Rainer Bauböck, "Political Boundaries in a Multilevel Democracy," contribution to a conference on "Identities, Affiliations and Allegiances," Yale University, October 3–5, 2003.

15 See Gerald Frug, *City Making* (Princeton, NJ: Princeton University Press, 2001); Iris Marion Young, *Inclusion and Democracy* (Oxford: Oxford University Press, 2000), Chapter 6.

16 The discussion that follows of problems with most versions of the two-state solution has benefited from reading the "Proposal for an Alternative Configuration in Palestine–Israel," Alternative Palestine Agenda, www.ap-agenda.org.

17 For details on the situation of Palestinian minority in Israel, see Adalah: The Legal Center for Arab Minority Rights in Israel, *The Palestinian Arab Minority in Israel: Economic, Social and Culture Rights*, 1998; Nadim N. Rouhana, *Palestinian Citizens in an Ethnic Jewish State: Identities in Conflict* (New Haven, CT; Yale University Press, 1997); Yossi Yonah and Ishak Saporta, "The Politics of Lands and Housing in Israel: A Wayward Republican Discourse," *Social Identities*, vol. 8, no. 1, 2002, pp. 91–117; Nimer Sultany, *Citizens without Citizenship* (Haifa: Mada–Arab Center for Applied Social Research, 2003).

18 For example, Seif Da'Na, "Single, Secular, Democratic," *Al-Ahram Weekly Online*, July 19–25, 2001, no. 543; Thomas L. Freidman, "One Wall, One Man, One Vote," *New York Times*, September 14, 2003; Ahmad Samih Khalidi, "A One-State Solution: A Unitary Arab–Jewish Homeland Could Bring Lasting Peace to the Middle East," *The Guardian*, September 29, 2003; Yakov M. Rabkin, "The One-State Prescription for Mideast Peace," *Montreal Gazette*, November 12, 2003; Daniel Lazare, "The One-State Solution," *The Nation*, November 3, 2003; Ali Abummah, "Palestine/Israel: One State for all its Citizens," *The Electronic Intifada*, October 16, 2003, www.electronicintifada.net. While he refers to his alternative as binational, Tony Judt's vision appeals to me of a singular, secular, individualist state; see Tony Judt, "Israel: The Alternative," *New York Review of Books*, vol. 50, no. 16, October 23, 2003; my reading leads me to think that two different visions come under the general label of "binationalism" in current discussions about the future of Palestine/Israel, corresponding to two of the alternatives I state here, one a singular state, the other a more federated conception. Responses to Judt by Abraham Foxman, Amos Elon, Michael Walzer, and Omer Bartov appear in the *New York Review of Books*, vol. 50, no. 19, December 4, 2003.

19 See, for example, Yoel Esteron's critical response to Judt's article, *Haaretz*, November 28, 2003.

20 Alternative Palestinian Agenda, www.ap-agenda.org.

21 Oren Yiftachel, *Ethnocracy: Land, Politics and Identities in Israel/Palestine*, Chapter 13, "Proposal for a Bi-national Capital Region for Jerusalem/Al-Quds," unpublished ms.

22 The Alternative Palestinian Agenda's "Proposal for an Alternative Configuration in Palestine–Israel" contains thought-through details about
discontiguous jurisdictions and how they might relate to one another. In
one of his columns arguing against the idea of separate sovereign states
of Palestine and Israel, Edward Said mentioned that enactment of a right
of self-determination for the groups might best be realized in "federated
cantons," but he gave no details. Edward Said, "The One-State Solution,"
New York Times, January 10, 1999.

23 Jeff Halper argues for a region-wide confederated system in the Middle
East that might function like the European Union; individuals would
hold citizenship in one unit, for example, but be able to move freely
among and reside in other units. "A Middle Eastern Confederation: A
regional 'two-stage' approach to the Israeli–Palestinian conflict," *Arabic
Media Internet Network*, December 15, 2002, available on line at
www.one-state.org.

**Chapter 4   Power, Violence, and Legitimacy: A Reading
of Hannah Arendt in an Age of Police Brutality and
Humanitarian Intervention**

1 Hannah Arendt, *On Violence* (New York: Harcourt, Brace, 1969). Page
citations below are to this work.

2 There are some exceptions. See Ted Honderich, *Violence for Equality*
(London: Routledge, 1989), and Sergio Cotta, *Why Violence?*
(Gainesville: University of Florida Press, 1985).

3 John McGowan does focus specifically on the concept of violence in
Arendt. See McGowan, "Must Politics be Violent? Arendt's Utopian
Vision," in Craig Calhoun and John McGowan, eds, *Hannah Arendt and
the Meaning of Politics* (Minneapolis: University of Minnesota Press,
1997), pp. 263–96; Bat-Ami Bar On, *The Subject of Violence: Arendtian
Exercises in Understanding* (Albany: State University of New York Press,
2003).

4 I am grateful to the following people for comments on an earlier version
of this essay that saved me from much wrong-headedness: David Alexander, Bat-Ami Bar On, Leah Bradshaw, Michael Geyer, Bonnie Honig,
Jeffrey Isaac, Patchen Markell, Martin Matustik, Nancy Rosenblum,
William Scheuermann, and Dana Villa.

5 Martha Minow, "Between Nations and Between Intimates: Can Law Stop
theViolence?" in Martha Minow, *Breaking the Cycles of Hatred: Memory,
Law, and Repair*, ed. Nancy L. Rosenblum (Princeton, NJ: Princeton
University Press, 2002), pp. 56–76.

6 See Robert Bernasconi, "The Double Face of the Political and the Social:
Hannah Arendt and America's Racial Divisions," *Research in Phenome-
nology*, XXVI, 1996, pp. 3–24; Anne Norton, "Heart of Darkness: Africa
and African Americans in the Writings of Hannah Arendt," in Bonnie
Honig, ed., *Feminist Interpretations of Hannah Arendt* (University Park:
Pennsylvania State University Press, 1995), pp. 247–62.

7 The best critique of Arendt's idea of the social and its separation from the political is Hanna Pitkin's. See Pitkin, *The Attack of the Blob* (Berkeley: University of California Press, 1999).

8 For the purposes of this essay, I am limiting discussion to physical forms of violence; their incidence is frequent and horrible enough to call urgently for inquiry. I recognize that there may well be phenomena of psychological violence, various ways that people are able to destroy the spirit of other persons without doing them bodily damage. Indeed, some of Arendt's other writings have rich veins to mine for such a concept of psychological violence. Because nonphysical forms of violence present more serious conceptual problems, and because the phenomenon Arendt seems most concerned with in this essay is violence that involves bringing physical pain to, wounding, or killing human beings, I limit my discussion here to that form.

9 Arendt, *The Human Condition* (Chicago: University of Chicago Press, 1958), especially Chapter 28.

10 Max Weber, "Politics as a Vocation," in H. H. Gerth and C. Wright Mills, eds, *From Max Weber* (New York: Oxford University Press, 1946), pp. 77–8; Jürgen Habermas contrasts Weber's instrumental and positivistic view of state power with Arendt's view, which he interprets as more normative and based in communication. See Habermas, "Hannah Arendt on the Concept of Power," in *Philosophical and Political Profiles* (Cambridge, MA: MIT Press, 1983), pp. 171–88.

11 See Arendt, "What is Authority?" in *Between Past and Future* (New York: Viking Press, 1968), pp. 91–142.

12 Compare Leah Bradshaw, "Political Authority and Violence," paper presented at the Canadian Political Science Association meetings, Quebec City, August 2000.

13 Nancy C. M. Hartsock suggests that in fact Arendt does undermine her concept of power by saying that power and violence often occur together. See Hartsock, *Money, Sex and Power* (New York: Longman, 1983), pp. 220–31.

14 Jeffrey Isaac, *Arendt, Camus and Modern Rebellion* (New Haven, CT: Yale University Press, 1992), p. 149.

15 See Pitkin, *The Attack of the Blob*.

16 Arendt, *On Revolution* (New York: Viking Press, 1965), p. 175.

17 Max Weber, "Politics as a Vocation," pp. 79–81; "The Social Psychology of World Religions," in Gerth and Mills, eds, *From Max Weber*, p. 294.

18 Minow, "Between Nations and Intimates," p. 67.

19 Ibid., p. 70.

20 Independent International Commission on Kosovo, *Kosovo Report: Conflict, International Response, Lessons Learned* (Oxford: Oxford University Press, 2000), especially Chapters 6 and 10.

21 Information about the conduct of the war and its aftermath drawn from the *Kosovo Report*, Chapters 3, 4, and 10.

Chapter 5 Envisioning a Global Rule of Law

1 http://www.9-11commission.gov.
2 The lower and upper estimations are reported from, respectively, the Project on Defense Alternatives and Marc Herold, University of New Hampshire. The latter report is available at http://www.cursor.org/stories/civilian_deaths.htm.
3 See Richard Falk, "In Defense of 'Just War' Thinking," *The Nation*, December 24, 2001, pp. 23–5.
4 Brian Knowlton, "How the World Sees the US: and Sept. 11," *International Herald Tribune*, December 20, 2001.
5 See Anne-Marie Slaughter, *A New World Order* (Princeton, NJ: Princeton University Press, 2004); notably Slaughter does not discuss international security issues in any detail.
6 See David Held and Mary Kaldor, "Justice in a Global Age," *Constellations*, vol. 9, no. 1, March 2002.
7 It is not surprising that the petition supporting the conflict as a just war and signed by a number of important American intellectuals never mentions Afghanistan. Not even this document could establish a clear link between the action (the terrorist attacks) and the reaction (the war against Afghanistan). *What We're Fighting For*, Institute for American Values, released February 2002 and available at http://www.propositionsonline.com/Fighting_for.html. Signatories include Amitai Etzioni, Francis Fukuyama, Samuel Huntington, Robert Putnam, and Michael Walzer.
8 Jean Bethke Elshtain, *Just War Against Terror* (New York: Basic Books, 2004).
9 Several international relations and international legal scholars have made this argument since 2001. See, for example, Philip B. Heyman, *Terrorism, Freedom and Security: Winning without War* (Cambridge, MA: MIT Press, 2003); Christopher Greenwood, "International Law and the 'War against Terrorism,'" *International Affairs*, vol. 78, no. 2 (2002), pp. 301–17; Mary Kaldor, "American Power: from 'Compellance' to Cosmopolitanism?" *International Affairs*, vol. 79, no. 1, 2003.
10 See David Zweshimo and Sebastian Rotella, "Interpol Hopes Terror Investigators Keep in Touch," *Los Angeles Times*, December 23, 2001.
11 In William H. Luers, ed., *Combating Terrorism: Does the UN Matter . . . and How?*, UNA-USA, New York, 2002, p. 5.
12 See Phil Williams, "Crime, Illicit Markets, and Money Laundering," in P. J. Simmons and Chantal de Jonge Oudraat, eds, *Managing Global Issues: Lessons Learned* (Washington, DC: Carnegie Endowment for International Peace, 2001), pp. 106–50.
13 The case is considered in Christopher Greenwood, "International Law and the 'War against Terrorism,'" *International Affairs*, vol. 78, no. 2, 2002, pp. 301–7.

14 Reported in the *International Herald Tribune*, November 16, 2001, p. 5.
15 Christopher Greenwood, "International Law and the 'War Against Terrorism,' " p. 317.
16 Data on world inequalities are scrutinized in the United Nations Development Program, *Human Development Report 2001* (New York: Oxford University Press, 2002). The ethical implications are addressed in an increasingly vast literature, including Thomas Pogge, ed., *Global Justice* (Oxford: Blackwell, 2001).
17 oecd.org.
18 Helmut Anheir, Marlies Glasius, and Mary Kaldor, eds, *Global Civil Society 2001* (Oxford: Oxford University Press, 2001).
19 oecd.org.
20 See, for example, David Held, *Democracy and the Global Order* (Cambridge: Polity, 1995); Richard Falk, *Law in an Emerging Global Village: A Post-Westphalian Perspective* (Ardsley, NY: Transnational Publishers, 1998).

Chapter 6   The Logic of Masculinist Protection: Reflections on the Current Security State

1 See Mary Kaldor, *New & Old Wars: Organized Violence in a Global Era* (Cambridge: Polity, 1999).
2 Earlier versions of this essay were presented at conferences at Washington University in St. Louis, and Lancaster University in England, and I have benefited from discussions on both occasions. I am grateful to David Alexander, Neta Crawford, Tom Dumm, Samantha Frost, Susan Gal, Sandra Harding, Anne Harrington, Aaron Hoffman, Jeffrey Isaac, Patchen Markell, John McCormick, Linda Nicholson, Lora Viola, Laurel Weldon, Alexander Wendt, and an anonymous reviewer for *Signs* for comments on earlier versions. Thanks to Anne Harrington and Kathy McCabe for research assistance.
3 See, for example, Joshua S. Goldstein, *War and Gender* (Cambridge: Cambridge University Press, 2001).
4 Compare Carol Cohn, "Wars, Wimps, and Women: Talking Gender and Thinking War," in Miriam Cooke and Angela Woolocott, eds, *Gendering War Talk* (Princeton, NJ: Princeton University Press, 1993).
5 Judith Stiehm, "The Protected, the Protector, the Defender," *Women's Studies International Forum*, vol. 5, nos. 3/4, 1982, pp. 367–76; Ann Tickner, *Gender in International Relations: Feminist Perspectives on Achieving Global Security* (New York: Columbia University Press, 1992); Ann Tickner, *Gendering World Politics: Issues and Approaches in the Post-Cold War Era* (New York: Columbia University Press, 1992).
6 Harry Brod and Michael Kaufman, eds, *Theorizing Masculinities* (London: Sage, 1992); Charlotte Hooper, *Manly States: Masculinities, International Relations, and Gender Politics* (New York: Columbia University Press, 2001).
7 Stiehm, "The Protected, the Protector, the Defender."

8 Catherine MacKinnon, *Feminism Unmodified: Discourses on Life and Law* (Cambridge, MA: Harvard University Press, 1987); Larry May, *Masculinity and Morality* (Ithaca, NY: Cornell University Press, 1998), Chapters 4, 5, and 6.
9 See Jean Bethke Elshtain, *Women and War* (Chicago: University of Chicago Press, 1987); and Elshtain, "Sovereignty, Identity, Sacrifice," in V. Spike Peterson, ed., *Gendered States: Feminist (Re)visions of International Relations Theory* (Boulder, CO: Lynne Rienner, 1995), pp. 141–54.
10 Stiehm, "The Protected, the Protector, the Defender," p. 372.
11 Carole Pateman, *The Sexual Contract* (Stanford, CA: Stanford University Press, 1988), Chapter 3.
12 Michel Foucault, "Technologies of the Self," in L. H. Martin, H. Gutman and P. H. Hutton, eds, *Technologies of the Self: A Seminar with Michel Foucault* (Amherst: University of Massachusetts Press, 1988), pp. 19–49; Foucault, "Omnes et Singulatim: Toward a Critique of Political Reason," in James D. Faubion, ed., *The Essential Works of Foucault, Vol. III, Power* (New York: New Press, 1994), pp. 298–325.
13 Thomas Hobbes, *Leviathan* (Indianapolis: Hackett, 1994), Chapter XVII, pp. 3, 4; Robert Nozick, *Anarchy, State and Utopia* (New York: Basic Books, 1974), Chapter 2.
14 Hobbes, *Leviathan*, Chapter XVII, p. 13.
15 Ibid., Chapter XXII, p. 135.
16 Compare Laurent Berlant, "The Theory of Infantile Citizenship," in Berlant, *The Queen of America Goes to Washington City: Essays on Sex and Citizenship* (Durham, NC: Duke University Press, 1997), pp. 25–54.
17 Elshtain, *Women and War*; "Sovereignty, Identity, Sacrifice."
18 Speech of George W. Bush, September 14, 2001.
19 Speech of George W. Bush, March 15, 2002.
20 David Firestone, "Are You Safer Today Than a Year Ago?" *New York Times*, November 17, 2002, section 4, p. 1.
21 John Keane, "Fear and Democracy," in Kenton Worcester, Sally Avery Bermanzohn, and Mark Ungar, *Violence and Politics: Globalization's Paradox* (New York: Routledge, 2002), pp. 226–44.
22 Karen O'Connor, "For Better or For Worse: Women and Women's Rights in the Post 9/11 Climate," in Dennis L. Dresang et al., *American Government in a Changed World* (New York: Longman, 2003), pp. 171–91.
23 Susan Rae Peterson, "Coercion and Rape: The State as a Male Protection Racket," in Mary Vetterling-Braggin, Frederick A. Elliston, and Jane English, eds, *Feminism and Philosophy* (Totowa, NJ: Littlefield, Adams, 1977), pp. 360–71.
24 See Tickner, *Gender in International Relations*, pp. 51–3.
25 Speech of George W. Bush, January 29, 2002.
26 Speech of Laura Bush to the United Nations Commission on Women, March 8, 2002.
27 Sharon Lerner, "Feminists Agonize over War in Afghanistan: What Women Want," *Village Voice*, October 31–November 6, 2001.

28 See Antoinette Burton, *Burdens of History: British Feminists, Indian Women and Imperial Culture, 1865–1915* (Chapel Hill: University of North Carolina Press, 1994).
29 Chandra Mohanty, "Under Western Eyes: Feminist Scholarship and Colonial Discourse," in Mohanty, Ann Russo, and Lourdes Torres, eds, *Third World Women and the Politics of Feminism* (Bloomington: Indiana University Press, 1991).
30 Uma Narayan, "Restoring History and the Politics of 'Third World Traditions,'" in Narayan, *Dislocating Cultures: Identities, Traditions and Third World Feminism* (New York: Routledge, 1997).
31 Kristie Reilly, "Left Behind: An Interview with Revolutionary Afghan Women's Associations' Shar Saba," *In These Times*, vol. 26, no. 11, April 29, 2002, pp. 16–18.
32 Iris Marion Young, "Autonomy, Welfare Reform, and Meaningful Work," in Eva Feder Kittay and Ellen Feder, eds, *Philosophical Approaches to Dependency* (Lanham, MD: Rowman & Littlefield, 2003).
33 Joan Tronto, *Moral Boundaries* (New York: Routledge, 1994); Eva Feder Kittay, *Love's Labor* (New York: Routledge, 1999); Nancy Hirschmann, *The Subject of Liberty: Toward a Feminist Theory of Freedom* (Princeton, NJ: Princeton University Press, 2002), Chapter 5.
34 Stiehm, "The Protected, the Protector, the Defende," p. 372.

Chapter 7   Decentering the Project of Global Democracy

1 This statement, along with a number of commentaries on it, is reprinted in Daniel Levy, Max Pensky, and John Torpey, eds, *Old Europe, New Europe, Core Europe: Transatlantic Relations after the Iraq War* (London: Verso, 2005), pp. 3–13; I cite page numbers for quotations in the text.
2 Enrique Dussel, *The Invention of the Americas*, trans. Michael D. Barber (New York: Conferences, 1995).
3 Dipesh Chakrabarty, *Provincializing Europe: Postcolonial Thought and Historical Difference* (Princeton, NJ: Princeton University Press, 2000), especially Introduction.

Chapter 8   Reflections on Hegemony and Global Democracy

1 On February 16, 2003, CNN reported that one hundred and ten million people had participated in demonstrations around the world in that one weekend. For one written confirmation that this figure was reported, see the Italian newspaper *La Republica*, February 16, 2003.
2 John Locke, *Second Treatise of Government* (Indianapolis: Hackett, 1980), pp. 8–17, Chapters II and III.
3 Here's an example of how bias can enter global governance under hegemony. In *Globalization and its Discontents* (New York: W.W. Norton, 2002), Joseph Stiglitz argues that the global economic system is currently run by a "dictatorship of international finance" (p. 247). The global

finance elites from the US and a few other G8 countries, from the IMF, World Bank, and WTO allied with private financial and investment interests, effectively set the major terms of international finance and capital movement. Stiglitz acknowledges that these governments, international organizations, and business officials believe that they have the general interest of the world's people in view. The problem is that their background, training, social positions, and those to whom they are most directly accountable induce them to define this general interest in particular ways that are biased against the interests of most of the world's poor.

4 See Iris Marion Young, *Justice and the Politics of Difference* (Princeton, NJ: Princeton University Press, 1990), Chapter 4; see also Donna Haraway, "Situated Knowledges: The Science Question in Feminism and the Privilege of Partial Perspective," in Haraway, *Simians, Cyborgs, and Women* (New York: Routledge, 1991).

5 On dialogic ethics, see for example, Jürgen Habermas, "Discourse Ethics: Notes on a Program of Philosophical Justification," in *Moral Consciousness and Communicative Action* (Cambridge, MA: MIT Press, 1990), pp. 43–115; see also David Ingram, *Reason, History and Politics: The Communitarian Grounds of Legitimation in the Modern Age* (Albany: State University of New York Press, 1995), Part III.

6 Iris Marion Young, *Inclusion and Democracy* (Oxford: Oxford University Press, 2000), especially Chapter 3.

7 This is the point of view taken, for example, by Paul Hirst and Grahame Thompson in *Globalization in Question: The International Economy and the Possibilities of Governance*, 2nd edn (Cambridge: Polity, 1999).

8 See Saskia Sassen, *Losing Control? Sovereignty in an Age of Globalization* (New York: Columbia University Press, 1996), especially Chapter 1.

9 For this critique of self-determination as noninterference, I draw on Philip Pettit's arguments against interpreting freedom as noninterference. See *Republicanism* (Oxford: Oxford University Press, 1997), Part I; see also *A Theory of Freedom* (Oxford: Oxford University Press, 2001), Chapter 6.

10 See Iris Marion Young, *Inclusion and Democracy* (Oxford: Oxford University Press, 2000), Chapter 6 and 7; Iris Marion Young, "Two Concepts of Self-Determination."

11 See Ayalet Shachar, *Multicultural Jurisdictions: Cultural Differences and Women's Rights* (Cambridge: Cambridge University Press, 2001), Chapters 5 and 6.

12 David Held, *Democracy and the Global Order* (Cambridge: Polity, 1995), especially Part IV; Daniele Archibugi and David Held, eds, *Cosmopolitan Democracy: An Agenda for a New World Order* (Cambridge: Polity, 1995).

13 James Tully, *Strange Multiplicity: Constitutionalism in an Age of Diversity* (Cambridge: Cambridge University Press, 1995), Chapter 5; although the context for Tully's account is primarily Canadian federalism, his

principles easily apply to regional and global interaction. See also Yael Tamir, *Liberal Nationalism* (Princeton, NJ: Princeton University Press, 1993), Chapters 3 and 7; Tamir argues for a form of regional federalism to respond to the legitimate aspirations of both Jews and Palestinians for self-determination; a weakness of her conception, in my opinion, is that she imagines self-determination as primarily cultural rather than involving economic opportunity.

14 Joshua Cohen and Charles Sabel, "Directly-Deliberative Polyarchy," *European Law Journal*, vol. 3, no. 4, December 1997, pp. 313–42; Oliver Gerstenberg and Charles F. Sabel, "Directly-Deliberative Polyarchy: An Institutional Ideal for Europe?" in Christian Joerges and Renaud Dehousse, eds, *Good Governance in Europe's Integrated Market* (Oxford: Oxford University Press, 2002), pp. 289–341; Joshua Cohen and Charles F. Sabel, "Sovereignty and Solidarity: EU and US," in Jonathan Zeitlin and David Trubek, eds, *Governing Work and Welfare in a New Economy: European and American Experiments* (Oxford: Oxford University Press, 2003).

15 James Bohman, "Constitution Making and Institutional Innovation: The European Union and Multisited Federalism," *European Journal of Political Theory*.

16 Gerald Frug, *City Making: Building Communities without Walls* (Princeton, NJ: Princeton University Press, 1999); Frug offers a model of metropolitan federalism whose theory and principles can apply to relations among units of any size.

17 Archon Fung, *Empowered Participation: Reinventing Urban Democracy* (Princeton, NJ: Princeton University Press, 2004); Fung's is also a model applied in his book to urban politics, but the principles can apply to any project of decentralized accountability.

18 Iris Marion Young, *Inclusion and Democracy* (Oxford: Oxford University Press, 2000), Chapter 6.

19 David Miller, *On Nationality* (Oxford: Oxford University Press, 1995); Thomas Hurka, "The Justification of National Partiality," in Robert McKim and Jeff McMahan, *The Morality of Nationalism* (Oxford: Oxford University Press, 1997), pp. 139–57; for a good critical review of arguments skeptical of a global scope of justice, see Darrell Mollendorf, *Cosmopolitan Justice* (Boulder, CO: Westview Press, 2002), pp. 69–77.

20 For useful analysis of the tensions and dilemmas between this position and a more cosmopolitan position, see Samuel Scheffler, *Boundaries and Allegiances* (Oxford: Oxford University Press, 2000).

21 Charles Beitz, *Political Theory and International Relations* (Princeton, NJ: Princeton University Press, 1979), Part 3, Chapter 1; Onora O'Neill, *Towards Justice and Virtue* (Cambridge: Cambridge University Press, 1996), Chapter 4; Thomas Pogge, "Priorities of Global Justice," in Pogge, ed., *Global Justice* (Oxford: Blackwell, 2001), pp. 6–24.

22 John Loxley, "International Capital Markets, the Debt Crisis and Development," in Roy Culpeper, Albert Berry, and Frances Stewart, eds, *Global Development Fifty Years after Bretton Woods: Essays in*

Honour of Gerald K. Helleiner (New York: St Martin's Press, 1997), pp. 137–68.

23 Martin Dent and Bill Peters, *The Crisis of Poverty and Debt in the Third World* (Aldershot: Ashgate, 1999); Mollendorf, *Cosmopolitan Justice*, pp. 92–7; Patrick Bond, *Against Global Apartheid* (Cape Town: University of Cape Town Press, 2003); Alison Jaggar, "Vulnerable Women and Neoliberal Globalizations: Debt Burdens Undermine Women's Health in the Global South," in Robin N. Fiore and Hilde Lindemann Nelson, *Recognition, Responsibility, and Rights* (Lanham, MD: Rowman & Littlefield, 2002), pp. 195–211.

24 Heikki Patomaki, *Democratising Globalisation: The Leverage of the Tobin Tax* (London: Zed Books, 2001); Joseph Stiglitz, *Globalization and its Discontents*, pp. 265–6.

25 Thomas A. Pogge, "A Global Resources Dividend," in David A. Crocker and Toby Linden, eds, *Ethics of Consumption: The Good Life, Justice, and Global Stewardship* (Lanham, MD: Rowman & Littlefield, 1998), pp. 501–36.

26 Leena Tikkila and Katarina Sehm Patomaki, eds, *Democracy and Globalization* (Helsinki: Network Institute for Global Democratization, 2002); Jose Seoane and Emilio Taddei, "From Seattle to Porto Alegre: The Anti-Neoliberal Globalization Movement," *Current Sociology*, vol. 50, no. 1, January 2002, pp. 99–122; Jai Sen, "On Building Another World: Or: Are Other Globalizations Possible?" paper presented at World Social Forum, February 2002; William F. Fisher and Thomas Ponnich, eds, *Another World Is Possible: Popular Alternatives to Globalization at the World Social Forum* (London: Zed Books, 2003).

27 See Heikki Patomaki and Telvo Telvainen, with Mika Ronkko, *Global Democracy Initiatives: The Art of Possible*, NIGD Working Paper 2/2002, Helsinki.

28 Mary Kaldor, *New & Old Wars: Organized Violence in a Global Era* (Cambridge: Polity, 1999), Chapters 6 and 7; Michael Doyle, "The New Interventionism," in Thomas Pogge, *Global Justice* (Oxford: Blackwell, 2001), pp. 212–35.

Chapter 9 Responsibility, Social Connection, and Global Labor Justice

1 Thanks to David Alexander, Daniel Drezner, David Owen, and Ellen Frankel Paul for comments on an earlier version of this essay. Thanks to David Newstone for research assistance.

2 I have begun analysis of global labor justice focusing on the antisweatshop movement in two previous papers: Iris Young, "From Guilt to Solidarity: Sweatshops and Political Responsibility," in *Dissent*, Spring 2003, pp. 39–45; and Iris Marion Young, "Responsibility and Global Labor Justice," *Journal of Political Philosophy*, vol. 12, no. 4, 2004, pp. 365–88.

3 John Rawls, *A Theory of Justice* (Cambridge, MA: Harvard University Press, 1999 (1971)), pp. 7–8.

4 John Rawls, *The Law of Peoples* (Cambridge, MA: Harvard University Press, 1999), section 1, pp. 11–22.
5 David Miller, *On Nationality* (Oxford: Oxford University Press, 1995).
6 Miller, *Principles of Social Justice* (Cambridge, MA: Harvard University Press, 1999), Chapter 1.
7 See Peter Singer, *Practical Ethics* (Cambridge: Cambridge University Press, 1993), Chapters 2 and 9; Peter Unger, *Living High and Letting Die: Our Illusion of Innocence* (New York: Oxford University Press, 1996).
8 See, for example, Samuel Scheffler, *Boundaries and Allegiances: Problems of Responsibility and Justice in Liberal Thought* (Oxford: Oxford University Press, 2001).
9 Immanuel Kant, "To Perpetual Peace: A Philosophical Sketch" (1795), in Ted Humphrey, trans., *Perpetual Peace and Other Essays* (Indianapolis: Hackett, 1983), pp. 107–44.
10 Charles Beitz, *Political Theory and International Relations* (Princeton, NJ: Princeton University Press, 1979).
11 Onora O'Neill, *Faces of Hunger* (London: Allen & Unwin, 1985); *Towards Justice and Virtue* (Cambridge: Cambridge University Press, 1996), Chapter 4; compare Robert Goodin, *Protecting the Vulnerable* (Chicago: University of Chicago Press, 1985); and Thomas Pogge, *World Poverty and Human Rights* (Cambridge: Polity, 2002), especially Chapters 1, 2 and 4.
12 Pogge, *World Poverty and Human Rights.*
13 Allen Buchanan, "Rawls's Law of Peoples: Rule for a Vanished Westphalian World," *Ethics*, 110, no. 4, 2000, pp. 697–721; Buchanan, *Justice, Legitimacy, and Self-Determination: Moral Foundations for International Law* (Oxford: Oxford University Press, 2004), especially pp. 83 and 84.
14 In April 2003, for example, the Milwaukee Common Council voted unanimously for an ordinance requiring the procurement of apparel for city staff from manufacturers that meet several labor rights conditions; see "Sweatfree Communities Gain Ground," Campaign for Labor Rights, www.clrlabor.org.
15 Lisa Featherstone, *Students Against Sweatshops* (London: Verso, 2000); Micha Gaus, "The Maturing Movement Against Sweatshops," *In These Times*, February 16, 2004, pp. 34 and 52.
16 Peter Kwong, "Forbidden Workers and the US Labor Movement," *Critical Asian Studies*, 31, no. 1, 2002, pp. 69–88; Edna Bonacich and Richard P. Appelbaum, *Behind the Label: Inequality in the Los Angeles Apparel Industry* (Berkeley: University of California Press, 2002).
17 See Kimberly Ann Elliott and Richard B. Freeman, *Can Labor Standards Improve Under Globalization?* (Washington, DC: Institute for International Economics, 2004), p. 55.
18 For an account of working conditions, see Ellen Israel Rosen, *Making Sweatshops: The Globalization of the US Apparel Industry* (Berkeley: University of California Press, 2002), Chapter 2; Naomi Klein, *No Logo* (New York: Picador, 2000), especially Chapter 9.
19 Most of the countries in which factories like those I am describing operate do have minimum wage laws, as well as regulation of other labor

conditions. In many cases these laws could be more comprehensive and stronger, of course. For a comprehensive country-by-country survey of labor regulation, see the Industrial Labor Organization, www.ilo.org. The primary problem with labor regulation in much of the world, however, including arguably the United States, is lack of enforcement rather than lack of standards.

20 "Garment Industry Subcontracting and Workers' Rights," Women Working World Wide, at www.cleanclothes.org.

21 See Saba Gul Khattak, "Subcontracted Work and Gender Relations: The Case of Pakistan," in Radhika Balakrishnan, ed., *The Hidden Assembly Line: Gender Dynamics of Subcontracted Work in a Global Economy* (Bloomfield, CT: Kumarian Press, 2002), pp. 35–62.

22 Andrew Ross, *Low Pay, High Profile: The Global Push for Fair Labor* (New York: New Press, 2004), especially Chapter 2.

23 Elliott and Freeman, *Can Labor Standards Improve Under Globalization?*, pp. 50–4.

24 Elisabeth Prugl and Irene Tinker, "Microentrepreneurs and Homeworkers: Convergent Categories," *World Development*, 25, no. 9, 1997, pp. 1471–82. Women Working Worldwide, "Garment Industry Subcontracting and Workers' Rights," text online at www.cleanclothes.org.

25 See John Miller, "Why Economists are Wrong about Sweatshops and the Antisweatshop Movement," *Challenge*, 46, no. 1, 2003, pp. 93–122; see also Robert Pollin, Justine Burns, and James Heintz, "Global Apparel Production and Sweatshop Labour: Can Raising Retail Prices Finance Living Wages?" *Cambridge Journal of Economics*, 28, 2004, pp. 153–171.

26 In previous work I have begun developing an account of structural injustice. See I. M. Young, "Equality of Whom? Social Groups and Judgments of Injustice," *Journal of Political Philosophy*, 9, no. 1, 2001, pp. 1–18; I. M. Young, *Inclusion and Democracy* (Oxford: Oxford University Press, 2000), especially Chapter 3; and I. M. Young, "Lived Body vs. Gender: Reflections on Social Structure and Subjectivity," *Ratio: An International Journal of Analytic Philosophy*, XV, no. 4, 2002, pp. 411–28.

27 Rawls, *A Theory of Justice*, p. 7.

28 For one catalog of uses by English language theorists through the mid-1970s, see Peter Blau, "Introduction: Parallels and Contrasts in Structural Inquiries," in Peter M. Blau, ed., *Approaches to the Study of Social Structure* (New York: Free Press, 1975), pp. 1–20.

29 Jeffrey Reiman, among others, uses this channel metaphor. See Reiman, *Justice and Modern Moral Philosophy* (New Haven, CT: Yale University Press, 1989), p. 213.

30 Peter Blau, *Inequality and Heterogeneity* (New York: Free Press, 1977), p. 4.

31 Pierre Bourdieu, *The Logic of Practice* (Stanford, CA: Stanford University Press, 1980), Book I.

32 Anthony Giddens, *The Constitution of Society* (Berkeley: University of California Press, 1984), p. 25.

33 Jean-Paul Sartre, *Critique of Dialectical Reason*, trans. Alan Sheridan-Smith (London: New Left Books, 1976), bk. 1, ch. 3.
34 Ibid., pp. 277–92.
35 See Joseph E. Stiglitz, *Globalization and its Discontents* (New York: W. W. Norton, 2002), Chapter 4.
36 Peter French, *Collective and Corporate Responsibility* (New York: Columbia University Press, 1984).
37 See George Fletcher, *Basic Concepts of Criminal Law* (Oxford: Oxford University Press, 1999), for a clear statement of this model of responsibility.
38 See, for example, Tony Honore, "Responsibility and Luck: The Moral Basis of Strict Liability," in *Responsibility and Fault* (Oxford: Oxford University Press, 1999), pp. 14–40.
39 As I discussed in a previous note, in most cases there are labor laws, and sweatshop conditions often violate them. Sometimes this is because the host countries make exceptions to their labor regulation standards in special manufacturing zones. In many other cases, the problem is that factory operators, distributors, retailers, and others are able to ignore labor law with impunity. See Bonacich and Appelbaum, *Behind the Label*, Chapters 2 and 8.
40 For an account of the constraints on actors in the global apparel industry, see Rosen, *Making Sweatshops*, Chapter 11; see also Bonacich and Appelbaum, *Behind the Label*, Chapters 2 and 5.
41 See Jill Esbenshade's discussion of sweatshops in the United States and Department of Labor reports concerning these conditions. Esbenshade, *Monitoring Sweatshops: Workers, Consumers, and the Global Apparel Industry* (Philadelphia: Temple University Press, 2004), Chapter 1.
42 See Henry S. Richardson, "Institutionally Divided Moral Responsibility," in Ellen Frankel Paul, Fred D. Miller, Jr, and Jeffrey Paul, *Responsibility* (Cambridge: Cambridge University Press, 1999), pp. 218–49; see also Robert Goodin, "Apportioning Responsibilities," in *Utilitarianism as a Public Philosophy* (Cambridge: Cambridge University Press, 1996), pp. 100–18.
43 See George Fletcher's discussion of the way that the assignment of criminal liability must distinguish between foregrounded deviations from background conditions assumed as normal, and the background conditions themselves. *Basic Concepts of Criminal Law* (New York: Oxford University Press, 1998), pp. 69–70.
44 See Hans Jonas, *Imperative of Responsibility* (Chicago: University of Chicago Press, 1984), pp. 90–120.
45 See Elliott and Freeman, *Can Labor Standards Improve Under Globalization?*, Chapter 3.
46 Larry May, *Sharing Responsibility* (Chicago: University of Chicago Press, 1993), Chapter 2. As formulated in this book, May's theory of shared responsibility remains backward looking; he is concerned to assign a responsibility for harms that have occurred and reached a terminus. Thus, his theory is more continuous with a liability model of responsibility than

the theory I am developing here. May also focuses more on subjective states such as attitudes for linking persons to responsibility for a wrong, and says little about more objective social structures that connect persons to moral wrong or injustice. See my paper "Responsibility and Global Labor Justice," *Journal of Political Philosophy*, vol. 12, no. 4, 2004, pp. 365–88.

47 Melanie Beth Oliviero and Adele Simmons recommend uses of civil society organizations for addressing issues of labor standards; see "Who's Minding the Store? Global Civil Society and Corporate Responsibility," in Marlies Glasius, Mary Kaldor, and Melmut Anheier, eds, *Global Civil Society 2002* (Oxford: Oxford University Press, 2002), pp. 77–107; John Braithwaite and Peter Drahos argue that, as transnational social structures impinge on state sovereignty, civil society organization gains increased ability to influence labor and other business practices. See Braithwaite and Drahos, *Global Business Regulation* (Cambridge: Cambridge University Press, 2000), Chapters 5, 6, and 26.

48 Esbenshade, *Monitoring Sweatshops.*

49 William Connolly makes a similar distinction between responsibility as blame and a more politically oriented responsibility. For him, the resentment and counter-accusation dialectic that accompanies blame in a discourse of public affairs makes political identity overly rigid and paralyzes action. Thus he recommends a notion of political responsibility without blame and with a more fluid and ambiguous understanding of the sources of wrong than the implicitly Christian identification of the sinner. See Connolly, *Identity/Difference* (Ithaca, NY: Cornell University Press, 1993), especially Chapter 4. Melissa Orlie also distinguishes between a sentiment of resentment exhibited in blaming and holding oneself and others political responsible. See Orlie, *Living Ethically, Acting Politically* (Ithaca, NY: Cornell University Press, 1997), pp. 169–73.

50 Joel Feinberg, "Duties, Rights, and Claims," in Feinberg, *Rights, Justice and the Bounds of Liberty* (Princeton, NJ: Princeton University Press, 1980), pp. 135–40. See also Larry May, *The Socially Responsible Self: Social Theory and Professional Ethics* (Chicago: University of Chicago Press, 1996), Chapter 5.

51 See Robert Goodin, "Apportioning Responsibilities," and Henry Richardson, "Institutionally Divided Moral Responsibility."

52 Liam Murphy develops a useful theory of moral responsibility under conditions of injustice. See *Moral Demands in Nonideal Theory* (Oxford: Oxford University Press, 2000).

53 See Michael T. Rock, "Public Disclosure of the Sweatshop Practices of American Multinational Garment/Shoe Makers/Retailers: Impacts on their Stock Prices," *Competition & Change*, vol. 7, no. 1, March, 2003, pp. 23–38.

54 See Pollin, Burns, and Heintz, "Global Apparel Production and Sweatshop Labour." They find that the amount that retail prices would need to rise to bring workers a living raise is small, and consistent with increases

North American consumers say they would be willing to pay if they could be assured of "sweat free" conditions.

55 Esbenshade, *Monitoring Sweatshops*. See also Robert J. Luibicic, "Corporate Codes of Conduct and Product Labeling Schemes: The Limits and Possibilities of Promoting International Labor Rights Through Private Initiatives," *Law and Public Policy in International Business*, vol. 30, no. 1, 1998, pp. 111–58.

56 Rainer Braun and Judy Gearhart, "Who Should Code your Conduct? Trade Union and NGO Differences in the Fight for Workers' Rights," *Development in Practice*, vol. 14, nos. 1 and 2, 2004, pp. 183–96; Ronnie D. Lipschutz, "Sweating it Out: NGO Campaigns and Trade Union Empowerment," *Development in Practice*, same issue.

57 Lance Compa, "Trade, Unions, NGOs, and Corporate Does of Conduct," *Development in Practice*, vol. 14, nos. 1 and 2, 2004, pp. 210–15; Dara O'Rourke, "Outsourcing Regulation: Analyzing Nongovernmental Systems of Labor Standards and Monitoring," *Policy Studies Journal*, vol. 31, no. 1, 2003, pp. 1–29.

58 Ruth Pearson and Gill Seyfang, "New Hope or False Dawn? Voluntary Codes of Conduct, Labour Regulation and Social Policy in a Globalizing World," *Global Social Policy*, vol. 1, no. 1, 2001, pp. 49–78; Archon Fung, "Deliberative Democracy and International Labor Standards," *Governance: An International Journal of Policy, Administration, and Institutions*, vol. 16, no. 1, 2003, pp. 51–71.

Index